Killing Atheism

Killing Atheism

Powerful Evidence and Reasons to Believe Jesus

KENNETH L. FREDRICKSON

RESOURCE *Publications* · Eugene, Oregon

KILLING ATHEISM
Powerful Evidence and Reasons to Believe Jesus

Copyright © 2021 Kenneth L. Fredrickson. All rights reserved. Except for brief quotations in critical publications or reviews, no part of this book may be reproduced in any manner without prior written permission from the publisher. Write: Permissions, Wipf and Stock Publishers, 199 W. 8th Ave., Suite 3, Eugene, OR 97401.

Resource Publications
An Imprint of Wipf and Stock Publishers
199 W. 8th Ave., Suite 3
Eugene, OR 97401

www.wipfandstock.com

PAPERBACK ISBN: 978-1-7252-8698-6
HARDCOVER ISBN: 978-1-7252-8699-3
EBOOK ISBN: 978-1-7252-8700-6

01/25/21

To Judith Ann, my loving and faithful wife, great companion, best friend and peerless mother and grandmother.

Contents

Introduction ... xi

PART I: THE PROBLEM AND THE SOLUTION

1. The Problem ... 3
   Demons of Unbelief
2. Traditional Apologetics ... 6
3. Setting the Stage ... 9
4. The Solution ... 12
   God's Powerful and Compelling Evidence
5. Collateral Questions ... 16
   Suffering, the Bible, Nature of God, Coming to Belief
6. Prayer ... 22
7. The Dilemma of an Incomprehensible God ... 27

PART II: EVIDENCE

8. Appearances by Mary ... 33
9. Our Lady of Fatima ... 36
   and The Miracle of the Sun
9.1. Our Lady of Fatima ... 43
   1917: The First Four Appearances

9.2	Our Lady of Fatima *The September 13th Miracle*	48
9.3	Fatima's Messages of Love	50
9.4	Our Lady of Fatima *The Effects of Her Appearances*	54
9.5	Fatima and Islam	59
9.6	Our Lady of Fatima *The Floundering Skeptic*	61
10	Our Lady of Lourdes	63
11	Our Lady of Knock	73
12	Our Lady of Zeitoun	82
13.1	Our Lady of Guadalupe *Crushing the Snake*	85
13.2	Our Lady of Guadalupe *Gilding the Lily*	93
14	The Shroud of Turin *A Brief Introduction*	100
14.1	The Shroud of Turin *Historical Documentation*	104
14.2	The Shroud of Turin *Facts that Compel Belief*	109
14.3	The Shroud of Turin *Evidence against the Shroud's Authenticity*	115
14.4	The Shroud of Turin *Proving the Supernatural*	119
15	The Sudarium Confirms the Shroud of Turin	121
16	Holy House of Loreto	126
17	Science and Evolution	132
18	Miraculous Healings	138
18.1	Jack Traynor	140
18.2	Marie Bailly and Nobel Laureate Alexis Carrel	148
18.3	Gabriel Gargam	158
18.4	Marion Carroll	161

18.5	Francis Pascal	163
19	Miraculous Events	166
19.1	Miracle of the Holy Fire	168
19.2	Hell's Fire Restrained *The Great Peshtigo Fire*	173
19.3	Our Lady of China	178
19.4	Cokeville, Wyoming	180

PART III: THE TRUSTWORTHY BIBLE

20	The Word of God?	185
21	The Resurrection	188
22	The Resurrection *Complementary Gospel Accounts*	192
23	The Unexpected, Imaginative, and Incongruous	198
24	The Apostles Conspire	201

PART IV: A GOD OF LOVE

25	God's Love	213
26	Evil and Suffering	216
27	Suffering and Unanswered Prayers	221
28	Alexandrina da Costa of Balasar	226
29	The Savior's Incredible Love	229
30	Why did Jesus have to Suffer and Die?	235
31	A Loving God and Eternal Punishment	239

PART V: PERSONAL EXPERIENCES

32	Glimpsing Eternity	249
33	To Heaven, Hell, and Back	252
34	*Heaven is for Real*	256
35	Waco, Texas	260

PART VI: QUO VADIS?

36	Portrait of Jesus, Ruler of All	265
37	One Christian Mansion	268
38	If Jesus Comes Tomorrow, What Then?	271

Bibliography   277
Subject Index   281
Scripture Index   289

Introduction

HELP IS ON ITS WAY

If you or someone you know is caught in the web of depression and struggling with life, or doubts the existence of God, or the Christian faith, or if you need support so that you can help others with these issues, this book will prove invaluable. It goes beyond traditional apologetics and delivers hard evidence and airtight common sense to help us see that we're not alone and that the story of Christ is true. This is a guidebook to which you can return time and time again when unbelief gnaws, or times get desperate.

THE DEMONS OF UNBELIEF

The unfortunate truth is that there is a relentless attack upon God, the Bible, and Christianity. The attacks generally are based upon a superficial examination of the Bible, the nature and character of our claimed God, evil, suffering, unanswered prayers and various doctrines of Christianity (including hell) and their variance from the current cultural (generally Western) setting. The main thrust always seems to be that evolution and an unbiased analysis demonstrate that we no longer need a manufactured god to explain things and that the Bible is self-contradictory, promotes a bizarre moral and social code, describes an unloving god, is of questionable sourcing and authorship, as well as a host of other problems. Finally, and most importantly, skeptics argue that there simply is no evidence that God exists. In fact, the hidden God is the number one reason for not believing.

THE INADEQUACY OF TRADITIONAL APOLOGETICS

Traditional apologetics will not adequately respond to these questions. When it comes to the question of God, argumentation and apologetics only seem to reinforce presently held beliefs. If we rely exclusively on traditional apologetics to believe, we will always doubt. There are just too many questions that can never be answered by pure reason or historical examination.

That is why we will by-pass traditional apologetics (which almost always can be manipulated to support the person's pre-determined belief) and instead compellingly describe verified events from all Christian traditions (Catholic, Orthodox, Protestant, and even Mormon) to deliver hard evidence showing that the story of Christ must be true. Finally, we add the one ingredient so often missing from traditional apologetics, and that is love. Any explanation of Christ without love is a dead duck.

CHRIST PLEADS FOR OUR ATTENTION

Unbelievers and skeptics maintain that there is no evidence for God. We will plainly show that this contention is false, and that God does not hide. In fact, the God described in the Bible has given us the means to find him in whatever age we live, wherever we live, and whatever our level of education or intelligence. He has given us tangible and verifiable proof in the form of miracles, heavenly visitations, miraculous cures, creation itself, and even the burial cloths of Jesus. It is this empirical evidence that will be the foundation for this book. We will introduce historical and contemporaneous facts and events which can be independently verified, as well as some analysis and insights to help us recognize the truths of such biblical events as the Crucifixion and Resurrection. Ours is not an academic endeavor; it is a spiritual and evidentiary journey, with only a few digressions into the world of traditional apologetics. We don't speculate or theorize but present tangible evidence and describe events that clearly could not have occurred without divine intervention.

We confront head-on other perplexing issues such as the presence of evil, suffering, unanswered prayers, the apparent conflict between God's omniscience and free will, questions about the Bible, and hell. We demonstrate that these issues should not deter the honest seeker once he recognizes that God has made his presence known. These problems become excuses, and not reasons to reject the God of Christian theology.

STEPPING ON THE DEMONS

Books and lectures might direct us toward God, but in the end, and whether your education stopped at the 4th grade or you received several doctorates in Biblical Theology and Philosophy from Cambridge, you can only ascertain God's presence by talking to him. The gap between the Eternally Perfect and his imperfect creatures is immense beyond measure but can be bridged by prayer. Even though you may not believe, you still need to address him as though you did, and he'll help you along with the rest. Success depends upon a real desire to find God and humility.

If you think you don't need God—well, then more than ever you do. Do you remember the story about how Jesus was unable to perform miracles in his hometown?[1] The locals thought they knew him and would not believe he could work miracles. In the exercise of their free will they thought they knew it all, but they were wrong. Their reliance on their own knowledge blinded them to the gift walking before them. Don't you make the same mistake. Instead, rely upon God for help, and when you do, you will discover that God has revealed himself throughout the ages, and continues to do so, in ways that can leave no doubt as to his existence and love for us.

OUR CHOICE

Jesus has promised heaven for those who love him. He also told us about the eternal destination for those who reject God's love, and he gave us the free will to choose. If we but open our minds and consider the many unambiguous proofs God has given for the humble seeker, our choice will be certain and clear. Sadly, there are many who simply do not want to believe, and nothing will convince them otherwise. Quite frankly, if after you have considered the events and issues discussed in this book you still do not believe, you need to search within for hidden biases that are so powerful that you wouldn't believe even if Jesus were to rise from the grave directly in front of you. One can always find reasons to not believe. If that's your situation, I can't help you—and you don't want to believe.

C.S. Lewis puts it all in perspective: *"Christianity, if false, is of no importance, and if true, of infinite importance. The only thing it cannot be is moderately important."* There is no middle ground. Christianity compels us to ignore, reject or accept Jesus. If your inclination is to ignore or reject, you *must* deal with the points made in this book. If you are wrong (are you infallible?) you may very well be facing an eternity in the absence of God and

---

1. Mark 6:1–6 and Matt 13:54–58.

suffering in the presence of pure Evil, knowing there will never be an exit. If you are right and I'm wrong (I'm not infallible), well, we'll never know because we will all have dissolved into nothingness.

God has given each of us, including the skeptic, a ticket to belief. Don't be stupid and lose it.

INSPIRATIONAL MUSIC

From time to time we will introduce hymns and sacred songs. If they are not useful for you, well, skip past them. For many, however, sacred songs can be profoundly inspirational. They can also help us recognize the unity in our diverse Christian sub-faiths.

One example is the Lord's Prayer, which has been described as a miniaturization of the entire gospel. When set to music it becomes even more powerful. Mormons and Catholics are not exactly on the same page when it comes to various aspects of Christian belief. Yet, here they are, joined by Andrea Bocelli and the Mormon Tabernacle Choir singing the Lord's Prayer,[2] the same prayer taught by Jesus as he proclaimed the Kingdom of God.

REFERENCES

Every fact asserted in this book can easily be confirmed by accessing the internet. I would only ask that you not be selective in the materials you source for verification. Review them all. Incidentally, you will be astounded by the abundance of misinformation and the level of hate directed towards Christianity.

Unless otherwise stated, the few biblical quotations are from the Revised Standard Version and can be accessed at www.biblegateway.com. Internet references are as of December 2020.

---

2. https://www.youtube.com/watch?v=PRTumFIfo8g (YouTube search words: Bocelli Lord's Mormon).

PART I

The Problem
and
The Solution

1

The Problem

Demons of Unbelief

The principal reasons given for rejecting the existence of God and denying Christ can be condensed to these four.

1. THE HIDDEN GOD

If God exists and loves us as Christianity proclaims, he would clearly show himself. The doubters ask, "Why doesn't God make himself visible and show up every now and then? What's the big secret?" And they answer, "Because he isn't there, and there's no evidence for the existence of such a wildly implausible thing, no longer necessary, called god." In fact, the hidden God is the number one reason for disbelief. And, besides, assuming there is a god (or gods), why should it be the Christian God? How about Allah, Yahweh, or the myriad of other gods worshiped?

2. SUFFERING, EVIL, UNANSWERED PRAYERS, AND HELL

We are told that God is love, and that everything is subject to his control. Yet, we look about us and see pain, evil, suffering, natural disasters, and the cruelty of nature. We suffer and pray for relief and nothing happens. Moreover, a God of love would not consign some or many of the very people he created to eternal suffering in a place or condition called hell.

Every now and then we hear about God's love being revealed through miraculous healings and other miracles. But we wonder if they really happened or, if an event did occur, how do we know it was not just the result of some presently unknown dynamic or that the so-called miracle was not just a coincidence. In other words, there are no true miracles or miraculous healings. Miracles are the products of wishful thinking.

3. THE BIBLE IS UNTRUSTWORTHY

Christians lean on the Bible as the word of God to prove their case. Yet, we know that it (and particularly the Gospels of Matthew, Mark, Luke, and John) is fictitious. Here are some reasons:

- Objective scholars and experts have thoroughly examined the accounts of Jesus in the Four Gospels and conclude they are fictional.
- There is no extrinsic evidence supporting the biblical stories about Jesus.
- The Four Gospels were written decades after the supposed events by unknown authors.
- The Resurrection accounts conflict with one another.
- Other gospel accounts were rejected because they contained events and teachings contrary to the preferred dogma.
- The God it reveals is capricious and mean (particularly in the Old Testament).
- The biblical teachings are inconsistent and many conflict with what we know is right.

4. SCIENCE ELIMINATES THE NEED FOR AN IMPOSSIBLE AND INCOMPREHENSIBLE GOD

To accept the notion of an eternal omniscient, omnipotent being, who is creator and in control of everything in the universe, from the tiniest microbe in our pond to immense galaxies billions of light years away, is preposterous and flies in the face of all that makes sense. Modern day science can now explain the previously unexplainable, thereby demonstrating that the God of the Bible or any other god was a magical entity created by man to help him through life and explain the otherwise unknowable. That need no longer exists, and we must not be enslaved by ancient superstitions.

God's supposed traits of omnipotence and omniscience defy logic. If he's omnipotent, could he create a boulder he couldn't lift? Could he un-create himself? If he's omniscient, then do we really have free will since he knows everything we're going to do, even all our thoughts.

These are fair observations and questions, and they are the demons that feed unbelief and undercut the faith of numerous Christians. We will tackle them, head-on.

2

Traditional Apologetics

THE VISION OF ST. AUGUSTINE

St. Augustine devoted more than thirty years working on a treatise to explain the mystery of the Holy Trinity. One day he was walking on the beach contemplating and trying to understand this great mystery when he saw a small boy repeatedly dipping a seashell into the ocean and then carrying and emptying it into a small hole in the sand. The boy said he was trying to empty out the ocean and pour it into the hole. Augustine told the boy the obvious: what he was attempting was impossible.

> "That is true," the boy said. "It would be easier and quicker to draw all the water out of the sea and fit it into this hole than for you to fit the mystery of the Trinity and His Divinity into your little intellect; for the Mystery of the Trinity is greater and larger in comparison with your intelligence than is this vast ocean in comparison with this little hole."
> And then the child vanished.[1]

As a preliminary matter, we need to acknowledge that the limits of human understanding preclude us from coming to a deep faith through traditional apologetics, relying exclusively on logic and analysis. The mysteries

---

1 Our Lady of Mercy website, "Mystery of the Trinity," lines 10–14.

of God are simply unknowable. Instead, we will see that God has not only provided ample evidence of his Being but possesses a love for us so profound and deep that we could spend the next thirty years trying to unravel God's mysteries and stand a better chance of emptying out the ocean. God understands our limitations and made our journey to him simple.

THE FUTILITY OF TRADITIONAL APOLOGETICS

There are countless websites, books, articles, etc. purporting to prove or disprove the existence of God. Their sheer numbers, multitude of arguments, and general ineffectiveness confirms St. Augustine's vision and tell us what should be plain by now: after centuries of philosophical debate and syllogisms, Christianity can never be proved or disproved by philosophical musings and recourse to traditional arguments. For most of us this debate only results in confusion, and the confused mind always says 'no.'

Now, imagine you are a lawyer presenting the case for Jesus to a jury. Would you rather argue a complex stream of logic and abstractions based upon the writings of, say, St. Thomas Aquinas and other theologians and scholars, as well as scientists (of course the other side has their experts who have reached the opposite conclusions) or would you prefer to present empirical evidence in the form of unassailable and multiple corroborative witnesses and even video and other tangible evidence that by any objective standard shows God revealing himself throughout the ages, and that this evidence powerfully leads us to conclude that the story of Christ is true?

Here are some simple facts that are mostly ignored. Intelligent people who have examined the issue of Christianity:

1. are not Christians;
2. are Christians; or
3. don't know.

What this tells us is that the concept of God is so magnificent and beyond our collective ability to comprehend or describe that we cannot put him in a box of syllogisms. Our attempts at logic and other traditional forms of persuasion will always be woefully inadequate. There are just too many questions that can never be answered by pure reason or historical and scientific examination.

A TENUOUS CONVERSION

For the most part, whoever is converted based exclusively upon arguments and logic has a shallow faith, easily unhinged. Whatever the argument there is always the counterargument. A person's conclusion as to which is correct quite often is a result of where and how he grew up and his underlying assumptions and prejudices, whether Christian or non-Christian. We are intellectually stumped because we are attempting to solve a problem that cannot be solved by traditional apologetics. We simply do not have the intellectual or language resources to grasp the mysteries of the universe. We might just as well try to spoon out the ocean into a hole in the sand. The easiest path is to go about our business and (1) ignore the eternal question or (2) opt for the easiest solution, which is a purely naturalistic explanation for all we see or speculate.

DON'T MUCK IT UP

As you read books and websites arguing for atheism and why the existence of God is a hoax, see if you can identify what it would take to make the author a believer. In most cases, the answer is nothing.

Can you imagine Jesus walking around two thousand years ago trying to prove God's existence to his apostles and listeners by using metaphysical, logical, empirical and subjective arguments? Can you visualize him engaging others by expanding on epistemology and ontology? How about trying to bring them on board by expounding upon a theory of value? What if he were to anticipate and explain St. Aquinas's five proofs?

No, these approaches are obtuse and boring. They are merely arguments. I think Jesus would prove his point through miraculous events witnessed by others, then and throughout history. That is what he did, and that's what we're going to show.

Jesus gave us empirical proof of who he is and what he did. Since we are not mere animals, but made in the image of God, he also gave us free will to accept or reject him. We are sadly mistaken if we think pure logic will take us inside the Christian mansion. Traditional apologetics may open the door by showing that belief is intellectually reasonable and for some, even compelling, but it can only be a beginning. A sturdy faith is available only to those who recognize their limitations and approach the Lord open-minded and with child-like humility. God made it pretty simple for us. Just look at the evidence. Don't muck it up.

3

Setting the Stage

DO YOU REALLY WANT TO BELIEVE?

Are you sure you want to believe? I can't explain it, but I know there are some, perhaps many, that would never accept the biblical Jesus even if he were to rise from the grave in front of them. Here's a good way to determine whether you are within this group of hard-core nonbelievers. Go to chapters 14–14.4 discussing The Shroud of Turin; chapter 29 ("The Savior's Incredible Love"); and chapters 9–9.6 discussing Fatima. When you are finished, click on any atheist or skeptic's website and read their arguments as to why you shouldn't believe. Examine their reasons in light of Fatima and the Shroud. Do they even talk about the Shroud or Fatima? If they do, do their arguments and alternative explanations address the undisputed facts relating to the Shroud or Fatima? For example, in the case of the Shroud of Turin do they address how the great bulk of the characteristics and physical features were only first revealed in 1898 and that they simply could not have been created by a medieval artist. In the case of the Miracle of the Sun at Fatima, do they even mention that beginning three months earlier the three children said that a miracle would occur at noon on October 13 at a specified location? If they do, does their explanation make sense? Notice also how the facts pertaining to the Shroud or Fatima are distorted in the websites attacking them.

LOGIC AND SURRENDER

Are you prepared to engage both your brain and heart? Christianity is not exclusively an intellectual exercise. That is just the beginning. As Brother Lawrence tells us, "It is not necessary to have either a keen intellect or a great knowledge to go to God, but simply a heart resolved to apply itself to Him and for Him and to love only Him."[1] Your brain may enter you into the race, but your heart carries you over the finish line.

CHRIST'S SUFFERING AND LOVE

Christians believe that Jesus gave himself completely, without reservation, and took the time to suffer and die on the cross for us. You need to bring that suffering and love into your heart and return it. If you see Christ hanging from the cross and only your intellect is affected, you need to restart your engines. I don't see how it's possible to be an enduring Christian unless you suffer with him on the cross and are moved by his love. It is on the cross that his love is revealed in no uncertain terms.

PRAYER

We need to humble ourselves and try to speak with the Creator, and prayer is our way of communicating with God. Any effort to find God without trying to talk to him (even if you do not believe) would be like surviving in an atmosphere without oxygen. Without prayer, Jesus will remain a mystery. You may catch an occasional glimpse, but it will be fleeting. Prayer is our starting, middle, and end point to believe and to live in the presence of God.

ATTACKING CHRIST

A question for your consideration: What motivates outspoken atheists and skeptics to vehemently attack Christ and his followers? What is the upside for the militant atheist to destroy someone's faith? How does he profit by making a believer into a non-believer? Can they possibly believe the world will be a better place if Christianity were to be eradicated? A possible answer for some unbelievers may be a hidden or unrecognized agenda for the believer to show him God. For others, I wonder if pride prevents them

---

1. Helms, *Brother Lawrence*, 70.

from believing. Can it be they reject God's amazing grace[2] because they cannot tolerate the concept of an Eternal Being to whom they must ultimately surrender?

UNCOVERING THE HIDDEN GOD

For most of us, philosophical musings, reason, and traditional apologetics won't lead us to a firm belief. There are always counter arguments. The arguers merely dance back and forth on the stage, convincing only themselves and others who believe the same. Apologetics on both sides seem to start off with the conclusion, followed by arguments to support the desired result. The primary objective seems to win the debate, and not to uncover the truth.

The overriding reason for nonbelief is that if God existed, he would show himself. He has not, thereby demonstrating he is a myth. All other skeptic arguments are subordinate. That is simply because if we can show by hard empirical evidence that God has revealed himself and, better yet, continues to do so, the remaining arguments such as the presence of evil, etc., simply dissolve. They in effect become statements of how we think God should have done his job. We substitute our ideas of right and wrong and how creation should unfold for those of the Creator. This is simply arrogant, irrelevant, and silly.

What should convince regular doubters (not the hard-core skeptics—they will never believe) is the empirical evidence that God has given us that HE IS. This is where we are going. Our approach is to introduce observable evidence outside the Bible to help the reader recognize the loving presence of Jesus Christ. This evidence, along with prayer (see chapter 6) and humility will lead to a sure and firm faith.

God has given us free will to accept, ignore, or reject Christ. We will try and help you make the right choice, and we begin in the next chapter by summarizing some of the evidence God has given us.

---

2. Perhaps the best known and beloved Christian hymn is *Amazing Grace*. If you feel down or need a spiritual lift listen to Andre Bocelli at https://www.youtube.com/watch?v=TF9jQNxJfyU (YouTube search words: Bocelli grace central).

4

The Solution

God's Powerful and Compelling Evidence

Nonbelievers argue (and it seems quite sensibly) that if God exists, he would show himself or at least give us some evidence of his presence and that he cares.

    I don't understand how the internet works; I can't see it, but it's there. If I could travel to the year 1830 and tell them about a future where we could instantly retrieve any book ever written, witness events any place in the world as they occur, listen to Mozart, view the earth from space to the most minute detail, and do all of this instantly and throughout the world simultaneously, I would be given a one-way ticket to the nearest looney bin. But we know we can do all of this. We can't see the internet, but it manifests itself and there can be no other explanation besides its presence.

    The same is true for God.

PART II: EVIDENCE
CHAPTERS 8-19

The mother of Jesus has appeared numerous times throughout the centuries and the fact of her appearances is quite unassailable. If you are still not convinced, maybe a photograph of Jesus at the instant of his resurrection will help, and for that we will go to Turin, Italy. How about documented healings and other events that have no explanation but the Divine Hand of God?

Here is a summary of the materials covered in Part II.

APPEARANCES BY MARY: CHAPTERS 8 THROUGH 13.2

If we have but one appearance by Mary that we know with absolute certainty occurred, the only intellectually honest conclusion would be that the story of Jesus is true; all other conclusions and religions are necessarily eliminated. Here, we report on not one, but five apparitions (there are others as well). There is no explanation for any of these except the intervening hand of God.

- Portugal 1917: Our Lady of Fatima and the Miracle of the Sun (chapters 9–9.6).
- France 1858: Our Lady of Lourdes (chapter 10).
- Ireland 1879: Our Lady of Knock (chapter 11).
- Egypt 1968–1971: Our Lady of Zeitoun (chapter 12).
- Mexico 1531: Our Lady of Guadalupe (chapters 13.1, 13.2).

PHYSICAL EVIDENCE FOR THE BIBLICAL JESUS: CHAPTERS 13.1 THROUGH 16

Except for Our Lady of Guadalupe, the above appearances by Mary are attested to by numerous witnesses. The 1531 appearance by Mary to Juan Diego in Mexico is confirmed by her image which appears on Juan Diego's tilma now enshrined in the Basilica of Our Lady of Guadalupe in Mexico City. Other physical evidence God has provided includes:

- The Shroud of Turin (chapters 14–14.4).
- The Sudarium (chapter 15).
- Holy House of Loreto (chapter 16).

SCIENCE AND EVOLUTION: CHAPTER 17

Evolution is merely a word, bandied about to provide a secular explanation for the variety and unfathomable complexity of life. Be sure to view the YouTube videos referred to in chapter 17 and ask yourself, "Can evolution explain the incredible complexity and synergism of the human body and mind?" It cannot. *Res ipsa loquitur* = the thing speaks for itself. For example, vision is but one of the numerous complex systems which grace our bodies. Ask yourself how a clump of inorganic material could self-assemble into diverse and completely different parts to enable vision. Because no survival advantage would be gained without the entire visual package being assembled, the construction would have to be immediate and simultaneous. The retina cannot function without the cornea; nothing works without the optic nerve; the brain first would have to have evolved to the point where it could interpret the data, create and direct actionable responses, etc., etc. There is no rational explanation other than a Creator.

MIRACULOUS HEALINGS: CHAPTERS 18 THROUGH 18.5

Lourdes, France is famous as a place of miraculous healings, both physical and spiritual. The voice of God speaks through and is verified by these healings. Miraculous healings, however, are not confined to Lourdes. They are just better documented there. After reading the accounts of instantaneous and inexplicable healings referred to below, try to find a naturalistic explanation. You will fail and the best you can do will be to say we don't know how or why these healings occurred, but someday we will. If that is your position, please recognize that your approach has devolved from scientific to faith in something you (and everyone else) know nothing about.

- Lourdes 1923: Jack Traynor (chapter 18.1).
- Lourdes 1902 and 1944: Marie Bailly and Nobel Laureate Alexis Carrel (chapter 18.2).
- Lourdes 1901: Gabriel Gargam (chapter 18.3).
- Knock 1989: Marion Carroll (chapter 18.4).
- Lourdes 1938: Francis Pascal (chapter 18.5).

MIRACULOUS EVENTS: CHAPTERS 19 THROUGH 19.4

Events can reveal God's love and presence. I can understand why some, such as the Great Peshtigo Fire, might be considered nothing more than spectacular coincidences. Others, however, lend themselves to no explanation other than God's love made manifest.

- Jerusalem, every Easter Saturday: Miracle of the Holy Fire (chapter 19.1).
- Wisconsin 1871: Great Peshtigo Fire (chapter 19.2).
- China 1900 and 1995: Our Lady of China (chapter 19.3).
- Wyoming 1986: Cokeville (chapter 19.4).

Since the materials discussed in Part II conclusively show that Christ lived, suffered on the cross, died, and rose from the dead as recorded in the New Testament, all the other objections against Christianity should dissolve. But as we know, they do not. Consequently, we need to address evil, pain, suffering, natural disasters, hell, an incomprehensible Divine Being and unexplained issues about the Bible and see if we can make sense of them.

We do this in Parts I, III, and IV, and the next chapter summarizes the material presented in these sections.

5

Collateral Questions

Suffering, the Bible, Nature of God, Coming to Belief

Apart from the hidden God argument, the principal objections to Christianity can be condensed to:

1. Science now eliminates the need for an impossible and incomprehensible God;
2. The presence of suffering, evil, unanswered prayers, and hell; and
3. The Bible is untrustworthy.

Here is how we will address these collateral questions.

PART I: SCIENCE AND THE NEED FOR GOD (CHAPTERS 7 AND 17)

Objection

Science explains, or will eventually explain, everything. To accept the notion of an eternal omniscient, omnipotent being, who is creator and in control of everything in the universe, from the tiniest microbe in our pond to immense galaxies billions of light years away, is preposterous and flies in the face of all that makes sense.

Summary response

The naturalistic explanation for the universe and life is addressed in Chapter 17, "Science and Evolution." The vastness and complexity of the universe and the incomprehensibility of God, as well as his omnipotence and omniscience are discussed in chapter 7, but only briefly, because that is all any of us are capable of. We need to sweep aside all pretensions. If we cannot understand the nature of God or the interplay between omniscience and free will, that is to be expected. Neither we, nor you, or any human or group of humans regardless of their level of intelligence, learning, and even spirituality, can ever satisfactorily resolve these issues. Do not use this lack of understanding as a crutch to deny the Creator. Of necessity, God and his characteristics are incomprehensible, meaning any attempt to describe or limit him is doomed. It may be fun to speculate about God, but whatever we think or say is mere speculation.

PART III: THE TRUSTWORTHY BIBLE (CHAPTERS 20—24)

Objection

Skeptics argue that the Bible is mostly fiction. They point to internal inconsistencies and numerous other reasons, including the questions of authorship, dates of writing and other corollary issues relating to the Four Gospels and other books of the Bible.

Summary response

This argument could be important if we did not have Jesus revealed to us as described in Part II. Nevertheless, to reinforce your faith in the reliability of Mark, Matthew, Luke, and John as faithful accounts of the life, teachings, suffering, death, and resurrection of Christ you should consider the Part III chapters:

- The Resurrection (chapter 21).
- The Resurrection: *Complementary Gospel Accounts* (chapter 22).

- The Unexpected, Imaginative, and Incongruous (chapter 23).
- The Apostles Conspire (chapter 24).

In Part III we will briefly look at the question of whether the four accounts of the Resurrection, the *sine qua non* of Christianity, are at odds with one another and we will show that a reasonable reading of these Gospels is that, on the contrary, they beautifully complement one another. Moreover, the stories within the four Gospels are (i) such a clear departure from Judaism, (ii) so imaginative, and (iii) contain a theological depth (particularly when read in the context of the Old Testament), that it belies logic and common sense to believe they were the work of some ancient fishermen (or their followers). We will provide examples of what I mean. Additionally, the objective evidence in the person of the man on the Shroud of Turin and the Sudarium (chapters 14–15) compel the conclusion that the Gospel accounts of torture and pain he endured are painfully accurate.

Put yourself in the shoes of the fishermen or their immediate followers and assess whether you could fictionalize such a masterful account of Jesus of Nazareth as is presented in the New Testament.

PART IV: A GOD OF LOVE (CHAPTERS 25—31)

Objection

We are told that God is love, and that everything is subject to his control. Yet, we look about us and see evil, suffering, pain, and terror imposed upon all his creatures. The most innocent of us, and even animals, are not exempt. Moreover, we are told a loving God would not send the very creatures he made into eternal torment called hell. A loving God would not permit any of this and would not leave our prayers unanswered.

Summary response

We have an imperfect and limited understanding of reality and our place in the eternal progression of God's plan of salvation. Just because we might have created a world order differently is not a legitimate reason to ignore Jesus.

Ask Aaron Arrogance.

A Brooklyn fire escape

"What do you mean there's only one fire escape?" Aaron Arrogance was speaking. He had just inherited a four-story walk-up apartment building in Brooklyn. Now he was on the fourth floor grilling the apartment supervisor and berating him for his insistence that in the event of a fire there was only one way out. Mr. Arrogance knew that was wrong. Logic and his life experiences had shown him that there must be at least two ways out. Anything else was senseless. Of course, he was only twenty-two years old and wasn't there when the building was constructed one hundred years earlier. Nevertheless, there simply had to be additional escape routes; that's the way he would have built it. And he was willing to bet his life on it, even as the smoke crawled up the stairwell. The supervisor wasn't listening anymore. He knew the gravity of the situation and was out the window and down the fire escape. The building was old and dilapidated. He reached the ground safely, but just as Mr. Arrogance decided that perhaps he better exit down the one route to safety, the fire escape collapsed and there was no exit. The heir's arrogance and procrastination cost him his life.

Even if we accept the principle embodied in this short story, it is still hard to reconcile all the pain and suffering we see and feel with a loving God. And then, to top it all off, are told that eternal fire awaits those who turn from God and we continue to wonder how this can be consistent with a loving God. So, we speculate about these issues (just as theologians, philosophers, scientists, and everyone else has done for millennia), and puzzle as to how we can make sense of this apparent inconsistency. These questions nag and their harshness is jarring. Consequently, we will consider these issues in Part IV:

- Evil and Suffering (chapter 26).
- Suffering and Unanswered Prayers (chapter 27).
- Alexandrina da Costa of Balasar (chapter 28).
- The Savior's Incredible Love (chapter 29).
- Why did Jesus have to Suffer and Die? (chapter 30).
- A Loving God and Eternal Punishment? (chapter 31).

When we consider what Jesus did, as described in "The Savior's Incredible Love" (chapter 29) and why, as explained in "Why did Jesus have to Suffer and Die?" (chapter 30), we can see that rejecting the existence of God because of our pain, suffering, etc. is an excuse and not a reason for nonbelief. The extent of God's love for us is demonstrably and unimaginably deep.

PART V: PERSONAL EXPERIENCES (CHAPTERS 32—35)

As summarized in chapter 32 God continues to reveal himself through personal experiences, including near-death experiences. While these personal experiences cannot be independently verified, many are compelling and deserve your attention.

Be sure to read about Father Jose's 1987 experience in India, "To Heaven, Hell, and Back" (chapter 33), and the independent visions of two four-year-old children in *"Heaven is for Real"* (chapter 34) living half a continent apart. These experiences ring powerfully true. In the case of Father Jose his more than thirty years of service to God as a Catholic priest and his healing ministry following his death and return to life speaks volumes. In the case of the two children, their testimony and the portrait of Jesus painted by one of the four-year-old children when she was eight called the *Prince of Peace*[1] validate their stories.

Finally, I'll bet if you sat down with family members or friends over a drink (or with anyone at the nearest tavern) and they opened up, other stories would emerge which have no explanation other than a divine intervention. I describe one such personal event in "Waco, Texas" (chapter 35).

PART VI: QUO VADIS? (CHAPTERS 36—38)

Jesus is not an ephemeral character/philosopher that lived thousands of years ago. He was a real person, and we think we know what he looked like. "Portrait of Jesus, Ruler of All" (chapter 36) describes the relationship and stunning similarity of three portraits of Jesus which almost certainly resulted from divine intervention. When you look upon the Shroud of Turin, *Christ Pantocrator*[2], and the *Prince of Peace* you are quite likely looking at the face of Jesus.

One final point: As explained in Chapter 37, "One Christian Mansion," if you are trying to figure out whether Christianity is real, don't discard your search because you feel that any faith with as many divisions or traditions

---

1. Ellis, *"Akiane, Jesus is for real,"* God Reports website.
2. Tour Egypt website, *Christ Pantocrator*.

as Christianity can't be true. Similarly, if you are trying to help others find and accept Jesus, try not to attack other Christian denominations because certain of their doctrines differ from yours. These disputes, and particularly the heated ones, can only repel honest seekers. Share your faith in a way that preserves and strengthens our Christian unity.

Chapter 38, "If Jesus Comes Tomorrow, What Then?" provides an overview of the facts and evidence discussed in the book. Even if you or the person you are talking to may have an uncertain faith now, by the time you finish this book (assuming you read it carefully and with an open mind) you or your loved one should be able to say "*I Came to Believe.*"[3]

---

3. *I Came to Believe* sung by Johnny Cash. https://www.youtube.com/watch?v=PCb-JJ7bPE4&t=17s (YouTube search words: Cash came believe gospel collection).

6

Prayer

The Lord uses diverse means to help us in our faith. Sometimes it is other people and sometimes books. The Catholic, Orthodox, and some Protestant denominations teach that he has given us Mary to help us in our journey to Christ. All Christians agree that he has given us the Bible.

ABSOLUTE NECESSITY OF PRAYER

But prayer trumps all. At the creation, God set in motion a history of love and salvation. He established a protocol, so to speak, of what he wants from each of us, including a powerful mechanism to approach him. That mechanism is prayer and it is the ultimate means of seeking and finding Him. This gift is available to everyone regardless of our age, culture, intelligence, or the church in which we were raised. As with any gift, it can be accepted, ignored, or rejected.

PRAYER AND THE UNBELIEVER

But you ask, what's the point in praying to a Creator that we're not even sure exists? The answer is that God will reveal himself to those who are seeking him in humility and a child-like demeanor. Proof? When we examine those events where provable claims are made of Mary's appearances such as Fatima, to whom does she appear? It is always children or the unlearned.

And we are back to the beginning. If you do not want to believe or if your approach is to rely upon your own intellect and resources, you never will. And any faith that emerges will be shallow and tenuous. You must be willing to believe and surrender to God. This may require a sustained effort on your part. If it would be helpful, consider repeating and dwelling upon the evening prayer of St Francis, "Who are you my God, and who am I?"

God will answer you. He wants our prayers, even in times of spiritual dryness or distraction, and even when we harbor a deep disbelief. Maybe we don't know what to say when we pray; maybe we feel hopelessly inadequate; or maybe we just may feel plain foolish praying to God when we're not sure he listens, or even exists. You may be assured that God has foreseen all these circumstances and he knows your situation. He is not looking for eloquence; he is looking for love, humility, desire, and commitment.

St Augustine and his mother might be able to provide some help.

ST. AUGUSTINE

St. Augustine is a great example of someone who initially rejected the gift of prayer, but eventually accepted. Prayer transformed his life. For his first thirty or so years, St. Augustine ignored the Lord and rejected prayer. God was in one place, and he was in another. His life consisted of carousing and illicit sexual relationships. He knew this was wrong but did not care. His mother, however, did, and she prayed, prayed, and prayed for his conversion.

Finally, Augustine sought God in earnest. While praying in a garden in Milan, Italy and repenting of his sinful life, he heard a voice say, "Take up and read." Augustine randomly selected chapter 13 of Romans: "Let us then cast off the works of darkness and put on the armor of light; let us conduct ourselves becomingly as in the day, not in reveling and drunkenness, not in debauchery and licentiousness, not in quarreling and jealousy. But put on the Lord Jesus Christ, and make no provision for the flesh, to gratify its desires."

St. Augustine was baptized in 388 at the age of thirty-four. His mother's prayers and his own led him to conversion and he became one of the greatest (if not the greatest) Doctor of the Church (that is, someone considered to be of particular importance regarding his contribution to theology or Christian doctrine). This man is synonymous with erudite scholarship and theology, but he found his faith because of prayer.

DRIFTING FROM THE SHORE

Everyone experiences periods of spiritual dryness. We might harbor a nagging doubt about the existence of God or his love for us. Perhaps our attention wanders when we pray and our prayers falter. Doubts and inattention may continue for days, weeks, months, or even years. Even Mother Teresa of Calcutta wrote how removed she felt from God for much of her life, even when she was most intensely submerged in God's work. In these times, follow her example and pray. There is no downside. It is not like eating contaminated herring. God understands—even when our mind wanders or unbelief knocks. Try, try, and try some more. Try always to enter prayer with the intent of drawing closer to God and trusting him. God always understands our weaknesses. If the Bible teaches nothing else, it is that he always forgives and strengthens—if that is what we want. We just need to ask in faith and be persistent.

PRACTICE, PRACTICE, PRACTICE

Perhaps you have tried prayer, with absolutely no success. "I keep chopping but the chips aren't flying." If you wish to excel at something you need to work, practice, train, and work some more. You need to spend long hours practicing the piano, studying the law, lifting weights in the gym to achieve your goal. If you aspire to be an NFL linebacker you will need to endure hundreds and thousands of hours practicing and training in the hot summer sun, enjoy Friday night triumphs in high school, suffer defeats, injuries, setbacks and conquer a lot of self-doubts. But to be successful, you need to put all the negatives aside and work to build on your talents.

Six years as an NFL linebacker makes all the preparatory pain and hard work worth it. A lifetime of playing and revealing to others the mastery and beauty of Mozart or Bach or Liszt makes the thousands of hours of practice and study worthwhile.

We would all like to be gifted with these athletic or artistic talents even though the payout may only last six years as a professional football player or a mere lifetime in the case of the piano virtuoso. Contrast that with the gift of prayer we have all received, regardless of culture, status in life, and religious heritage, and with a payout for all eternity. Unfortunately, it now appears that the vast majority deny the presence of this gift or ignore it.

SIMPLICITY AND PERSISTENCE

It is not surprising, then, that our spiritual direction can become muddled and prayer difficult. Allow me to make a suggestion. When you don't know how to pray or what to say or how to say it, try reverting to the most basic, shortest, and simplest of prayers, and that is nothing more than repeating the Savior's name: *Jesus, Jesus, Jesus . . .*: If you do nothing more than meditate upon His name with gratitude and love, additional guidance will come. If we keep trying, we will get on track. We just need to enter prayer with the intent to pray sincerely and never give up.

PRAYER—NEVER TOO LATE

In 1972, a prayer was published that had been found in the pocket of a dead World War II Soviet soldier, Aleksander Zacepa. He had been rigorously raised as an atheist in this communist regime. He composed this prayer just before the World War II battle that would take his life:

> Hear me, oh God! In my lifetime, I have not spoken with you even once, but today I have the desire to celebrate. Since I was little, they have always told me that you don't exist. And I, like an idiot, believed it.
>
> I have never contemplated your works, but tonight I have seen from the crater of a grenade the sky full of stars, and I have been fascinated by their splendor. In that instant I have understood how terrible is the deception.
>
> I don't know, oh God, if you will give me your hand, but I say to you that you understand me. Isn't it strange that in the middle of this frightful hell, light has appeared to me, and I have discovered You?
>
> I have nothing more to tell you. I am happy, because I have known You. At midnight, we have to attack, but I am not afraid. You see us.
>
> They have given the signal. I have to go. How good it was to be with You! I want to tell You, and You know, that the battle will be difficult. Perhaps this night, I will go to knock on your door. And even though up to now I haven't been your friend, If I go, will You allow me to come in?
>
> But, what's happening to me? I cry? My God, look at what has happened to me. Only now, I've begun to see clearly.

> Farewell, my God, I am going. It's scarcely possible that I'll return. Strange; Death now has no fear for me.[1]

It's never too late—as long as you have enough time left.

THE CRUCIAL ELEMENT

We can come to some knowledge about God and Jesus' love through reason and study, but the fact is God is so far above us that we can never come to belief by trying to understand. We need to surrender in prayer and ask for his help. When we do, Jesus will abide within us. It is only when we believe that we will understand.

God humbled himself and became man, to be carried for nine months in the womb of the Blessed Virgin Mary. In humility she accepted his will and agreed to bring us the Savior. Thirty years later, Jesus humbly trudged to Calvary and bore all our sins through a most agonizing death. For us to emulate the Creator of time and the universe, his Son, and Mary (the most favored of all his creatures) by humbling ourselves in prayer should not be all that hard.

DID YOU THINK TO PRAY?

Christians believe that Jesus gave himself completely, without reservation, and took the time to suffer and die on the cross for us. Maybe we can take some time for him. Even though God already knows what we need, he wants us to stay in touch and rely upon him. This morning, *Did You Think to Pray?*[2] Finally, be sure to listen to the prayer that Jesus taught, sung by Andrea Bocelli.[3] Prayer is our starting and end point to find and live in the presence of God.

---

1. Grace Gateways website, "Prayer of a Soviet Soldier."
2. *Did You Think to Pray* sung by Charley Pride https://www.youtube.com/watch?v=rROtyA6MtWU&ab_channel=BrentE (YouTube search words: think pray Pride).
3. *The Lord's Prayer* sung by Andrea Bocelli https://www.youtube.com/watch?v=PRTumFIfo8g (YouTube search words: Lord's Prayer Bocelli).

7

The Dilemma of an Incomprehensible God

By definition, God is incomprehensible. Maybe when we cross the river we will understand how he could exist from all eternity, be the creator of all, and hold the universe and all its components in the palm of his hand (and still exist within the womb of Mary for nine months). Right now, that is all way beyond us, but that's not a reasonable argument against the existence of God. Inability to understand the incomprehensible is not an argument; it is an excuse.

FIRST CAUSE

Quite frankly, it is counterproductive to speculate about issues which are not within our ability to understand. I recall a discussion about the age-old question of First Cause. Since science tells us that something could never come from nothing, matter could never be created or brought into existence. Nevertheless, here we are in our endless variations of electrons, protons, and other subatomic particles—creation which of necessity, or so it would seem, must have emerged from nothing. Therefore, God was required as creator. But that begs the question of how did God come into existence? There can never be a satisfactory answer to these questions, regardless of how erudite and wise the philosopher is, because we are limited by our human condition of experience, points of reference, senses, pride, and brain power. The best answer came from an eleven-year-old boy who was not at all perturbed by the question of First Cause. He merely reminded us that God is God, and, as such, completely beyond our realm of understanding. Essentially, his message was, "God is eternal with no beginning because God is God—so what's the problem?"

EXPERTS AND AMATEURS

The problem is that we are too quick to rely on "experts." Carl Sagan boldly proclaimed there is no God (Mr. Sagan is now dead). Stephen Hawking (now dead) boldly proclaimed there is no God. After all, they were famous and articulate astronomers and physicists, and a lot smarter than you and me. Only a fool would not believe them. That, however, is not the case.

Astronomy is for astronomers and physics is for physicists. When they attempt to transfer their knowledge and skills into the non-scientific region called God and the supernatural, they quietly and quickly become struggling amateurs—just as we are. Stephen Hawking knew a lot about finding answers posed by science, but he did not know any more than you about finding God—probably less.

GOD'S OMNISCIENCE AND OUR FREE WILL

Two of God's attributes we assign to him are omniscience and omnipotence. That God is omnipotent seems fairly easy to understand. Whatever God chooses to do, he can, since everything is under his dominion, and the concept of omnipotence does not conflict with any other Christian teaching. The attribute of omniscience, however, seems to be at odds with the fundamental Christian doctrine of free will. If God, who knows everything, knows what our future actions are going to be, including our innermost thoughts, it would seem free will is an illusion.

While there is no easy answer to this apparent dilemma, there is an answer (possibly two or three). Let me explain. Our thought processes and actions are enslaved by the sequential timeline. We have yesterday, today, and tomorrow. One follows the other, and what happens today and tomorrow is dependent and built upon what has preceded. Our argument that God's omniscience precludes free will simply ignores that God, the creator of time, is not limited by it. He can see what happened a thousand years ago, what is happening now, and what is going to happen a thousand years into the future as an event or events as though he were viewing it all at once. This is heady stuff, and I defer to C.S. Lewis:

> Everyone who believes in God at all believes that He knows what you and I are going to do tomorrow. But if He knows I am going to do so-and-so, how can I be free to do otherwise? Well, here once again, the difficulty comes from thinking that God is progressing along the Time-line like us: the only difference being that He can see ahead and we cannot. Well, if that were true, if God *foresaw* our acts, it would be very hard to understand how we could be free not to do them. But suppose God is outside and above the Time-line. In that case, what we call 'tomorrow' is visible to Him in just the same way as what we call 'today'. All the days are 'Now' for Him. He does not remember you doing things yesterday; He simply sees you doing them, because, though you have lost yesterday, He has not. He does not 'foresee' you doing things tomorrow; He simply sees you doing them: because, though tomorrow is not yet there for you, it is for Him. You never supposed that your actions at this moment were any less free because God knows what you are doing. Well, He knows your tomorrow's actions in just the same way—because He is already in tomorrow and can simply watch you. In a sense, He does not know your action till you have done it: but then the moment at which you have done it is already 'Now' for Him.[1]

This explanation is similar (if not identical) to the Catholic position that when we receive communion, we receive the body and blood of Christ at Calvary. When we attend Mass and receive the Holy Eucharist, God reaches back in time (from our standpoint but not from God's) and brings to us the sacrifice of the Son of God. In much the same way, Jesus reached forward in time at the Last Supper and gave his apostles his sacrificial body and blood.

How about that!?

Here is a third reference point. What if God, in his omnipotence, elects not to see what you are going to do tomorrow? He would know if he wished to but has elected not to. He is omniscient, but in your case decided not to pay attention to your activities unless, of course, you ask him to. I suppose we could say he has bigger fish to fry.

If this chapter brings you closer to God, that's great. If it does not, drop it. The whole issue is way beyond our pay grade. Focus on Fatima, Lourdes, the Shroud of Turin, miraculous healings, and the other events

---

1. Lewis, *Mere Christianity*, 170.

to be discussed in the following chapters. Above all, keep talking to God through prayer

You won't go wrong.

Believe and you will understand.

PART II

Evidence

8

Appearances by Mary

History is full of purported appearances by Mary, the mother of Jesus. Some undoubtedly are the product of highly imaginative minds and some are faked. But there are others which offer no explanation other than real Marian apparitions. We will explore some of these in chapters 9 through 13.2. Each must be assessed individually and evaluated based on their particular facts. For example, if someone tells you that Our Lady of Fatima can't be real because it has been shown that other supposed Marian appearances have been exposed as fraudulent you can be sure they are struggling to make secular sense of what can only be described as God revealing himself.

We must not reject the picture God started to paint thousands of years ago with the ancient Jews and that he brought into sharp relief with Jesus. He has written his love and commandments in all our hearts and he is asking us to open the door for him. As you will see, he has commissioned the Blessed Virgin to help in this task.

OUR LADY OF FATIMA AND THE MIRACLE OF THE SUN

Fatima may well be the most important event in the twentieth century, yet one largely ignored. The upshot is that if you had been in 1917 Fatima, Portugal you would have known with absolute certainty that Mary was in heaven, thereby conclusively confirming the biblical narrative that Jesus had lived among us, was crucified, died, and rose from the dead. There were seventy thousand witnesses to this extraordinary event. Chapters 9–9.6.

OUR LADY OF LOURDES

Jesus helps us believe by giving us miraculous healings. While the Resurrection is the ultimate miracle, he also proclaimed who he was and his power throughout his three-year ministry by instantly healing a multitude of sick. Those miracles helped the witnesses believe. His miracles continue today, and there is no better place to look than Lourdes, France where, in 1858, a Heavenly Lady self-identified as the Immaculate Conception appeared to the fourteen-year-old Bernadette eighteen times. The Heavenly Visitor was Mary, the mother of Jesus, and is known as Our Lady of Lourdes. Chapter 10.

OUR LADY OF KNOCK

In 1879 Knock, Ireland the silent apparition of Mary, Joseph, and the Apostle John was witnessed by fourteen villagers. No words were spoken but as you will see, the silent messages delivered by this visitation were quite profound. As was the case with the parables spoken by Jesus, to understand you must first desire understanding. Chapter 11.

OUR LADY OF ZEITOUN

Appearances by Mary are not limited to Catholics, but such apparitions receive little publicity in the West. That is probably why you haven't heard about the Marian apparitions on the Coptic Orthodox Church in Cairo, Egypt from 1968 to 1971. This church is built on the location where tradition holds that Mary, Joseph, and the baby Jesus stayed when they fled to Egypt to escape Herod. There are even fuzzy photographs of what was seen by Christians, Muslims, Jews, atheists, and everyone else that was there when she appeared numerous times. Chapter 12.

OUR LADY OF GUADALUPE

The famous image on the tilma in Mexico City known as Our Lady of Guadalupe has long been thought to bear the image of Mary miraculously impressed upon the tilma in 1531. What emerges, however, is the high likelihood that the portrait appeared in two stages: the first of direct divine origin impressed by Mary herself, and the second by indirect divine origin through a human instrument which transformed the already miraculous image into an even more powerful expression of God's love. The messages within Our Lady of Guadalupe spoke forcefully to the Indian natives at the time and speaks just as forcefully to us today. The process is similar in concept to the gospel story authored by Jesus, first directly, and then indirectly through the teachings of his apostles and later generations. Chapters 13.1 and 13.2.

FINDING JESUS

These Marian apparitions provide clear and verifiable evidence of God's presence and love for those who seek him. As you consider the overwhelmingly credible stories about Fatima, Lourdes, Knock, Guadalupe, and Zeitoun, how is it possible to dismiss the Incarnation, Passion and Resurrection? Just as she did two thousand years ago, Mary presents Jesus to the world. When we turn towards Mary we turn toward her son. She does not divert. She magnifies. She delivers.

9

Our Lady of Fatima

and The Miracle of the Sun

Fatima may well be the most important event in the twentieth century. It is a treasure chest full of God's graces, yet an event largely ignored outside Catholic circles. God in his eternal love never ceases speaking to us. We just have to listen. If you had been in 1917 Fatima, Portugal you would have known that Mary was in heaven, thereby conclusively confirming the biblical narrative that Jesus had lived among us, was crucified, died, and rose from the dead.

It's time to visit 1917 Fatima, Portugal.

FATIMA BACKGROUND

Fatima is a small Portuguese village located about 80 miles north of Lisbon. In 1917 three peasant children, ages seven, eight, and ten (Jacinta, Francisco, and Lucia) claimed they saw and spoke with a beautiful lady from heaven who came to be known as Our Lady of the Rosary or Our Lady of Fatima.

Jacinta, Lucia, and Francisco

October 13, 1917 was her final appearance, and it was then that the Miracle of the Sun occurred, precisely when and where the children said it would. The predicted event can only be described as miraculous and was so described in the secular atheistic press at that time.

The children said a beautiful Lady from heaven appeared to them six times (May 13, June 13, July 13, August 19, September 13, and October 13, 1917). Beginning directly after the first appearance on May 13, the children reported these apparitions. They were generally greeted with disbelief and skepticism, and often with scorn and hate. During these visitations, she gave them messages and, beginning in July, promised to perform a miracle on October 13, 1917 so that everyone could believe. On September 13, a preliminary miracle occurred, and the Lady promised that the October 13 miracle would take place at noon. The children were quite unequivocal. They were confident something spectacular was going to take place and the word spread throughout the region.

FATIMA—1917

We know beyond a shadow of a doubt that the Miracle of the Sun and other miracles occurred. There were thousands upon thousands of witnesses to the events on that day as well as contemporaneous reporting by a hostile secular press. The most readable and comprehensive study is given us by

Father John de Marchi who devoted more than three years in Fatima researching the events which, at the time of his investigation, had occurred less than thirty years earlier. He spoke with a number of witnesses, including family members of the three children and in 1947 his book exhaustively chronicling the Fatima appearances was published. Over three million copies of his book, *The True Story of Fatima*,[1] have been printed. All quotations and page references which follow are to Father de Marchi's book. I would also encourage you to visit the official Fatima website[2] for a much more detailed account of the 1917 events, as well as the earlier 1916 visitations and the subsequent appearances to Lucia.

THE MIRACLE OF THE SUN

Despite the official opposition and even persecution, on October 13, 1917 seventy thousand faithful, unfaithful, skeptics, and press gathered at the site where the little children said a noon miracle was to occur. The entire area was a muddy bog because it had rained continuously the night before and throughout the morning. Of the thousands that gathered, many were there simply to gloat when the promised miracle failed to materialize. They were certain that the whole episode would be revealed as a Catholic fraud.

The rain continued throughout the morning and into early afternoon, beyond the time the Lady had promised the miracle. The fraud was beginning to be apparent. What the crowd failed to realize was that Our Lady speaks in celestial time, not the artificial time increments created by man. The sun didn't reach its zenith until after one o'clock, local time.

By one o'clock the entire area had become a muddy bog. It was then that the rain stopped.

There are numerous contemporary accounts as to what happened next. Some of these accounts are quoted in Father de Marchi's book. The Lisbon newspaper, *O Seculo*, a major Portuguese anti-clerical newspaper, reported in detail the Miracle of the Sun:

> From the height of the road where the people parked their carriages and where many hundreds stood, afraid to brave the muddy soil, we saw the immense multitude turn towards the sun at its highest, free of all clouds. The sun called to mind a plate of dull silver. It could be stared at without the least effort. It did not burn or blind. It seemed that an eclipse was taking

---

1. Available online at https://fatima.org/wp-content/uploads/2017/03/The-True-Story-of-Fatima.pdf.

2. https://fatima.org/.

place. All of a sudden a tremendous shout burst forth, 'Miracle, miracle! Marvel, marvel!'

Before the astonished eyes of the people, whose attitude carried us back to biblical times, and who, white with terror, heads uncovered, gazed at the blue sky, the sun trembled and made some brusque unheard-of-movements beyond all cosmic laws; the sun danced, is the typical expression of the peasants.

> Immediately afterwards the people asked each other if they saw anything and what they had seen. The greatest number avowed that they saw the sun trembling and dancing; others declared that they saw the smiling face of the Blessed Virgin Herself; they swore that the sun turned around on itself as if it were a wheel of fireworks and had fallen almost to the point of burning the earth with its rays. Some said they saw it change colors successively.[3]

Another eyewitness (Dr. Almeida Garrett, professor at the University of Coimbra) gave his account of the events, which took place at "two o'clock wartime or about noon, sun time." His testimony reads, in part:

> The sun had broken jubilantly through the thick layer of clouds just a few moments before. It was shining clearly and intensely. . . . It looked to me as a luminous and brilliant disc, with a bright, well-defined rim. It did not hurt the eyes. The comparison (which I heard while still at Fatima) with a disc of dull silver, did not seem right to me. The color was brighter, far more active and richer than dull silver, with the tinted luster of the orient of a pearl.
>
> Nor did it resemble the moon on a clear night. Everyone saw and felt that it was a body with life. It was not spheric like the moon, neither did it have an equal tonality of color. It looked like a small, brightly polished wheel of iridescent mother-of-pearl. It could not be taken for the sun as though seen through fog. There was no fog at that time (The rain and fog had stopped). The sun was not opaque, veiled or diffused. It gave light and heat and was brightly outlined by a beveled rim. The sky was banked with light clouds, patched with blue here and there. Sometimes the sun stood out alone in rifts of clear sky. The clouds scuttled along from west to east without dimming the sun. They gave the impression of passing behind it, while the white puffs gliding in front of the sun seemed to take on the color of rose or a delicate blue.
>
> It was a wonder that all this time it was possible for us to look at the sun, a blaze of light and burning heat, without any

---

3. Marchi, *True Story of Fatima*, 57.

> pain to the eyes or blinding of the retina. This phenomenon must have lasted about ten minutes, except for two interruptions when the sun darted forth its more refulgent, lightning-like rays that forced us to look away.
>
> The sun had an eccentricity of movement. It was not the scintillation of a celestial body at its highest power. It was rotating upon itself with exceedingly great speed. Suddenly, the people broke out with a cry of extreme anguish. The sun, still rotating, had unloosened itself from the skies and came hurtling towards the earth. This huge fiery millstone threatened to crush us with its weight. It was a dreadful sensation.
>
> During this solar occurrence, the air took on successively different colors. While looking at the sun, I noticed that everything around me darkened. I looked at what was nearby and cast my eyes away towards the horizon. Everything had the color of an amethyst: the sky, the air, everything and everybody. A little oak nearby was casting a heavy purple shadow on the ground.[4]

These are just samples of numerous contemporaneous testimonies. Karl Keating tells how a priest described the Miracle of the Sun as he saw it as a boy from his home in the Azores (a group of Islands in the Atlantic Ocean about 700 miles west of Portugal). Keating tells us, "None of his relations believed him when he explained what he witnessed in the sky. They presumed it was a childish fantasy. Weeks later the accounts from Fatima filtered in, and only then did his family understand that he had been granted a special privilege."[5]

THE HOLY FAMILY

As further reported in Father John de Marchi's account:

> The sun was now pale as the moon. To the left of the sun, Saint Joseph appeared holding in his left arm the Child Jesus. Saint Joseph emerged from the bright clouds only to his chest, sufficient to allow him to raise his right hand and make, together with the Child Jesus, the Sign of the Cross three times over the world. As Saint Joseph did this, Our Lady stood in all Her brilliancy to the right of the sun, dressed in the blue and white robes of Our Lady of the Rosary.

---

4. Marchi, *True Story of Fatima*, 57–59.
5. Keating, *Catholicism and Fundamentalism*, 262.

Meanwhile, Francisco and Jacinta were bathed in the marvelous colors and signs of the sun, and Lucia was privileged to gaze upon Our Lord dressed in red as the Divine Redeemer, blessing the world, as Our Lady had foretold. Like Saint Joseph, He was seen only from His chest up. Beside Him stood Our Lady, dressed now in the purple robes of Our Lady of Sorrows, but without the sword. Finally, the Blessed Virgin appeared again to Lucia in all Her ethereal brightness clothed in the simple brown robes of Mount Carmel.[6]

CONFIRMATION

Then came the follow-up miracle: "As the miracle came to its end and the people arose from the muddy ground, another surprise awaited them. A few minutes before, they had been standing in the pouring rain, soaked to the skin. Now they noticed that their clothes were perfectly dry."[7]

After long study and careful interrogations of many witnesses, the Bishop of Leiria wrote:

> The children long before set the day and hour at which it was to take place. The news spread quickly over the whole of Portugal and although the day was chilly and pouring rain, many thousands of people gathered ... They saw the different manifestations of the sun paying homage to the Queen of Heaven and Earth, who is more radiant than the sun in all its splendor. This phenomenon, which no astronomical observatory registered, was not natural. It was seen by people of all classes, members of the Church and non-Catholics. It was seen by reporters of the principal newspapers and by people many miles away.[8]

EVERYONE WAS ASKING FOR A SIGN AND THEY GOT IT

The Fatima appearances and the contemporaneous records have been merely summarized here and in the next few chapters simply to introduce the reader to Fatima and help him understand how this whole phenomenon

---

6. Marchi, *True Story of Fatima*, 55–56.
7. Marchi, *True Story of Fatima*, 60.
8. Marchi, *True Story of Fatima*, 60.

developed and that it could not have been fabricated to trick the gullible. The Miracle of the Sun and related events were freely given by God so that we may believe. Everyone was asking for a sign and they got it.

Salvation history is rich with examples of God's continuing grace to us all, and Fatima is but one example. Fatima tells us that Mary, the mother of Jesus, lives, and since she lives and interacts with us it can only be at the direction of Jesus. There can be no other conclusion. Without the resurrected Jesus of the Bible, there could have been no Fatima. This little town in Portugal provides unequivocal evidence of the Risen Lord. We just need to open our hearts.

9.1

Our Lady of Fatima

1917: *The First Four Appearances*

October 13, 1917 was the Heavenly Lady's final appearance, and it was then that the Miracle of the Sun occurred, precisely when and where the children said it would. What follows in this chapter is an account of her visits on May 13, June 13, July 13, and August 19. Her visitation on September 13, 1917 is described in the next chapter.

MAY 13—FIRST VISITATION

The Lady first appeared to them on May 13, 1917 after the children had just completed praying the Rosary together. Her appearance was preceded by a bright light. All three of the children saw this shaft of light on two successive occasions, but when she first appeared Francisco did not see or hear her. When Lucia told the Lady that Francisco did not see her, she answered, "Let him say the Rosary and in that way he too will see me." Shortly after he started the Rosary the Lady became visible to him "with almost blinding splendor."

    The Lady told Lucia (age ten) and Jacinta (age seven) that they would go to heaven, but that Francisco (age eight) would first have to say many Rosaries. The Lady also told them, "Say the Rosary every day to earn peace for the world and the end of the war."

Despite a vow of secrecy among the three children not to reveal the visitation, seven-year-old Jacinta could not contain herself and immediately revealed the details to her parents that evening. Francisco and Jacinta were brother and sister, and Francisco confirmed everything Jacinta had said. The next morning, the mother relayed the story to her neighbors, and within a short time circled back to Lucia. She reluctantly affirmed everything Francisco and Jacinta had said. Lucia's mother was much more skeptical and concluded that her daughter was a liar and treated her as such. The story, nevertheless, circulated throughout the village and to the local pastor.

On May 13, the Lady had told the children to appear at the same spot on the 13th day of the month for the next five months, and that she would appear to them through October 13, 1917.

JUNE 13— SECOND VISITATION

On June 13, the children were accompanied by a small contingent from the village and a couple of neighboring towns. The Lady told the children to pray the Rosary, and either on this visitation or the July 13th (or both) to insert the following prayer between the mysteries: "O my Jesus, forgive us our sins, save us from the fires of Hell, lead all souls to Heaven, especially those most in need." This has come to be known as the Fatima Prayer and has been incorporated into the Rosary throughout the world.

Again, following the June 13 apparition, skepticism was the general order of the day—especially on the part of the parish pastor. Lucia was directed by her parents to have a session with the pastor in the hopes of her recanting her stories of the apparitions. The pastor did not believe that the Lady was Our Lady of the Rosary and told her that what she was seeing and hearing could be a trick of the devil.

JULY 13— THIRD VISITATION

The third apparition occurred on July 13. This time a crowd accompanied the children to the Cova da Iria, where the visitations took place. During this visit the Lady provided the children with a graphic image of hell. Lucia later described the vision:

> She opened Her hands again as She had done the two previous months. The light reflecting from them seemed to penetrate into the earth, and we saw as if into a sea of fire, and immersed

in that fire were devils and souls with human form, as if they were transparent black or bronze embers floating in the fire and swayed by the flames that issued from them along with clouds of smoke, falling upon every side just like the falling of sparks in great fires, without weight or equilibrium, amidst wailing and cries of pain and despair that horrified and shook us with terror. We could tell the devils by their horrible and nauseous figures of baleful and unknown animals, but transparent as the black coals in a fire.[1]

To save sinners the Lady said that God wants to establish throughout the world the devotion to Her Immaculate Heart (see chapter 9.3). It was also on this date that Our Lady asked for the Consecration of Russia and the whole issue of what was to become known as the third secret emerged.

Lucia was severely upset about what her pastor had said— that this whole series of events and visitations could be the work of the devil— and so she asked the Lady to tell them who she was and to perform a miracle so that everyone could see that she had appeared to them. The Lady responded, "Continue to come here every month. In October, I will say who I am and what I desire and I will perform a miracle all shall see, so that they believe."

Many within the village had asked the children to petition the Lady for favors and cures. But even when the requests for favors and cures were not going to be granted, the Lady pointed to a higher duty and the need to say the Rosary, "Some I will cure and others not. As to the crippled boy, I will not cure him or take him out of his poverty, but he must say the Rosary every day with his family."

Following the July 13 visitation, all three children continued to be ridiculed and Lucia's life became even more distressing because her mother refused to believe her. Crowds continued to follow the children, with a severe disruption of the parents' agriculture livelihood; their garden was trampled, etc. The children would not reveal most of the messages that the Lady had given them and took comfort among themselves. A few priests believed them, but most did not. The apparitions had been reported in the newspapers and the newspaper accounts accused the children of being duped by priests and heaped ridicule upon the children and those that believed them.

---

1. Marchi, *True Story of Fatima*, 30.

AUGUST 19—FOURTH VISITATION

The fourth apparition occurred on August 19th, not the 13th. Why?

At that time, the village of Fatima was under the jurisdiction of an Administrator, or Chief Magistrate. He had tremendous power. All administrative, political, and sometimes even judicial power was in his control. He had left the Catholic faith as a young man and founded and became head of a Masonic Lodge. He was also a newspaper publisher by which he endeavored to undermine the faith of the people in the Church and its priests.

This was a powerful man with the strength to intimidate and spread terror among the locals. He realized the effects that the apparitions of Fatima might have among the people and that these visitations would strengthen the faith and the Church. He needed to destroy the children's credibility. To keep them from kneeling at the place where the apparitions had taken place (which was always the 13th day of the month) and through plain old trickery he had the children kidnapped on the morning of August 13. He took them to his house and subjected them to intense interrogation. The children spent the night in confinement, and then on the morning of the 14th they were taken to the County House where they were subjected to relentless questioning. Finally, they were incarcerated in jail with criminals and told that they would be thrown into a tank of boiling oil if they did not reveal their lies.

Let us not forget that Jacinta was seven, Francisco was now nine, and Lucia was ten. Later, they were returned to the County House and the threats continued. They were told that the oil was boiling, and one by one—beginning with Jacinta—they were led out and told they would be plunged into boiling oil. Of course, none recanted (How could they? They knew what they had seen and heard) even though each was convinced they would soon be dying a horrible death.

They were eventually released and on August 19, 1917 the children went to the Cova da Iria, the scene of the previous appearances. Again, the Lady appeared, and told them, "I want you to continue to come to the Cova da Iria on the 13th and to continue to say the Rosary every day." She also told them, "In the last month, in October, I shall perform a miracle so that all may believe in My apparitions. If they had not taken you to the village, the miracle would have been greater. Saint Joseph will come with the Baby Jesus to give peace to the world."[2]

Quotations and page references are from *The True Story of Fatima*.

---

2. Marchi, *True Story of Fatima*, 41.

INTRODUCTION TO SEPTEMBER 13

Despite the August 19th terror imposed upon them by the Administrator, the children were not deterred. They followed the Heavenly Lady's instructions and returned to the Cova da Iria on September 13 and it was there at that time and place that the underreported September 13th miracle occurred.

9.2

Our Lady of Fatima

The September 13th Miracle

While Fatima is best known for the October 13, 1917 Miracle of the Sun, most people are unaware of the other Fatima miracles that took place on that date, as described in chapter 9. Even fewer know about the miraculous events of September 13.

Let's return to Fatima. When it came time for the children to leave for the Cova da Iria on September 13th, there were so many people following that Lucia later wrote, "that we could hardly move a step." When they arrived at their usual place, the children started the Rosary with the crowds surrounding them responding. When the Lady appeared to the children, a globe of light appeared before the crowd. This luminous globe was seen by many. One of those present on September 13 was a priest, Monsignor John Quaresma. He came because he didn't know what to believe—whether the children were lying, being duped, hallucinating or telling the truth. Monsignor Quaresma was accompanied by another priest and they chose a spot overlooking Cova da Iria. They could easily see, without coming too close, the place where the children prayed as they waited for the heavenly apparition. Here is his personal account of what he witnessed:

> At noontime, silence fell on the crowd, and a low whispering of prayers could be heard. Suddenly, cries of joy rent the air, many

voices praising the Blessed Virgin. Arms were raised to point to something above, "Look! don't you see?" . . .

"Yes, I see it!"

I, too, raised my eyes to probe the amplitude of the skies, hoping to see what the other more fortunate eyes were seeing before me. There was not a single cloud in the whole blue sky, yet to my great astonishment, I saw clearly and distinctly a luminous globe, coming from the east to the west, gliding slowly and majestically through space. My friend also looked up, and had the happiness of enjoying the same unexpected but enchanting apparition. Suddenly, the globe with its extraordinary light, disappeared before our eyes.

There was a little girl near us, dressed like Lucia and about the same age. She was excited with joy and kept saying, "I still see Her. . .now She is coming down." A few minutes later the child exclaimed again, pointing to the skies, "Now she is rising again," following the globe with her eyes until it disappeared towards the sun.[1]

The priest and his friend were convinced that they had been in the presence of Our Lady and that the three children had seen the Mother of God herself. The priests had been given the grace of seeing the chariot that had borne her from Heaven. Everyone around them had seen the same as they. "For on all sides were heard manifestations of joy and greetings to Our Lady. Some, however, saw nothing; for one good and pious soul nearby wept bitterly for not having seen."

During the apparitions in July, August and September, Our Lady promised the children that the last time she would appear would be in October and that she would effect a miracle that everyone would see and thereby believe. A great miracle was promised to take place at a specific place (Cova da Iria) at a specific time (noon) on a specific date (October 13th). On September 13, 2017, the Lady added, "Our Lord also will come to bless the people. . . ." The stage was being set and we can easily understand why an estimated 70,000 came to see and then witnessed the October 13th miracles.

All quotations and page references are to Father de Marchi's book, *The True Story of Fatima*. As in earlier chapters, I would also encourage you to visit the official Fatima website[2] for a much more detailed account of the 1917 events, as well as the earlier 1916 visitations and subsequent appearances.

1. Marchi, *True Story of Fatima*, 49.
2. https://fatima.org/

9.3

Fatima's Messages of Love

At Fatima, God was pleading for our attention. And he was placing his stamp of approval on the claims of the three innocent children, saying, "Listen to them!"

And what did Our Lady tell them? During her six appearances, the Heavenly Lady delivered a series of messages that continue to resonate today and will forever. While a lot of publicity has been generated as to the various secrets the Lady gave the children and the vision of hell, the central message delivered at all six visitations was direct, profound, and simple: "Pray the Rosary!"

PRAY THE ROSARY

Since praying the Rosary was the nexus of each visit, we need to make certain the reader understands what this devotion is. The Rosary proclaims that Jesus Christ is Lord and Savior. It condenses Salvation History as presaged in the Old Testament and as finally revealed in the New. When we pray the Rosary, we recall and pray the gospel, and we call upon the Lord's Blessed Mother to help us find and keep Jesus in our heart. Of necessity, praying the Rosary involves opening our hearts to Mary, and we can petition the Mother of Jesus, referred to as the Mother of God or the Theotokos, to help us with our individual needs and the needs of those we pray for by asking her to advocate before her Son on our behalf. It is both the simplest and yet the most profound of prayers. As Pope John Paul II tells us in his Apostolic Letter, *Rosarium Virginis Mariae* [*Rosary of the Virgin Mary*], dated October 16, 2002: "With the Rosary, the Christian people sits at the school of Mary and is led to contemplate the beauty on the face of Christ and to experience the depths of his love. Through the Rosary the faithful receive abundant grace, as though from the very hands of the Redeemer."[1]

This message of praying the Rosary probably explains why a great preponderance of non-Catholic Christians ignore Our Lady of Fatima. She tells us to engage in a prayer which they simply do not understand. If more Christians understood how the Rosary could deepen their faith, the news about Our Lady of Fatima would be more widely distributed and with a far greater intensity and accuracy than now is the case.

THE IMMACULATE HEART OF MARY

Sometimes other Christians avoid thinking about Our Lady of Fatima or view her as a fraud because some of her messages or requests seem to fly in the face of their faith tradition. Mary's request for devotion to her Immaculate Heart comes to mind. Devotion to a heart!? And why to Mary's? For many, this is indeed a puzzling request and seems unchristian, wrong, and misdirected.

Here's the brief answer:

Perhaps nothing reveals the loving God more than Mary's request for devotion to her Immaculate Heart. That is because the Immaculate Heart of Mary is pure love. It is love directed toward God the Father, who created all things and sent us His Son. It is love directed toward the Holy Spirit, which in turn is pure love. It is the same Holy Spirit which overshadowed Mary and led to the conception of Jesus. It is love directed to Jesus, her son, who loved so much he was willing to die for us and reposed within her for nine months. It was her blood and nourishment that flowed through her heart and through him. It was his blood that flowed through his heart back to hers. It was not possible for there to be a more intimate and loving communion. Who among us from the beginning of time could possibly have a greater and more intimate relationship with Jesus than his mother? Her love for him is pure and unabated.

This is the Immaculate Heart of Mary—a limitless physical and spiritual love for God with no expectation of receiving anything in return.

---

1. Pope John Paul II, *Rosarium*, par 1.

Unlike the love exchanged between us and Jesus which is the love generated by Jesus toward us, and then our response in love, the love from the Immaculate Heart of Mary to God is a love (insomuch as it is possible) initiated by Mary not as a response but as an uncompelled and unrestrained act. When we devote ourselves to the Immaculate Heart of Mary we join her pure love directed toward God, recognizing that our love flows through and joins Mary in praise and honor. Our devotion does not stop at Mary's heart. There is no fence or barricade terminating its journey. Instead, her soul "proclaims the greatness of the Lord," and we join in that proclamation so that all our love and her love is directed toward God. I suppose one way of expressing the difference is that each of us is a capillary of love and devotion which reaches a central limitless magnifying transmitter, the Blessed Mother. She magnifies and joins our devotion to hers and they become a mighty river coursing towards God.

What a beautiful way to enter and remain in the presence of Jesus! And if she did not instruct the children for a devotion to her Immaculate Heart, then Lucia, Francisco, and Jacinta were some pretty imaginative and astute child theologians, ages seven, nine, and ten.

FATIMA: MESSAGES OF LOVE

We need to look at the totality of messages delivered by our Heavenly Visitor. The complete narratives are available in *The True Story of Fatima*. I urge you to slowly read through these accounts. As you do you will see that what ties all the visitations and messages together is love. Undisguised and profound is its presence.

Finally, you should note that Mary almost always is shown with her hands folded in prayer and holding the rosary. She is directing attention to heaven; she does not want the focus to stop with her, but to continue heavenward— and to Jesus.

The story of Fatima is not complete without referring to some more messages, both explicit and implicit, delivered by the Blessed Virgin. They confirm and strengthen our faith.

- God loves us with an eternal love. His love was so intense that he sent his only begotten son so that whoever believes in him would not perish but have everlasting life. The mere presence of Mary at Fatima and her messages confirm this central doctrine of Christianity.

- God continuously makes himself available to us.

- We cannot understand God and what, why, or how he exists and created us. We can only accept and respond to his love. This is what he expects from us. Mary didn't just appear to the children and say, "Here I am, the mother of our Lord. You should be happy." No, she gave specific instructions as to what they were to do—and they did it. She even told Francisco that he needed to pray many Rosaries. His response was positive and obedient. That is how our relationship with Jesus should be. We know what he did and taught, and now we need to respond.
- Mary showed the three children a vision of hell. It was a gruesome and horrifying sight, thereby confirming what Jesus taught—more than anyone—that hell is very real.

The overarching message conveyed by Our Lady of Fatima was gentleness, love, beauty, and truth. The next time you see the initials GLBT in the news think not of their contemporary meaning but think instead of Our Lady and that all of her and what she represents and proclaims is available to those who are humble and rely upon God. That is not a new message, but it is one we tend to forget. The ancient Jews who relied upon their own resources when they battled the Philistines, the Arabs and others invariably lost. When their king humbled himself before the Lord and did not turn away from him, the Jews would prevail. Why would anything be different now with his new Chosen People?

Most importantly, these visitations give us proof positive that Jesus loves us with an undying commitment for our salvation. If with full knowledge of the facts, you reject or ignore the appearances by the mother of Our Lord who was sent to us help us find and keep Jesus—well, then you're not so smart.

9.4

Our Lady of Fatima

The Effects of Her Appearances

THE HISTORICAL JESUS

It would appear that the September 13 and October 13 phenomena were heaven's way of confirming to the world the appearances by Mary to the three children. Still, the doubts continue. What can we do or say to help others recognize that the appearances by Our Lady of Fatima (also known as Our Lady of the Rosary) were very real and that she is none other than the mother of Jesus? Sometimes the best way, and on occasion the only way, to assess the reality, importance and source of an event is to examine its aftermath and effects—its fruits. A sterling example would be the effects that flowed from the life, death, and resurrection of Jesus. We will examine those first, and then describe the immediate and long-term effects of the visitations at Fatima.

Non-Christians sometimes assert that Jesus never even existed, and that the Gospel accounts are self-serving and not to be trusted. To support their contention, they tell us that there are no non-Christian writers living at the time of Jesus or shortly thereafter that recorded what he said and did. No one said that they reviewed reports about this Nazarene who taught that the Kingdom of God had arrived, that Jesus was crucified and rose from the dead.

That's not quite true.

Jewish and Roman historians and others who lived living shortly after Jesus wrote about a rapidly increasing group called Christians. Paul Barnett's book *Is the New Testament History?* summarizes some of the verified effects of Jesus having lived.

Pliny. Around A.D. 110 an experienced administrator by the name of Pliny was sent by the Roman Emperor Trajan to be governor of Bithynia, a Roman province located just south of the Black Sea. He wrote to the emperor asking what to do about a group called Christians who were becoming powerful and "spreading like a disease." Many had been imprisoned and Pliny wanted advice on how to conduct their trials. What punishments were appropriate? Should the punishments be the same for young and old? Would renunciation of Jesus earn them a pardon? Pliny wrote Trajan that these Christians maintained that they assembled on a fixed day before sunrise and recite a "form of words to Christ as a god." After this their custom was to depart, and to meet again to take food, "but ordinary and harmless food." Some of the prisoners maintained that they had rejected Christ at least 20 years earlier and so were innocent. Barnett concludes: "Based on what Pliny wrote there can be no doubt about the existence in about A.D. 110 of a substantial body of Christians in remote Bithynia. This is a fact of history. But how do we explain this fact? How did they come to be there? Their presence was an historical *effect* for which there was some *cause*. What was it?"[1]

Tacitus. Tacitus was made governor of another Roman province at about the same time Pliny was appointed to Bithynia. Tacitus was also an historian. In his *Annals of Imperial Rome* Tacitus described how the Emperor Nero blamed the Christians for the fire that destroyed Rome in A.D. 64. Tacitus confirmed that "Christus" lived during the time of the Emperor Tiberius; that Pontius Pilate was the Roman governor when Christ died; that he was executed in Judea; that a "deadly superstition" broke out which spread from Judea to Rome. "An arrest was first made of all who confessed, then, upon their information, an immense multitude was convicted, not so much of the crime of arson, as of hatred of the human race."[2] Tacitus, as was the case with Pliny, hated these Christians.

Suetonius. Suetonius lived from A.D. 69–140. Referring to A.D. 49 he writes that, "Since the Jews constantly made disturbances at the instigation of Chrestus, he [Claudius] expelled them from Rome." Suetonius described the Christians as a "class of man given to a new and wicked superstition."[3]

---

1. Barnett, *New Testament History?* 19.
2. Barnett, *New Testament History?* 20–21.
3. Barnett, *New Testament History?* 23.

Josephus. Josephus was a Jewish historian born in A.D. 37. He wrote *Jewish Antiquities*. All scholars agree that Josephus confirmed in his writings that Jesus was called Christ and that his brother James was delivered up by the Jewish authorities and stoned because he had transgressed the law. There is less agreement that he wrote the following passage (the content would be troubling to non-Christians), although it exists in all manuscripts:

> About that time there lived Jesus, a wise man, if indeed one ought to call him a man. For he was one who wrought surprising feats and was a teacher of such people as accept the truth gladly. He won over many Jews and many of the Greeks. He was the Messiah. When Pilate, upon hearing him accused by men of the highest standing among us, had condemned him to be crucified, those who had in the first place come to love him did not give up their affection for him. On the third day he appeared to them restored to life, for the prophets of God had prophesied these and countless other marvelous things about him. And the tribe of the Christians so called after him, has still to this day not disappeared.[4]

Except for Josephus, none of these wrote directly about Christ; they wrote about the effects that Christ had upon others and how his followers within this Jewish sect kept growing despite the horrors and persecutions visited upon them. In view of these non-Christian letters and documents can there be any doubt but that a very real and extraordinary person named Jesus Christ lived. What flowed from Christ's life are undeniable.

Similarly, the effects of Fatima are irrefutable.

EFFECTS OF FATIMA

Fatima tells us that God continues to reveal himself and his teachings through instruments chosen by him, whether the instrument is the mother of Jesus or three small children. Earlier in salvation history, he chose fishermen, uneducated Jews and a tyrant persecuting the Church. All of them labored to help the Savior fulfill his work. Two thousand years ago in ancient Israel he used Mary to introduce God the Son to the world. He continues to use her as a doorway to his love. She in turn uses the most humble and simplest of human instruments to evangelize with hard proofs and evidence for even the most skeptical—if they open their hearts. Fatima tells us that in 1917 the door to heaven was opened and, using the instrumentality of Mary,

---

4. Barnett, *New Testament History?* 28.

God said, "Here I am. Open your eyes and your hearts!" Although Fatima was a private revelation, it was made in a very public setting. Her appearances and messages quite simply should help some find belief and others to sustain it. Let's see if she was successful.

- The lives of three illiterate and pious children were changed forever as foretold by Mary. After October 13, 1917 Jacinta was interested only in prayer for the conversion of sinners. She wanted to make herself like Jesus and suffered very much. She never complained, accepting the suffering with happiness for she believed it would help many souls escape the terrible fire of hell. She died in 1920 at the age of nine. Francisco's only desire was to console Our Lord and Our Lady who seemed so sorrowful because of the ingratitude and sins of man. After Fatima he would devote the greater part of each day in church praying the Rosary. His last request was to receive his first communion. He died in 1919 at the age of ten. Lucia became a nun and lived to the age of ninety-seven. She died in 2005 and her story has brought the wonder of God to millions.

- A focus on the apparitions and what they mean have continued unabated since 1917. Jesus reveals himself to those who are searching and, in this day of the internet and easy access to information, failure to know Jesus and his continuing search for us is inexcusable and means that we just don't care enough about the love God has given us and asks from us in return.

- Millions have been brought to Jesus Christ, either by an outright conversion or a deepening of their faith.

- Our Lady of Fatima requested that a chapel be built in her honor. The civil authorities were opposed to the construction of a chapel. Nevertheless, from the offerings made to the children a small chapel was constructed in 1917–1918. On March 6, 1922 two bombs were planted, one in the chapel and the other at the holm oak tree where the Lady had appeared. The roof of the chapel was blown off, but the bomb at the oak tree failed to explode.[5] By 1958 and after twenty-five years of construction, Our Lady of Fatima Basilica was completed and consecrated. Then, on October 12, 2007 the Church of the Most Holy Trinity[6] was consecrated and is reported to be the eighth largest Christian church in the world. As is always the case, the honor

---

5. Marchi, *True Story of Fatima*, 77.
6. *Wikipedia*, "Basilica of the Holy Trinity."

accorded to Mary gathered itself, was magnified and found its real destination—the Holy Trinity.

- Fatima is a major shrine where millions of faithful and not so faithful flock every year and from whence even more millions of faithful depart. The little chapel that was constructed immediately following the appearances in 1917 is today a basilica with a central tower 213 feet high, flanked by colonnades linking it with convent and hospital buildings.

Maybe one of Fatima's effects will be your conversion or the strengthening of your faith—or someone you love.

9.5

Fatima and Islam

FATIMA'S GENESIS

The story of Fatima did not begin in 1917. It began some 700 years earlier, and possibly reflects a deeper underlying significance of why Our Lady appeared in Fatima. And this history reveals the possibility that Our Lady of Fatima may eventually (or maybe even now) be an instrument to convert Muslims to Christianity. You be the judge of what God's amazing grace can do.

Fatima is the name of the Islamic prophet Muhammad's favorite daughter. Consequently, many Muslim women are named Fatima. In the late 1100's a party of Moorish (Muslim) occupiers were ambushed and taken captive. The prisoners included a young woman whose name was Fatima and they were taken to the Portuguese king in Santarem, which is about 40 miles south of the present site of Fatima.

The leader of the Christian knights fell in love with her. She converted to Christianity and, with the king's permission and blessing, was joined in marriage to the knight. She was given the name Oureana—the Golden One. The king's wedding gift was a village which was then renamed Oureana in her honor (now known as Ourem, located about 6 miles northeast of Fatima).

Oureana died young and her grieving husband eventually had her body moved, and there he built a small commemorative chapel which (probably because her Christian name had already been used to rename the village) became known by her former Muslim name, Fatima. And this is where, in 1917, Our Lady of Fatima appeared.

One more important detail: Of all women, Islam considers Mary to be the most favored by God. As quoted by Monsignor Pope on October 12, 2015, Archbishop Sheen tells us that the Koran:

> has many passages concerning the Blessed Virgin. First of all, the Koran believes in her Immaculate Conception, and also, in her Virgin Birth ... The Koran also has verses on the Annunciation, Visitation, and Nativity. Angels are pictured as accompanying the Blessed Mother and saying, Oh Mary, God has chosen you and purified you, and elected you above all the women of the earth. In the 19th chapter of the Koran there are 41 verses on Jesus and Mary. There is such a strong defense of the virginity of Mary here that the Koran in the fourth book, attributes the condemnation of the Jews to their monstrous calumny against the Virgin Mary.[1]

The name, Our Lady of Fatima, takes on a completely different meaning and significance when we understand that Fatima is more than a place. She is Our Lady for both Christians and Muslims, and Muslims already know about and revere Mary. Is it possible that Our Lady of Fatima may be a bridge from Islam to Christianity? If you are a skeptic, please consider the possibility that God knows what he is doing, even if his timeline does not match yours. As Archbishop Sheen tells us, "Since nothing ever happens out of Heaven except with a finesse of all details, I believe that the Blessed Virgin chose to be known as 'Our Lady of Fatima' as pledge and a sign of hope to the Moslem people, and as an assurance that they, who show her so much respect, will one day accept her divine Son too."[2]

FINDING JESUS

In view of the overwhelmingly credible stories about Fatima, how is it possible to dismiss the Incarnation, Passion and Resurrection? Once again, just as she did in Bethlehem, Mary presents Jesus to the world. When we turn towards Mary we turn toward her son. She does not divert. She magnifies. She delivers. God has written his love and commandments into all our hearts and he is asking us to open the door for him. He has commissioned the Blessed Virgin to help in this task. Maybe she can deliver Islam to Christ.

---

1. Pope, "Fatima," sixth par.
2. Pope, "Fatima," sixth par.

9.6

Our Lady of Fatima

The Floundering Skeptic

Nonbelievers maintain that all the events of Fatima can be explained as an elaborate hoax, sundogs, unusual weather, atmospheric anomalies, other natural phenomena, mass hysteria, optical effects caused by prolonged staring at the sun, retinal distortion, collective hallucination, or other psychological trickery such as people submitting to the power of suggestion.

As you read the complete story of Fatima it should be apparent that none of these explanations, either separately or together, can account for what occurred. For example, beginning in July 1917 the three children, ages seven, nine, and ten, said that the Heavenly Lady told them she would effect a miracle on a specific date (October 13th) at a specific site (the Cova da Iria where the apparitions took place), and at a specific time (noon). At noon on October 13th at the Cova da Iria the historical event we call the Miracle of the Sun occurred, just as the children had said. Indeed, the fulfillment of the children's prediction is itself a miracle. If you are a nonbeliever, please explain how they came by this specific knowledge of future events unless the Heavenly Lady told them.

This foretelling by the three children is ignored (and indeed must be ignored) by those attacking Fatima. Another event on that October 13th ignored by the nonbelievers is the instantaneous drying of water-soaked clothing by the witnesses.

When you read websites and books offering naturalistic explanations you will find they are full of misstatements and false and incomplete narratives of the events—all manipulated to fit whatever naturalistic explanation is being proposed.

Another tactic is to throw Fatima into the same barrel as the hundreds of other purported visions of Mary and other heavenly beings, including Jesus, that are obviously ridiculous such as the image of Mary on a piece of bread, or a melted candle, or a darkened oval knot in a wooden fence that looked like Mary, or a reflection on a window pane that resembles the typical representation of Mary. These are, of course, quite irrelevant to Fatima's legitimacy. Their intent is merely to mock and thereby delegitimize all things supernatural.

Once you scratch the surface of these anti-Fatima websites you see how their arguments are not really arguments, but conclusions clothed in the garb of arguments. For the most part the conclusions/arguments are premised upon a false narrative (I'm not sure for any particular article or website whether the misstatements are intentional or reflect shoddy research) of what occurred at Fatima. Be sure to google the sites that try to belittle or naturalistically explain Fatima. Try using the search words: Fatima hoax; Fatima fraud; etc. Be alert to false narratives, and when you are finished and thoroughly discouraged, come back here and read the chapters on Fatima.

The truth is that the good-faith skeptic does not understand the complete story of what happened at Fatima. Once understood, the skeptic or unbeliever must flounder and resort to explanations that cannot possibly explain Fatima. And if he can delude himself into believing he has a rational explanation for the Miracle of Sun, he still must cope with the September 13th heavenly visitation witnessed by others. Of course, the ultimate fallback position is that we may not understand now, but someday we will. When all the non-miracle explanations are exhausted and the atheist is still arguing against Fatima you can be sure he is not interested in the truth; he is interested only in winning a debate. As everyone agrees, on October 13, 1917 something incredibly spectacular and other-worldly occurred. Mass hysteria, suggestion, or atmospheric or cosmological events are illusory explanations and have no substance. What was witnessed was a special vision (not a natural event) granted to those present at the site, and even to some many miles away—even seven hundred miles on an island in the Atlantic Ocean.

How about that!

10

Our Lady of Lourdes

The village of Lourdes, France is famous as a place of miraculous healings. On February 11, 1858, fourteen-year-old Bernadette Soubirous said that a Heavenly Lady appeared to her in a grotto near this remote town at the foot of the Pyrenees Mountains. There were a total of eighteen apparitions, and she alone was able to see and hear them. The heavenly visitor was Mary, and she told Bernadette to scratch out a spring, ask the parish priest to build a church, and requested processions. Bernadette did all this, the priest eventually complied, and the processions began. Out of this spring flowed clear running water, followed by thousands of miraculous healings. The processions continue to this day—as do the miraculous cures.

MIRACULOUS HEALINGS AND LOURDES

There have been literally thousands of cures at Lourdes which can only be described as scientifically and medically inexplicable, but only seventy have been declared miraculous by the Catholic Church. Claimed cures are most rigidly examined by a commission of physicians and scientists who operate with great caution and circumspection. The alleged cure must be immediate and permanent to be regarded as a miracle. Medical records prior to the trip are studied, as well as the patient's subsequent medical history.

The examination and evidence gathering may continue for years, and even decades. Very few cures stand up against these rigid tests or even begin the process of verification, but there are uncounted more that have never been subjected to a controlled analysis. We do not know how many cures can be considered miraculous, but all it takes is just one to demonstrate the loving hand of God.

Did the Blessed Virgin Mary appear to Bernadette or did this little French girl hallucinate or concoct a series of intricate lies for reasons unknown? The miracle themselves should answer that question, and four of them are discussed in chapters 18.1 through 18.3 and chapter 18.5. But if you are on the fence, it might be helpful to visit 1858 Lourdes and see if there is any confirming evidence. Are Bernadette's actions and demeanor consistent with the visions she claimed, or would they also make sense in the context of hallucinations or an elaborate hoax? Are there witnesses who can be described as objective, even skeptical, that can provide us with unbiased contemporaneous reports? There are, and one in particular is Jean-Baptiste Estrade.

JEAN-BAPTISTE ESTRADE

Jean-Baptiste Estrade was a government employee living in 1858 Lourdes. He oversaw the tax division responsible for collecting certain taxes and knew the police commissioner well. In fact, Estrade lived on the second floor of a building and above the police commissioner's residence. They were friends. Estrade belonged to a men's club consisting of local dignitaries. Shortly after Bernadette's first vision members began to hear of the extraordinary claims Bernadette was making. The local common folk tended to believe her, but Estrade and his friends knew better. These were simply superstitious tales believed by the unsophisticated. Nevertheless, as the days progressed and after Bernadette's sixth vision, Estrade and some others decided to join villagers who followed Bernadette to the grotto or were already there in anticipation of the heavenly lady's appearance. Estrade and his friends thought the whole affair was a child's delusion and wished to see for themselves why anyone would believe such outrageous claims.

TUESDAY, FEBRUARY 23; THE SEVENTH APPEARANCE

Bernadette arrived shortly after 6 a.m., and here is how Estrade described the event:

We men made use of our elbows and cleared a way to the little girl's side. From this moment she was under our closest observation; our eyes were riveted upon her and did not leave her for an instant.

Bernadette knelt down, took her rosary out of her pocket and made a profound reverence. She did it all without the least shade of awkwardness or self-consciousness, just as simply and naturally as of she had gone into the parish church for her ordinary devotions. Whilst she was passing the beads between her fingers she looked up towards the rock as though waiting for something. Suddenly, as in a flash of lightning, an expression of wonder illuminated her face and she seemed to be born into another life. A light shone in her eyes; wonderful smiles played upon her lips; an unutterable grace transformed her whole being. The seer's soul within the narrow prison of the flesh seemed to be trying to reveal itself to the outward sight and to proclaim its joy and happiness. Bernadette was no longer Bernadette; she was one of those privileged beings, the face all glorious with the glory of heaven, whom the Apostle of the great visions has shown us in ecstasy before the throne of the Lamb.[1]

And we men who stood there, spontaneously, without a thought of our dignity, took off our hats and bent our knees even as the humblest peasant women. The time of argument and discussion was past for ever, and we, like all those present at this heavenly scene, looked from the ecstatic to the rock and from the rock to the ecstatic. We saw nothing, we heard nothing, but what we could and did see and understand was that a conversation was going on between the mysterious Lady and the child upon whom our gaze was fixed.

After the first transports of joy caused by the Lady's arrival the seer's attitude was that of a listener. Her movements and gestures and the play of her features quickly gave evidence of all the characteristics of a conversation. Sometimes smiling, sometimes grave, at one time the child would show her approval by an inclination of the head, at another she would appear to be asking a question. When the Lady spoke a thrill of joy seemed to convulse the girl's body; when on the contrary Bernadette made a request she would bow herself down to the ground and

---

1. During the fifth apparition on February 20 Bernadette's mother accompanied the girl to the grotto for the second time. As was the case when her mother was present at the preceding visitation, she was stunned by the change in her daughter's appearance during her ecstasy, "A superhuman grace transfigured all her movements and her own mother, who was kneeling at her side, said with tears of emotion, 'I must be out of my mind, for I simply can't recognize my daughter.'" Estrade, *Appearances*, 53–54.

be moved almost to tears. We could see that at certain moments the conversation was broken off, and then the child would return to her rosary but with eyes still fixed upon the rock. She seemed afraid to lower her eyes lest she should lose the vision of the ravishing object which she contemplated.

* * * * *

The ecstasy lasted for an hour; at the end of that time the seer went on her knees from the place where she was praying to just below the wild rose tree hanging from the rock. There, concentrating all her energies as for an act of worship, she kissed the earth and returned still upon here knees to the place which she had just left. A last glow of light lit up her face, then gradually, almost imperceptibly, the transfiguring glory of the ecstasy grew fainter and finally disappeared. The seer continued praying for a few moments longer but it was only the face of the little peasant child which we saw. At last Bernadette got up, went to her mother, and was lost in the crowd.

After the scene which I have just described I felt like one in a dream and I left the grotto without remembering the ladies for whom I was responsible. I could not shake off my emotion and a crowd of thoughts invaded my soul. The Lady of the rock might hide herself from my bodily eyes, but I had felt her presence and I was convinced that she had looked on me with maternal love. It was indeed a solemn hour of my life and deeply was I moved to think that I, the omniscient and superior person who had mocked and scoffed at such things had been allowed to come so near to the Queen of Heaven.[2]

Estrade was no longer a skeptic. He knew that the visions were real and immediately began recording his observations. He gathered statements from other witnesses and became close friends and a confidant of Bernadette. He sat in on the interrogation conducted by the police commissioner and recorded word by word the questions and Bernadette's answers. Over the years he continued speaking to those who had been in 1858 Lourdes. Estrade had no intention of publishing this material; he was only gathering it for his own personal edification. Forty years later, at the importuning of the local clergy, he reluctantly gathered his notes and thoughts and, in 1899 at the age of seventy-eight, completed his manuscript, *The Appearances of the Blessed Virgin Mary at the Grotto of Lourdes: Personal Souvenirs of an Eyewitness*. Estrade died in 1909.

2. Estrade, *Appearances*, 75–77.

Estrade was an eyewitness and otherwise uniquely qualified to provide the most complete and detailed description of the events surrounding the eighteen appearances by the Blessed Virgin Mary from February 11 to July 16. As we explore some of the evidence and details of a few of the visitations ask yourself whether Bernadette's actions and demeanor could be anything but her reaction to what she saw and heard. Any honest reading must conclude that they are neither fabrications nor hallucinations. When you consider the events of 1858 along with the subsequent miraculous healings it is certain that Mary lives and continues to guide us to Jesus.

THURSDAY, FEBRUARY 11: THE FIRST APPEARANCE

The Lady's initial appearance was quite unexpected. On February 11, 1858, Bernadette, along with Toinette, her eleven-year-old sister, and a friend, Jeanne Abadie, set off to gather firewood. When they came to the Gave River, Toinette and Jeanne decided to search for firewood on the other side. Bernadette was asthmatic and while the current was not strong, the river was cold and she feared an asthma attack. Her two companions crossed the Gave and picked up some firewood near the Massabielle grotto and then walked along the river away from the grotto searching for more. Bernadette then decided to cross the river and had begun to take off her stockings when she heard a noise "like the sound of a storm."

> I looked to the right, to the left, under the trees of the river, but nothing moved; I thought I was mistaken. I went on taking off my shoes and stockings, when I heard a fresh noise like the first. Then I was frightened and stood straight up. I lost all power of speech and thought when, turning my head towards the grotto, I saw at one of the openings of the rock a bush, one only, moving as if it were very windy. Almost at the same time there came out of the interior of the grotto a golden-coloured cloud, and soon after a Lady, young and beautiful, exceedingly beautiful, the like of whom I had never seen, came and placed herself at the entrance of the opening above the bush. She looked at me immediately, smiled at me and signed to me to advance, as if she had been my mother. All fear had left me but I seemed to know no longer where I was. I rubbed my eyes, I shut them, I opened them; but the Lady was still there continuing to smile at me an making me understand that I was not mistaken. Without thinking of what I was doing I took my rosary in my hands and went on my knees. The Lady made with her head a sign of approval and herself took into her hands a rosary which hung on

her right arm. When I attempted to begin the rosary and tried to lift my hand to my forehead my arm remained paralysed, and it was only after the Lady had signed herself [made the sign of the cross] that I could do the same. The Lady left me to pray all alone; she passed the beads of her rosary between her fingers but she said nothing; only at the end of each decade did she say the 'Gloria'[3] with me.

When the recitation of the rosary was finished the Lady returned to the interior of the rock and the golden cloud disappeared with her.[4]

As soon as the Lady disappeared, Toinette and Jeanne Abadie returned to find Bernadette still on her knees where they had left her. The mocked her, but later as they returned home she told them what had happened, but only against a vow of secrecy. Naturally, the young sister told their mother who said they were illusions and instructed Bernadette not to return to Massabielle.

An interesting detail is that except for the Glory Be, the Lady did not articulate the words of the Rosary with Bernadette. She merely passed the rosary beads through her fingers in synchrony with the girl. The only prayer the Lady verbalized was the Glory Be, which praises the Father, Son, and Holy Spirit. The other prayers in the Rosary would have been the Hail Mary and the Our Father (the Lord's Prayer). It takes no great imagination to understand that she would not be praying to herself and that she would have no need for the Lord's Prayer as she was already in heaven in the presence of the Father. It stretches common sense to believe that the fourteen-year-old Bernadette who could barely read and write would have mendaciously crafted these theological details.

When Bernadette's companions returned, she was still on her knees at the spot where they had left her. Remaining in a kneeling position for some twenty to thirty minutes (generally the length of time to pray the Rosary) while on a mission to find firewood seems a bit strange.

While space does not permit a detailed account for each of the other seventeen visions, I would like to draw your attention to several appearances which are particularly important. I strongly urge you to read Estrade's book, which is readily available online[5] for a summary of his background and a more complete description of all eighteen visitations.

3. This is known as the "Glory Be" and is repeated six times in the Rosary. "Glory be to the Father, and to the Son, and to the Holy Spirit. As it was in the beginning, is now, and ever shall be, world without end. Amen."

4. Estrade, *Appearances*, 34–35.

5. https://archive.org/stream/appearanceofmaryooestruoft?ref=ol#mode/2up?ref=ol.

DRINK AT THE SPRING

During the ninth appearance on February 25, Bernadette was kneeling in prayer, got up, and took two or three steps toward the Gave River.

> Suddenly she stopped abruptly, looked behind her as one who hears herself called, and listened to words which seemed to come to her from the side of the rock. She made a sign of assent, began to walk once more, but towards the grotto this time, not towards the Gave, to the left corner of the evacuations. After having gone about three-quarters of the way she stopped and cast a troubled look around. She raised her head as though to question the Lady; then she resolutely bent down and began to scratch the earth. The little cavity which she hollowed out became full of water; after having waited a moment she drank of it and washed her face; she also took a blade of grass which grew on the soil and raised it to her mouth. All the spectators followed the phases of this strange scene with a painful feeling and a sort of stupor. When the child raised herself to return to her place here face was still smeared with muddy water. Seeing this a cry of disappointment and pity rose from the lips of all: "Bernadette is out of her mind! The poor child has become insane!"
>
> Bernadette returned to her place without seeming moved and even without taking notice of the exclamations sounding in her ears. After her face had been cleaned she resumed her contemplation of the heavenly vision, happier than ever, and with an angelic smile upon her lips.[6]

Estrade and indeed the entire crowd thought they had been duped or, at best, the child was hallucinating or insane. Later, she was asked to explain her bizarre actions. Bernadette replied:

> "Whilst I was in prayer, the Lady said to me in a friendly but serious voice, 'Go, drink and wash in the fountain.' As I did not know where this fountain was, and *as I did not think the matter important,* I went towards the Gave. The Lady called me back and signed to me with her finger to go under the grotto to the left; I obeyed but I did not see any water. Not knowing where to get it from, I scratched the earth and the water came. I let it get a little clear of mud, then I drank and washed."
>
> "You also ate some grass. Why did you do that?"

---

6. Estrade, *Appearances*, 82.

"I do not know. The Lady urged me to it by an interior impulse."[7]

By the afternoon the muddy rut started flowing, first as a trickle, then a small stream flowing to the river. The next day the abundant fountain was flowing from Bernadette's muddy dig. It continues today and is the focal point for pilgrims and those seeking a miraculous cure.

THE IMMACULATE CONCEPTION

During the eleventh appearance on February 27 the Lady told Bernadette to tell the priests to build a chapel at the scene of the appearances. The village priest, Father Peyramale, had heard of these visitations but did not believe. Bernadette said that she was actually afraid of him; apparently he had a rough manner and could be quite intimidating. Bernadette gave the message to the Father and he asked Bernadette who this mysterious lady was. Bernadette said she did not know, and Peyramale told Bernadette to find out because he doesn't deal with people he doesn't know.

The Lady would not identify herself and, instead, on March 1 added to her request for a chapel to be built, by saying that she wished people to come in procession. The next day Bernadette again approached Father Peyramale to convey the Lady's request for a chapel, now augmented by asking for processions. Same result. Peyramale again said he must know her identity.

That is where matters stood until the sixteenth apparition on March 25. This day is precisely nine months before Christmas and is celebrated as the day the Angel Gabriel appeared to Mary. At the Annunciation, Mary said "yes" and would agree to bear the Son of God. Precisely nine months later, Jesus was born. In 1854, four years before the Lourdes visitations, the Catholic Church had infallibly proclaimed that Mary was free from original sin from the moment of her conception. This is known as the Immaculate Conception.

Bernadette tells us what happened during that sixteenth visitation. While on her knees and after pouring out her heart to the Lady she took up her rosary.

> Whilst I was praying, the thought of asking her name came before my mind with such persistence that I could think of nothing else. I feared to be presumptuous in repeating a question she had always refused to answer and yet something compelled me to speak. At last, under an irresistible impulsion, the words

7. Estrade, *Appearances*, 83–84.

fell from my mouth, and I begged the Lady to tell me who she was. The Lady did as she had always done before; she bowed her head and smiled but did not reply. I cannot say why, but I felt myself bolder and asked her again to graciously tell me her name; however, she only bowed and smiled as before, still remaining silent. Then once more, for the third time, clasping my hands and confessing myself unworthy of the favour I was asking her, I again made my request.

When the child reached this point in her story she was overcome by emotion. She continued as follows:

"The Lady was standing above the rose-tree, in a position very similar to that shown in the miraculous medal. At my third request her face became very serious and she seemed to bow down in an attitude of humility. Then she joined her hands and raised them to her breast . . . she looked up to heaven . . . then slowly opening her hands and leaning forward towards me, she said to me in a voice vibrating with emotion,

"'I AM THE IMMACULATE CONCEPTION'"

In pronouncing these last words, Bernadette lowered her head and and reproduced the Lady's gesture.[8]

Bernadette had no idea what these words meant, but she knew it referred somehow to the Blessed Virgin Mary. She told Father Peyramale. The chapel was built, and processions have continued to this day.

The foregoing is but a summary of the highlights from the eighteen visitations. There are many more incredible details and I again encourage you to read Estrade's account.

LIFE AFTER LOURDES

Bernadette reaped no earthly rewards because of these visions. Following the events at Lourdes in 1858, Bernadette became a nun and lived a life of suffering and pain. Her vocation was to pray. The Virgin had said to Bernadette: "I promise to make you happy, not in this world, but in the next." These words of the Virgin were fulfilled fully in our saint. She suffered much during her life until her death at the age of thirty-five.

---

8. Estrade, *Appearances*, 122–123.

POSTSCRIPT

Clearly, the Lady of Lourdes was the Mother of God, sent or sanctioned by Jesus to bring all of us closer to him. The miraculous spring still flows in Lourdes and people come by the millions each year.

This is the story of Bernadette and Lourdes, but, as you will see in chapters 18–18.3 and 18.5, it was just the beginning.

THE VILLAGE OF ST. BERNADETTE

In 1959 Andy Williams recorded *The Village of St. Bernadette*[9]. It reached #7 on the Billboard music chart. I wonder how popular this song would be if released today?

DESCRIPTIONS OF THE APPROVED SEVENTY MIRACULOUS CURES

- **Miracles one through sixty-seven.** http://www.miraclehunter.com/marian_apparitions/approved_apparitions/lourdes/miracles1.html
- **Miracle sixty-eight.** https://fsspx.news/en/news-events/news/france-official-recognition-68th-miracle-lourdes-22600
- **Miracle sixty-nine.** https://www.catholicnewsagency.com/news/lourdes-officially-records-69th-miracle
- **Miracle seventy.** https://www.catholicnewsagency.com/news/its-a-miracle-lourdes-healing-officially-declared-supernatural-84194

---

9. https://www.youtube.com/watch?v=vYRL5sJLFfY

11

Our Lady of Knock

At Lourdes and Fatima, the Blessed Virgin appeared on multiple occasions to one or a few children. She spoke and gave them messages. But just when you think you have it all figured out, along comes the 1879 silent apparition of Mary, Joseph, and John witnessed by fourteen Irish villagers living in Knock, Ireland.

When we first examine this event, it is a bit troubling. Apparently, there are no messages. Yet, as we explore with more intensity, the messages delivered by this visitation subtly begin to emerge. As you meditate upon them, they become quite profound.

THE VISITATION

The following summary is taken from the depositions of fifteen villagers in October 1879. Apart from those villagers who were still alive in 1936 at the time of the second official investigation into the events that took place on the evening of August 21, 1879, we don't know what happened to them. Certainly nothing extraordinary. Apparently, they just continued to live their lives the same way everybody else did at that time in rural Ireland.

The Knock apparition began at about 7 p.m. or a little later when Mary McLoughlin (age forty-five), the housekeeper to the parish priest, Father

Cavanagh, was passing by the chapel. It was still light and she noticed some "strange figures or appearances" at the south gable (A gable is the triangle wall just under where two sloping roofs join). These figures appeared to be the Blessed Virgin Mary, St Joseph, an unidentified bishop and an altar. She thought the priest had obtained them and left them outside. She saw a white light "about them" and thought it all a bit strange but didn't give it much thought and continued to the widow Byrne's house where, among others, the widow Byrne's daughter Mary Byrne (age twenty-nine) was present.

In the meantime, and at around 7:30 p.m. and when it was still light, Margaret Byrne (age twenty-one), the sister of Mary Byrne, went to the chapel and locked it. Upon returning home she noticed something luminous or bright at the south gable. She did not pay much attention and continued home.

McLoughlin stayed at the widow Byrne's house for about one-half hour or so and then returned to the Parish priest's house accompanied by Mary Byrne. As they approached the chapel the two women saw the figures. They stopped just west of the school at a ditch and a low wall, about thirty yards south of the figures. After gazing for a while Mary Byrne returned to her mother's house to tell others. Mary McLoughlin remained at the scene. McLoughlin stated that "It was now about a quarter past eight o'clock, and beginning to be quite dark. The sun had set; it was raining at the time."

News of the apparition spread and within a short time about fourteen witnesses were gathered around the ditch or wall fronting the gable. Evening and darkness fell, and it was raining. Later, during the investigation, these witnesses described in varying detail what happened and what they saw. The most detailed description comes from eleven-year-old Patrick Hill (It seems that the best witnesses to any event are boys between the ages of nine and twelve. It was no different in 1879 Knock).

> I am Patrick Hill; I live in Claremorris; my aunt lives at Knock; I remember the 21st August last; on that day I was drawing home turf, or peat, from the bog on an ass.
>
> While at my aunt's at about eight o'clock in the evening, Dominick Byrne came into the house; he cried out: 'Come up to the chapel and see the miraculous lights, and the beautiful visions that are to be seen there'. I followed him; another man by name Dominick Byrne, and John Durkan, and a small boy named John Curry, came with me; we were all together; we ran over towards the chapel.
>
> When we, running southwest, came so far from the village that on our turning, the gable came into view, we immediately beheld the lights; a clear white light, covering most of the gable,

from the ground up to the window and higher. It was a kind of changing bright light, going sometimes up high and again not so high. We saw the figures— the Blessed Virgin, St. Joseph and St. John, and an altar with a Lamb on the altar, and a cross behind the lamb.

At this time we reached as far as the wall fronting the gable: there were other people there before me; some of them were praying, some not; all were looking at the vision; they were leaning over the wall or ditch, with their arms resting on top. I saw the figures and brightness; the boy, John Curry, from behind the wall could not see them; but I did; and he asked me to lift him up till he could see the "grand babies," as he called the figures.

It was raining. Some, amongst them Mary McLoughlin, who beheld what I now saw, had gone away; others were coming. After we prayed a while I thought it right to go across the wall and into the chapel yard. I brought little Curry with me; I went then up closer; I saw everything distinctly. The figures were full and round as if they had a body and life; they said nothing; but as we approached they seemed to go back a little towards the gable.

I distinctly beheld the Blessed Virgin Mary, life size, standing about two feet or so above the ground clothed in white robes which were fastened at the neck. Her hands were raised to the height of the shoulders, as if in prayer, with the palms facing one another, but slanting inwards towards the face; the palms were not turned towards the people, but facing each other as I have described; she appeared to be praying; her eyes were turned as I saw towards heaven.

She wore a brilliant crown on her head, and over the forehead where the crown filled the brow, a beautiful rose; the crown appeared brilliant, and of a golden brightness, of a deeper hue, inclined to a mellow yellow, than the striking whiteness of the robes she wore; the upper parts of the crown appeared to be a series of sparkles, or glittering crosses. I saw her eyes, the balls, the pupils and the iris of each. (The boy did not know the special names for those parts of the eye, but he pointed to them, and described then in his own way).

I noticed her hands especially, and face, her appearance.

The robes came only as far as the ankles; I saw her feet and the ankles; one foot, the right, was slightly in advance of the other.

At times she appeared, and all the figures appeared, to move out and again to go backwards; I saw them move; she did not speak; I went up very near; one old woman went up and embraced the Virgin's feet., and she found nothing in her arms and hands; they receded, she said, from her.

I saw St. Joseph to the Blessed Virgin's right hand; his head was bent, from the shoulders, forward; he appeared to be paying his respects; I noticed his whiskers; they appeared slightly grey; there was a line or dark mearing between the figure of the Blessed Virgin and the spot where he stood. I saw the feet of St. Joseph, too. His hands were joined like a person at prayer. The third figure that stood before me was that of St. John the Evangelist. He stood erect at the side of the altar, and at an angle with the figure of the Blessed Virgin, so that his back was not turned to the altar, nor to the Mother of God. His right arm was at an angle with a line drawn across from St. Joseph to where Our Blessed Lady appeared to be standing.

St. John was dressed like a bishop preaching; he wore a small mitre on his head; he held a Mass Book, or a Book of Gospels, in his left hand; the right hand was raised to the elevation of the head; while he kept the index finger and the middle finger of the right hand raised; the other three fingers of the same hand were shut; he appeared as if he were preaching, but I heard no voice; I came so near that I looked into the book. I saw the lines and the letters. St. John did not wear any sandals.

His left hand was turned towards the altar that was behind him; the altar was a plain one, like any ordinary altar, without any ornaments. On the altar stood a lamb, the size of a lamb eight weeks old—the face of the lamb was fronting the west, and looking in the direction of the Blessed Virgin and St. Joseph.

Behind the lamb a large cross was placed erect or perpendicular on the altar. Around the Lamb I saw angels hovering during the whole time, for the space of one hour and a half or longer; I saw their wings fluttering, but I did not perceive their heads or faces, which were not turned to me.

For the space of an hour and a half we were under the pouring rain; at this time I was very wet; I noticed that the rain did not wet the figures which appeared before me, although I was wet myself. I went away then.

Patrick Hill said that an old lady approached the figure to embrace the Blessed Virgin's feet. This would have been Bridget Trench, age seventy-four. She reported:

I went in immediately to kiss, as I thought, the feet of the Blessed Virgin, but I felt nothing in the embrace but the wall, and I wondered why I could not feel with my hands the figures which I had so plainly and so distinctly seen. . . .

It was raining very heavily at the time, but no rain fell where the figures were. I felt the ground carefully with my hands and it was perfectly dry. The wind was blowing from the south, right against the gable of the chapel, but no rain fell on that portion of the gable or chapel in which the figures were.

The fifteenth recorded witness was Patrick Walsh who was about one-half mile from the chapel that evening. His deposition reads:

My name is Patrick Walsh; I live in Ballinderrig, an English mile from the chapel at Knock. I remember well the 21st August, 1879. It was a very dark night, it was raining heavily. About nine o'clock on that night I was going on some business through my land, and standing a distance of about half a mile from the chapel; I saw a very bright light on the southern gable end of the chapel; it appeared to me to be a large globe of golden light; I never saw, I thought, so brilliant a light before; it appeared high up in the air above and around the chapel gable and it was circular in its appearance; it was quiet stationary, and it seemed to retain the same brilliancy all through.

The above is a summary of what occurred that evening. The complete testimony of all fifteen witnesses can be accessed at the Knock Shrine website[1]. The vision eventually faded and never reappeared. Later, in 1880, a reporter for the London *Daily Telegraph*[2] interviewed a policeman who said he saw only "a rosy sort of brightness, through which what seemed to be stars appeared. I saw no figures . . . but some women who were praying there, declared that they beheld the Blessed Virgin," he said. Asked whether he looked around to see where the brightness came from, the policeman replied, "I did, but everything was dark. There was no light anywhere, except on the gable."

EXPLANATIONS

This is how it started, and this is what the witnesses saw. But could it be a hoax? There are several possible explanations for the appearance of Our Lady, St Joseph, St John, the altar, the Lamb, and the Cross.

1. Knock website, "Witness Accounts."
2. Encyclopedia.com, "Knock."

1. All fifteen witnesses and the policeman could be lying or were delusional.
2. The priests that conducted the 1879 investigation and who published the results of that investigation were all lying. The villagers either were too fearful to correct the priests' fabrications or they played along with it.
3. The witnesses were tricked into believing they saw a supernatural event when it in reality was a hoax played on them. The only explanation offered for how someone could have perpetrated such a hoax was for them to employ a magic lantern which would project the images upon the church wall.

   - The problem is that realistically there were two possible locations to place the projector. There was the wall where most of the witness stopped or the school some distance away and situated at an angle. The wall location doesn't work because that's where the witnesses were and they would have seen it. The school location is similarly deficient because there was no facing aperture from the school which could have been used.
   - Additionally, for the magic lantern to be effective, it had to be dark. The visions began while it was still light. Later in the investigation attempts were made to reproduce the images and they failed.
   - Moreover, the magic lantern required an effective light source to project an image the distance required. There was none except candlelight. The apparition took place in 1879, the same year Thomas Edison finally invented a light bulb that now lasted up to forty hours. There was no electricity in the Irish village of Knock in 1879.
   - The perpetrators would have had to possess the artistic and technological skills to create a slide of the image for projection onto the side of the building. The suspects named are two boys who some 50 years later apparently claimed to have perpetrated the hoax, a policeman, or the priest himself. There is no evidence to support these alternative theories by theorists who reject out of hand the notion of heavenly intervention.
   - It was raining during the apparition and so whatever projection was used the light would have had to penetrate the rain with no visible beam.

4. There is no natural explanation for the evening of August 21, 1879. The only explanation can be the apparition occurred as described by the witnesses ranging in age from five to seventy-four, or these fifteen (or more) diverse witness conspired and fabricated the entire story, all with the blessing of the investigating priests.

5. None of the witnesses ever changed their testimony. They knew what they saw and went to their graves with their stories intact. In 1936 a follow up investigation took place. Mary Byrne, now eighty-six years of age, was interviewed again and reaffirmed what happened with the statement: "I am clear about everything I have said and I make this statement knowing I am going before my God."

THE MESSAGES

But then we wonder about the purpose of such an apparition. There apparently were no messages delivered—just some static figures. In fact, however, there were indeed some extraordinarily beautiful and majestic messages given.

- **Message 1.** God lives. He reveals his glory and majesty through means of his own choosing, and the apparition on that 1879 night in Knock makes it easy for us to believe.
- **Message 2.** In the apparition Joseph is to the right of Mary, bending to her in a gesture of respect. Nearly nineteen hundred years earlier, when the Word became flesh, Joseph was there. In Bethlehem, and except for Mary, he was the first to hold the Lord. St John is to Mary's left. Except for Mary he was the last to be with the Lord at the foot of the cross. In the center, and dominating both Joseph and John, is the Blessed Virgin who bridges the first and the last. To John's left is the Lamb and the Cross. The Lamb is the pure sacrifice of Our Lord and the cross is the ultimate symbol Jesus' conquest of death. When we see the cross, we see the victory of Jesus.
- **Message 3.** The overall scene presents a message of salvation that can be understood by Christians of every tradition and culture.
- **Message 4.** John holds the written word. Yet we know from John himself that the written word contains only a small part of what Jesus taught. The rest comes through the apostles and their successors. John teaches as a Bishop using both the written and spoken word.
- **Message 5.** The scene presents a powerful image of the Eucharist. The altar is present and upon it the Lamb of God. The Lamb is Jesus and

- **Message 6.** Above the altar are what the visionaries assumed were angels. And perhaps that is what they were meant to be. None could see their faces, however, and maybe what they were really seeing was the 1879 equivalent of the dove at Jesus' baptism. Maybe they were witnessing the presence of the Holy Spirit.

GOD'S GIFT

Logic, scholarly research, and Bible study all play an important role to help us recognize and understand God's Plan of Salvation. But we will always flounder if we elect to confine our examination of eternity to our intellect. God makes his love available to all, and quite independent of our intellectual qualifications. And he uses diverse avenues to present us with this gift. It may be presented to us through the Church and its Sacraments or as we study the Bible and pray.

Or it may be given through the eyes of fourteen Irish villagers in 1879. Or God's love may be shown through the miraculous healing of one Marion Carroll, delivered one hundred and ten years after St Mary, St Joseph, St John, the Lamb of God, his Altar and the angels illuminated God's love. Our Lady of Knock delivers the gospel plainly and simply, trumping all scholarly discussions and analyses. She does not demand intellectual sophistication; she merely asks for faith. And when we have that faith, the messages delivered that evening in 1879 become clear. They are the gospel messages.

LADY OF KNOCK

Another gift given to us at Knock was the inspirational song *Lady of Knock* written more than one hundred years later. A great version is the recording by Daniel O'Donnell.[3] Another equally inspiring rendition is the one sung by the composer, Dana Rosemary Scallon.[4]

---

3. https://www.youtube.com/watch?v=N7p1HmcoRVo (YouTube search words: Lady Knock O'Donnell).

4. https://www.youtube.com/watch?v=Fm6ss1PBC1Q (YouTube search words: Lady Knock Scallon).

MARION CARROLL'S MIRACULOUS CURE

Knock demands our attention. Well, one may ask—what about miracles. Aren't these Marian apparitions supposed to be accompanied by miracles? In truth, the parish priest recorded a number of unexplained miracles, but there was no scientific documentation. Unlike Lourdes, Knock is not generally known as a place of inexplicable healings. Yet, as Marion Carroll (chapter 18.4) can attest, they occur.

12

Our Lady of Zeitoun

The problem with miracles is that there are just too many. Internet research will disclose a never-ending stream of stories and claims about the miraculous. Some or many may be a fortuitous coincidence explainable as natural events. Unexplained medical cures may in fact be a spontaneous remission of the disease. That does not rule out divine intervention; it just makes it more difficult to classify as a miracle. Ironically, too many inexplicable events would make them commonplace and thereby undermine the miracle of God.

A CROSS IN THE SKY

On the other hand, it would seem that if there were one totally inexplicable event that the whole world simultaneously witnessed, we would have universal proof certain that God exists and loves us. For example, assume for a moment that at 1200 Greenwich time a spectacular cross appeared in the heavens and was simultaneously viewed throughout the world from Greenland to Antarctica. Day or night, cloud coverage or no, everyone could see the blazing cross. Fifteen minutes later it disappeared.

I think it would be safe to speculate that the following Sunday there would be an upsurge in church attendance. Media would concentrate on the event—for a while. Soon talking heads would appear on television explaining the event as something which although can't be explained right now, when you think about it and in view of the billions and billions of stars and galaxies it was perhaps inevitable that sooner or later such a coincidence would occur. Moreover, if this were really a message from God, the words "Jesus Saves" would have been written above the cross.

The television program would then be interrupted by a news bulletin that a prostitute has proof that fifteen years earlier the President of the United States was her customer. The dominating news event would then shift to things more understandable and earthy. Adios God and hello beloved scandal. Memory and news coverage of the cross would diminish and recede until it was unofficially categorized as one more, among many, unexplained events such a UFO flying over Phoenix or an image of Jesus on a piece of toast.

OUR LADY OF ZEITOUN

The cross in the sky is of course completely fictitious. That is not the case with Our Lady of Zeitoun—a completely inexplicable event that was witnessed by thousands, and perhaps millions, complete with photographs. Over a three-year period, they saw what appears to have been Mary on a Coptic Orthodox Church in Cairo, Egypt. She moved among the domes of the church, sometimes bowing before a cross. Hovering above her were unidentified phenomena that appeared to be doves (in the New Testament, doves are associated with the Holy Spirit). This church is built on the location where tradition holds that Mary, Joseph, and little Jesus stayed when they fled to Egypt to escape the murderous treachery of Herod. There are even photographs of what was seen by Christians, Muslims, Jews, atheists, and everyone else who was there when she appeared on numerous occasions from 1968 to 1971. The apparition is now known as Our Lady of Zeitoun. The skeptics online encyclopedia, *The Skeptics Dictionary,* analyzed these appearances but was unable to offer a rational explanation of the image and its movement. The article concludes, "I don't know what caused the Zeitoun lights[1], but last on my list of plausible possibilities would be the hypothesis that it was the 2,000-year-old ghost of a virgin who gave birth to a god."

Return for a moment to the hypothetical cross that appeared in the heavens as postulated above. One can easily imagine a successor to Carl Sagan (who is dead) analyzing the event and then pronouncing his well-considered and objective conclusion, "I don't know what caused the image

---

1. Carroll, "Zeitoun," final sentence.

of the cross that was in the sky, but last on my list of plausible possibilities would be the hypothesis that it has anything to do with a 2,000 year old myth of a godman being nailed to it."

Why are so many afraid to acknowledge the possibility of God, even in the face of millions of witnesses? Why is a Supreme Creator cavalierly dismissed as an impossibility?

The number and diversity of miracles and visions granted by Our Lord is staggeringly high, and this book is only bringing you a few of them. Others are easily accessible on the internet. Read about them with an open mind and heart.

13.1

Our Lady of Guadalupe

Crushing the Snake

The Catholic Church unequivocally asserts that in 1531 the Blessed Virgin Mary appeared and spoke to a poor native in present-day Mexico City named Juan Diego (now a Saint). As proof, it is claimed that her image suddenly and inexplicably appeared on his burlap cloak (tilma). She is now known as Our Lady of Guadalupe.

To understand the significance of Our Lady of Guadalupe we need to travel to Mexico in the early sixteenth century.

THE AZTECS AND THE CULTURE OF DEATH

When Hernan Cortes and his band landed in Central America in 1519, they encountered a culture which was truly demonic.

The stone serpent was the center of the primary Aztec temple where massive human sacrifices were carried out. The temple was enclosed by a serpentine wall. The victims would be sacrificed by laying them on their back on the altar at the top of the temple. The Aztec priest would push his dagger into the chest of the conscious victim and extract the beating heart. The body would then be discarded by throwing it down the side of the temple where it would slither down the length of the steps in a grotesque display of evil. The flesh of the victims would be consumed. These activities occurred on such a massive scale that when the conquistadores journeyed inland they came across walls built of human skulls and stone. The skulls were thought to harbor the soul and by so constructing the wall the residual power within the skulls would strengthen it. In one wall there were over one hundred thousand skulls.

The temples were covered with representations of snakes and as the beating hearts were lifted up and carried away drummers would beat on snakeskin drums. A principle god was the feathered serpent, along with the sun god and the moon god. Every day was a struggle between the two. The moon god was trying to keep the sun god from dispelling the night as it rose from the east every morning because it was trying to bathe the earth in eternal blackness. The jaguar was the symbol of the night predator and because of its powers was worshipped. The sun god was aided by the eagle and together they were in constant battle against the moon god and its allies. As the moon god was defeated it would enter phases such as the crescent moon, thereby showing that the sun god was once again dismembering it. But the sun god and the eagle needed help. That assistance would come from the hearts and souls of the sacrificial victims which would be released to and strengthen the eagle as he vied against the jaguar, and thus help to ensure the dawning of a new day. This meant they needed a lot of sacrifices. In one festival alone in 1487 more than eighty thousand were sacrificed. Over one thousand would fall each day to the sacrificial priest. Twenty percent of Aztec children were sacrificed.

This was how they ensured the continuation of the earth and life; their function was to postpone the final day of reckoning when the sun god, if defeated, would remain in the earth and darkness would reign. The Aztecs believed the earth was flat and that the sun would emerge from mother earth every morning. Mother earth was made of snakes and she gave birth to the sun. The one that assisted the sun as it rose each morning was Quetzalcoatl, the feathered serpent. He was the one who gave them life.

The Mayans had their own system of sacrifices. While less extensive than the Aztec, their sacrifices were also centered on their version of the feathered serpent, called Kukulkan.

In 1521, with this panorama of human misery and evil gods confronting them, Cortes made his way into Mexico City and confronted Montezuma, the Aztec leader. Montezuma had long expected the arrival of a white king from the east because, according to Central American legend, he had visited them centuries before, taught arts and crafts and had actively introduced the concept that God didn't require human sacrifices. He sailed off to the east and said he would return some day. Well, here he was, some five hundred years later.

Montezuma sacrificed five people and offered their flesh to Cortes.

Cortes spent the next two years rounding up help from other Indian tribes. He laid siege against Mexico City, and Montezuma and the Aztecs were finally defeated.

ENTER THE SPANIARDS

The Spanish put a halt to the sacrifices, but then comes evidence of what happens when too much unchecked power falls into the hands of the wrong people. They started abusing the locals, even pressing them into slavery. The efforts of the padres to convert were meeting a solid wall of resistance. The Christian god was perceived as heartless and unjust as theirs. The tyranny of the Spanish rulers became so bad that Bishop Zumarraga put Mexico City under interdict. This meant that the sacraments could no longer be administered except on the death bed. The situation was tense, and an uprising seemed imminent.

We cannot emphasize enough the horror that the Spanish found in 1521. Cortes came and liberated the natives from their slavery to Satan, but very few converted to Catholicism in the first decade of Spanish rule because of the corruption of the Spanish rulers and the Aztec's attachment to polygamy and other pagan practices. Moreover, there was a real concern that the conversions were shallow and, given the right circumstances, the natives could easily revert to their former ways, and reinstate worship of their gods.

THE BLESSED VIRGIN APPEARS

The above discussion is well settled and free of controversy. Now we enter the arena of dispute. What follows is a condensation of the traditional narrative surrounding the claimed appearance by Mary, the mother of Jesus. I think it can be safely said that those who believe the image to be a regular painting would reject this narrative as being a fictitious account fabricated long after the claimed event—perhaps more than a hundred years later—to give the image divine credibility.

Juan de Zumarraga, Mexico's first bishop, could do little to convert the Aztecs and he prayed to the Blessed Virgin for help on tending to the spiritual needs of his flock and the conversion of the natives. Then he asked her to acknowledge his prayers by sending him some Castilian roses.

The earliest and most widely published written account of the Guadalupe events is the *Nican Mopohua,* written in Nahuatl, the native language. It is believed to date from around 1550 (give or take ten years) and can easily be accessed on the internet.[1]

On December 9, 1531, a simple fifty-seven-year-old convert with the Christian name of Juan Diego was on his six-mile walk to Mass when he approached the hill known as Tepeyac. This was the hill of an Aztec goddess by the name of Tonantzin. He first heard beautiful music and when it stopped a woman's voice was heard from the top of the hill saying, "Juan, Dearest Juan Diego!" When he arrived at the summit a young maiden was standing there.

> Her clothing was shining like the sun, as if it were sending out waves of light, and the stone, the crag on which she stood, seemed to be giving out rays; her radiance was like precious stones, it seemed like an exquisite bracelet (it seemed beautiful beyond anything else); the earth seemed to shine with the brilliance of a rainbow in the mist. And the mesquites and nopals and the other little plants that are generally up there seemed like

---

1. For example, the University of California San Diego website, http://pages.ucsd.edu/~dkjordan/nahuatl/nican/NicanMopohua.html.

emeralds. Their leaves seemed like turquoise. And their trunks, their thorns, their prickles, were shining like gold.[2]

Then she spoke to him, identifying herself as the Ever-Virgin Holy Mary and asked that a church be built at that site so that she could bring the Lord to her children. She directed Diego to go to the bishop and tell him all that he had seen and heard.

He did so, and Bishop Juan de Zumarraga received him, heard him and did not believe him. Juan Diego returned to the hill where the Lady had appeared early in the morning. The Blessed Virgin appeared again, and Juan Diego told her that the bishop did not believe him and for her to entrust this mission to someone of more importance. She replied that she had many messengers and servants, but she had chosen him to deliver this message and that through his intercession her message would be complied with. She told him to speak to the bishop again, "and carefully tell him again how I, personally, the Ever Virgin Holy Mary, I, who am the Mother of God, am sending you."[3]

The next day the bishop still did not believe Diego and told him that a sign was necessary to show that he had truly seen the Blessed Virgin. Juan Diego returned to Mary and relayed what the bishop had told him. She told him to return the next day and she would provide a sign so that the bishop would believe.

On December 11th when Juan Diego was to carry a sign to the bishop, he failed to return to the hill as instructed by Mary because when he had reached his home the night before, his uncle had become gravely ill. By nightfall, his uncle requested that early the next morning (December 12th) Diego summon a priest, to prepare him and hear his confession, because he was certain it was time for him to die, and that he would not arise or get well.

On December 12, 1531, before dawn, Juan Diego went to summon a priest. As he approached the road which joins the slope to Tepeyac hilltop, he deliberately avoided his normal route so that he would not see the Lady. He did not want to be delayed because his uncle was near death and needed a priest. When Diego rounded the hill, he saw her descend from the top of the hill and that she was looking toward where they previously met. She approached him at the side and asked where he was going.

Diego was extremely contrite and told her of his uncle and how he was going to summon a priest to hear his uncle's confession and prepare him for death. The Most Holy Virgin assured him that neither this illness nor any other harmful thing was cause for fear. She was his heavenly mother and

---

2. *Nican Mopohua,* lines 017–021.
3. *Nican Mopohua,* line 062.

would protect him. She told Juan Diego that his uncle would not die, and that he was already well.

And at that very moment his uncle became well, as he later found out.

THE CREATION OF THE TILMA IMAGE

She then directed him to climb to the top of the hill and gather the diverse flowers that would be growing there.

> And when he reached the top, he was astonished by all of them, blooming, open, flowers of every kind, lovely and beautiful, when it still was not their season, because really that was the season in which the frost was very harsh. They were giving off an extremely soft fragrance; like precious pearls, as if filled with the dew of the night. Then he began to cut them, he gathered them all, he put them in the hollow of his tilma. The top of the little hill was certainly not a place in which any flowers grew; there are only plenty of rocks, thorns, spines, prickly pears and mesquite trees. And even though some little herbs or grasses might grow, it was then the month of December, in which the frost eats everything up and destroys it.[4]

He brought the flowers to Our Lady, who then took them in her hands and returned them into the hollow of his tilma. She told him to open the tilma only in the presence of the bishop, telling him everything that happened. These flowers would be his requested sign "so that he will then do what lies within his responsibility so that my temple which I have asked him for will be made, will be raised."

Juan Diego immediately went to see the bishop. Again, after long delays and much skepticism he was finally admitted. Diego told the bishop what had just happened and stood in front of him and opened the tilma. The flowers scattered on the floor and the imprinted image of the ever-virgin Holy Mary was revealed on the tilma. The bishop believed and very soon thereafter a church was built as directed by the Lady.

---

4. *Nican Mopohua*, lines 128–133.

Juan Diego's uncle was instantly cured and in fact said that the Lady had appeared to him and told him that she should be known as the ever-virgin Holy Mary of Guadalupe.

DOES THE TILMA AND EARLY HISTORY SUPPORT THIS STORY?

I know that here in the twenty-first century all this sounds pretty far-fetched and much like a successful Mexican/Catholic legend created to bring the natives under control. But then, we have the tilma. If it can be shown to have characteristics which could not be the result of standard human artistry in the context of the time and age, we would have powerful evidence and reason to believe the hand of God as the artist. If on the other hand the tilma is nothing more than a very clever and beautifully composed portrait, then for hundreds of years the Mexican people and in fact all of Catholicism and much of Christianity may have been barking up the wrong tree.

The problem is that the evidence does not appear to be conclusive one way or the other. Moreover, the issue is compounded by unfounded (or at least non-verifiable) claims by proponents of certain qualities of the tilma which, if true, would conclusively prove its divine origin. On the other hand, those that hold steadfastly to the notion that miracles are fictitious events have promulgated their share of misrepresentations.

The next chapter provides clarification.

FURTHER RESEARCH

There are countless references to Guadalupe that can be accessed on the internet and through traditional print media. An excellent detailed, scholarly, and very readable history of Guadalupe is the beautifully written *Historiography of the Apparition of Guadalupe*, by Daniel J. Castellano, available online.

13.2

Our Lady of Guadalupe

Gilding the Lily

OUR DILEMMA

The three most famous Marian apparitions are Fatima, Lourdes, and Guadalupe. As confirmation, Fatima presents us with the Miracle of the Sun while Lourdes gives us inexplicable and carefully researched physical healings. Our senses and logic demand that we believe Fatima and Lourdes. That is not quite the case for Guadalupe. Belief in the divine origin of Our Lady on the tilma takes a subtler route. Certainly, there is hard physical evidence in the tilma and the image itself supporting the divine origin of Our Lady of Guadalupe, but there are gaps and questions. To resolve those questions by reading what others have said about the physical characteristics of the tilma and its history is an excruciatingly difficult task (if not impossible) because we are compelled to choose between competing claims that cannot be independently confirmed. We end up where we started: we believe if we wish to believe, and doubt if we wish to doubt.

FINDING OUR PATH

Because there are so many uncertainties concerning the tilma, and even if you believe the iconic portrait to be from heaven, it is a mistake to accept all the claims intended to prove its divine origin. To do so could be an invitation to a searing disappointment in the event they are proved incorrect. Instead, consider the very real possibility that the Lord used a two-step process to bring us the portrait of his beloved mother that we now see on the tilma.

GOD DELEGATES

God sometimes works directly to the completion of a salvation event, as was the case when Jesus uttered his last words on the cross, "It is finished." Other times God seems to start the ball rolling and then follows up by selecting certain men or women to continue his work. The establishment and growth of his church following Pentecost is an example. In the case of Our Lady of Guadalupe I believe the evidence strongly supports the conclusion that (1) God instantly imprinted the image of Mary on the tilma, and (2) subsequently used a human instrument(s) to complete the image as we now see it.

Step 1. Under this scenario, the portrait would initially have been a simple image of the face, hands, tunic (without the black bow) and mantle (without the stars)—in other words we would have received an unembellished and beautiful image of the Blessed Virgin as she appeared to Juan Diego. When Juan Diego opened his tilma in front of Bishop Zumarraga on December 12, 1531 and the flowers spilled out, this simple portrait of Mary is what the bishop saw. The image on the tilma was so unexpected, beautiful and so compelling that within a couple of weeks (December 26, 1531) the bishop led a procession to a small chapel or hermitage which he had hastily built to house this simple image. Mary had told Juan Diego that this is what she wanted, her image confirmed the message, and the good bishop complied.

Step 2. The second step occurred when at some unknown date, but certainly within a few years, someone decided (there is no record) to embellish the image, to gild the lily so to speak, so that it would deliver an even more powerful message to the natives. The remainder of the image as we now see it (except for a crown upon her head which was removed in the 1800s) was added. It is generally believed that a gifted native artist (generally identified as Marcos Cipac de Aquino) added these details and embellishments which sent a message that the native Indians understood as proof that she was there to crush the false hideous snake and carry them with motherly love to the religion of the padres.

Despite the two-step process, the image with all its embellishments would become and remain an incredibly rich and divine gift from God.

EIGHT MILLION CONVERTED

From 1531 to 1540 it is estimated that about eight million natives were converted to Christianity, and there appears to be no explanation for this sudden surge except Our Lady of Guadalupe. Once she appeared, the Aztec culture was doomed. Just as was the case at Lourdes, the opposition had no chance when the mother of the Lord enters the picture.

THE ORIGINAL VERSUS THE ADDITIONS

Interestingly, it is almost universally accepted by those who have examined the tilma that there is no sizing, undercoating, or other preparation of the surface where the original image appears. Moreover, the original part of the image has not suffered any deterioration and the colors have retained their luster and brilliance despite the passage of nearly five hundred years. The additions, however, have flaked and needed restoration and repair over the years. It's as though the image was saying that the Eternal Son within the mother could never pass away, but his creation, including the sun's rays, the moon, and the remainder of the painting could. It reminds us of what Jesus told us, when he said that the heavens and earth will pass away, but his word would remain forever.

INCULTURATION

How the Lord reveals himself and sustains his presence within us may well depend on the culture and time in which we live. The Creator of the universe makes himself understandable to all and to the extent necessary to share in the great mystery of Christ. Sometimes the recognition of who Jesus is and what he did appears to come upon us dramatically, while other times this knowledge takes place gradually with one piece of knowledge building gracefully upon the preceding one. Sometimes this knowledge is best understood by borrowing or incorporating the truth or tradition of a particular culture and applying or extending it to the gospel. One example which is often used by skeptics to attack Christianity is our designation of December 25 as the birthday of Jesus which they mockingly claim was nothing more than the winter solstice holiday celebrated by the ancient Romans. That could very well be the case, but the point is that we celebrate Christ's birthday, not a particular date, and since we don't really know what that date was, a day most familiar to the culture to assist in the transition from a pagan belief to Christianity would seem to make a lot of sense.

Viewed in this context, Our Lady of Guadalupe and how she came to us may be a perfect example of how inculturation works. Consider how the Savior is introduced to the Aztecs. First, they know of an ancient legend which stated that a white god from the east would return after having taught them some five hundred years earlier. The natives ultimately rejected his teachings, including the teaching that sacrifice of humans was evil, and perverted their culture by offering human sacrifices and the worship of hideous gods. Then the priests came in 1519 and began to lay the foundations for the Christian faith, but these foundations were shaky. The idea of God among them was completely alien to the Aztec culture. But then the iconic image of Our Lady of Guadalupe appears and with such symbols and in a manner that swept aside a religious history and culture which had smothered them for centuries. The symbols of the blue-green mantle, the black sash, etc. mean nothing to us today, but to the Aztec meant everything. The name Guadalupe suggested to the Spanish priests the statue of the Virgin and her Divine Son buried for centuries near the Guadalupe River in Spain. To the Aztec, however, it sounded like "she who crushes the stone serpent." Our Lady's immediate message to the Spaniards and the Aztecs was different, but the truth she was offering was identical.

Consider the image of Our Lady as a picture in a very real and literal sense as Mary, the mother of Jesus. Additionally, consider it a book of revelation and instruction intended primarily and initially for the natives. They did not use writing in the sense that we do, i.e., letters and words to convey ideas and facts. They used paintings, hieroglyphics, or symbols. And this is some of what God told them:

1. The blue-green mantle draped over her and covered with stars symbolized heaven and royalty. The Lady is from heaven and because the heavenly being at the bottom grasped both the mantle signifying heaven and her robe, which represented earth, they were joined. Yet, she herself was not divine because her head is bowed reverently, and her hands clasped in prayer.

2. Her face is gentle and compassionate and conveys love, mercy and peace which would conquer the Aztec gods of punishment and death.

3. Over the past few years troubling events had occurred in the Aztec culture, including the appearance of a comet. Aztec seers had foretold the beginning of the end for their civilization beginning in 1519, and this was the year that Hernando Cortez arrived on the east coast of Mexico. The black sash around her waist signified to the Aztec that she is with child. She is offering a heavenly child to the Aztecs who

would bring love, mercy, and peace and introduce a new era. While she was not divine, the child she bore would be. Her clothing was neither Spanish nor Aztec but from another culture. Thus the child she was carrying would be neither Spanish nor Aztec, but from elsewhere. Yet he will become one of them.

4. On her neck is the emblem of the religion preached by the new priests—a cross. She was, therefore, connected to them and was a messenger from their god.

5. The greatest Aztec god was the sun god, who was in constant battle with the moon god—the god of darkness. The Lady of Guadalupe was standing in front of the sun and blotting it out; she was standing atop the moon, putting it under her authority. She was greater than the sun god and the moon god. The image on the tilma told the natives that the Lady had stripped the Aztec gods of their power.

OUR INTERCEDING AND GUIDING MOTHER

In fact, the image with all its embellishments now speaks to everyone. She is the Lady in Revelations 12:1, the woman clothed with the sun and the moon under feet. At the same time the message delivered to Juan Diego (and to us) in 1531 was the same message Jesus gave to John at the foot of cross (and to us): Mary is our mother. But this mother is God's most favored and she was favored to bring Jesus to us, just as she did two thousand years ago in Nazareth and five hundred years ago in Mexico.

TWENTIETH CENTURY UNBELIEF

It is claimed that the tilma should have deteriorated centuries ago, and the fact that it has not is proof of its divine origin. I am not sure where the idea came that God cannot use his perishable creation to reveal himself, but it is interesting that over the centuries witnesses have stated unequivocally that the tilma was perfectly preserved. But towards the end of the nineteenth century there seems to be a shift and it is reported that the tilma is showing deterioration. And that returns us to Our Lady of Fatima.

You will recall from chapter 9.1 ("Our Lady of Fatima 1917: The First Four Appearances") that on August 13, 1917 the three children were kidnapped by the town authorities in an attempt to discredit them and their claimed visions of Our Lady of the Rosary. It did not work. The

Heavenly Lady told the children that the miracle they were to witness October 13th would have been greater if not for the disbelief shown by the authorities. This seems a bit strange, but her statement reflects a central theme of Christianity. We are all members or parts of the Body of Christ. Whatever we do, good or bad, as individuals affects the remainder of the Body. If someone jams a knife into your arm, your whole body suffers. That is why in Christian theology there is no such thing as a private sin. Whatever one of us does in defiance of God affects us all.

Beginning in the nineteenth century faith was declining. Science was pushing aside what it considered superstition. All smart people knew how foolish it was to believe in this mythical being called god. As faith diminishes, so does God's grace. The lack of faith at Fatima resulted in more subdued miracles on October 13th. Similarly, as mankind draws away from God, as we did beginning in the nineteenth century, it seems that God would inevitably withdraw his favors and grace. Could this be the reason why the tilma began to deteriorate as we moved into the twentieth century?

Don't know—just asking. Something to keep in mind.

ATTACKING CHRIST

The efforts to destroy Our Lady of Guadalupe have never ceased. Once again, let us return briefly to Fatima. On March 6, 1922, two bombs were planted, one in the church and the second on the oak tree on which the Heavenly Lady appeared. The bomb in the church blew the roof off the small chapel that had been built. The effect was to build a newer, bigger church, which has now grown into the Church of the Most Holy Trinity, the eighth largest Christian church in the world. The second bomb planted on the oak tree failed to detonate. It is hard to demolish a place that Mary, the mother of God, has touched.

On November 14, 1921, in Mexico City, a man placed a bomb in a bouquet of roses on the altar just a few feet from the tilma bearing the image of Our Lady of Guadalupe. Shortly thereafter and during Mass it exploded shattering the altar and breaking windows 450 feet from the explosion. Every stained-glass window in the Basilica was shattered and chunks of marble were blasted out of the sanctuary. Even though a brass crucifix near the altar was severely twisted by the explosion, both the tilma and the glass which enclosed it escaped unscathed and without a mark. None present in the Basilica at the time of the explosion was injured. There is no scientific explanation as to why the tilma survived and why this ferocious explosion did not hurt anyone. As was the case at Fatima, the treachery of God's opponents was converted into one more miraculous story to confirm Mary's 1531 appearances in Mexico City.

OUR NEVER-ENDING BATTLE

The world of the Aztec was a world of fear and death. Twenty percent of the Aztec children were sacrificed. Christ brought hope and life. Just as she did fifteen hundred years earlier, Mary once again intervened in the affairs of the world in a way which we can all understand, and she intervened to rout Satan from the New World.

It seems, however, that our battle is never-ending. Despite the United States of America being founded as a country under God you can see it falling away, even now as it happens. The Aztecs sacrificed 20 percent of their children. Not to be outdone, 20 percent of our children are sacrificed in the womb. Another example—we all recognize the *Ave Maria* composed by Schubert in 1825. The Barbara Streisand YouTube version is a sad commentary of self-involvement that permeates today. The *Ave Maria* words are there, but the images that accompany the song are various poses of Barbara Streisand[1] (I think you will agree that these images are extravagantly and egoistically silly). We need to pray and ask Our Lady to help us return our nation to one that is truly under God in spirit as well as in words.

MOTHER MARY

We need to remember the message of Guadalupe. Mary is our mother so that whenever we're having a rough time, we ought to meditate on what she told Juan Diego: "Do not be troubled or weighted down with grief. Do not fear any illness or anxiety. Am I not here? I, who am your mother. Are you not under my protection? Do I not hold you in the folds of my mantle? Am I not here—I who am your mother?" Is she not the Ark of the New Covenant, the New Eve, the daughter of the Father, the bride of the Holy Spirit, the mother of the Son? She is all these and more because God granted these most singular privileges to her. She who is most favored can help us along as well. What mother wouldn't?

---

1. https://www.youtube.com/watch?v=0wFtXvt8TOQ

14

The Shroud of Turin

A Brief Introduction

JESUS' PHYSICAL SUFFERING

The Bible offers an understated description of how Jesus physically suffered on that Holy Weekend two thousand years ago.[1] It merely summarizes his passion in a series of one word descriptions or terse phrases: he was seized, bound, spat upon, beaten, blindfolded, mocked, reviled, contemptuously treated, crowned with thorns, a reed placed in his right hand, stripped, arrayed in a purple robe, falsely accused, scourged, forced to drag his own cross to the hill where he would be taunted and crucified. Finally, a spear was run through his side to confirm he was in fact dead.

But did all of this really happen? It is said that a picture is worth a thousand words. If only we had a picture!

We do.

INTRODUCING THE SHROUD OF TURIN

There is overwhelming evidence, which by any objective standard should be considered conclusive, that the Shroud of Turin is this sacred picture. If it is, we are looking at the image of Jesus Christ at the instant of his resurrection. The Shroud provides us not only with a photographic-like image of the Savior's face, but a full front and rear bodily picture as well. The negative of the image is incredibly detailed. It shows a man severely abused and scourged with the distinctive markings of a Roman whip. It depicts bodily wounds that correlate with the biblical accounts of the crucifixion. The man on the bloodied Shroud was whipped, nails were driven into the base of his hands (exiting through his wrists) and into his feet, and he suffered a wound the size of a Roman spearhead in his side. The man suffered lacerations, contusions and scalp punctures. His face shows that he was beaten, there is swelling under the eye, and parts of his beard appear to have been ripped from his face. Medical technology and our understanding of Roman crucifixion techniques and Jewish burial traditions all conform to the man on the Shroud.

A DRAMATIC AND UNANTICIPATED REVELATION

Since 1578 the Shroud of Turin has been kept in the Cathedral of St John the Baptist in Turin. It is approximately fourteen feet long and four feet wide.

---

1. The complete accounts of the Passion and Crucifixion are contained in Matt 26:36—Chapter 27; Mark 14:32— Chapter 15; Luke 22:39—Chapter 23; and John 17—19. See also John 20:24–29.

Look at a photograph of the full Shroud as it appears to the naked eye.[2] You can see it bears the faint, almost indistinguishable, front and back image of a nude man, joined at the crown of the head. Interestingly, the more you concentrate on the image, the clearer it becomes. Its appearance is otherwise quite unremarkable and is dominated by intense repaired burn marks from a 1532 fire. To the naked eye the image is almost non-existent, particularly as you draw close. Nevertheless, the Shroud has always been venerated as the burial shroud of Jesus, and until 1898 the Shroud appeared only as a vague shadowy image.

In 1898 this all changed. It was photographed for the first time, and a completely unexpected negative plate revealed a stunning positive image. For the first time, crucifixion details were dramatically revealed, and we see the positive image of a man brutally tortured and crucified.

ALTERNATIVE EXPLANATIONS

If the Shroud is the burial cloth of Jesus, we have been granted the grace of seeing the Second Person of the Trinity. If it is a medieval fake, it is the most incredible forgery of all time —a forgery that no one, including the most fervent atheist, can explain how it was created. If it is a forgery, the perpetrator never cashed in on his creation. We don't know who he is and he never produced anything else.

STURP

In 1978 a team of scientists was granted special permission and for five days analyzed and tested the Shroud using the latest scientific and technological equipment and taking sticky tape samples. This was the first time such in-depth access and analysis had been permitted and is known as the Shroud of Turin Research Project (STURP). In October 1981 STURP issued its final report on their investigation, *The Shroud of Turin: A Critical Summary of Observations, Data and Hypotheses*, (*Shroud Critical Summary*) and concluded:

> We can conclude for now that the Shroud image is that of a real human form of a scourged, crucified man. It is not the product of an artist. The bloodstains are composed of hemoglobin and also give a positive test for serum albumin. The image is an ongoing mystery and until further chemical studies are made,

---

2. The full image can be accessed on numerous websites, including www.shroud.com.

perhaps by this group of scientists, or perhaps by some scientists in the future, the problem remains unsolved.[3]

Except for the now discredited 1988 carbon 14 dating (see Chapter 14.3, "Shroud of Turin: Evidence against the Shroud's Authenticity"), nothing has changed since then which would undermine this essential conclusion. In fact, all the evidence has solidified the conclusion that this must be Jesus's burial cloth at the instant of his resurrection (See Chapter 14.2, "Shroud of Turin: Facts that Compel Belief " and Chapter 14.1, "Shroud of Turin: Historical Documentation;" see also Chapter 14.4, "Shroud of Turin: Proving the Supernatural"). Still, we can never prove that the image is that of a resurrected man because to do so would take the inquiry out of the current definition of science. Nevertheless, the evidence powerfully demands that it is, but our belief in the Passion and Resurrection comes to us by faith and prayer.

REVERSING THE EVIDENCE

If the amount and credence of the evidence were reversed the Shroud of Turin would have long ago been dismissed as the burial shroud of Christ. But because science is proving that the Shroud is in fact the burial cloth of a man crucified in Palestine two thousand years ago and that his image precisely matches the biblical accounts of Jesus' crucifixion, those who wish not to believe have recourse only to speculative and disproven arguments.

GOD'S ETERNAL LOVE

Think of God's mercy and love that permits us to put our fingers in the Lord's wounds just as Thomas did. The Shroud dismantles the argument that God doesn't exist because he never shows himself. Nevertheless, if the unbeliever doesn't want to believe, the Shroud will never persuade. Hopefully, however, it will help break down some barriers to permit the entrance of grace, even for the most ardent skeptic.

---

3. *Shroud Critical Summary*, 43–44.

14.1

The Shroud of Turin

Historical Documentation

Skeptics argue that the Shroud was created in 1355 (the date it is universally agreed that the Shroud as we now see it was first revealed) or shortly before by an unknown artist or craftsman. Consequently, and to prove their point, they assert that there are no prior historical documents referring to the Shroud.

In view of the early persecution of Christians and the later, sometimes brutal repression by iconoclasts (the Shroud could have been perceived as an icon and thus subject to destruction), it is not surprising that the Shroud would have been hidden or only cryptic references made to it. But there is documentation and we will look at some of them in chronological order. Before we do so, however, we should note what the Bible may say about the possibility of the existence of Christ's burial cloth or cloak.

POSSIBLE BIBLE REFERENCES

1. The Gospel of John introduces us to the possibility of the Shroud. After Peter and John were informed that the tomb was empty and that Jesus was risen, they ran to the tomb. "Then Simon Peter came, following him, and went into the tomb; he saw the linen cloths lying, and the napkin, which had been on his head, not lying with the linen cloths but

rolled up in a place by itself. Then the other disciple, who reached the tomb first, also went in, and he saw and believed;"[1]

2. From his Roman prison, knowing that he would soon be executed, Paul writes Timothy and asks him to "bring the cloak that I left with Carpus at Troas, also the books, and above all the parchments."[2] Troas was approximately eight hundred miles from Rome. See "Elijah, Paul, the mantle and the cloak," following this timeline for the possible significance of this request.

PRE-1355 HISTORICAL TIMELINE

The following timeline is a chronology of recorded events and documents relating to the Shroud prior to its public display in 1355. Reference is also made to the *Shroud Critical Summary*.[3] This scholarly work contains a comprehensive and detailed narrative tracing the evidence and documents of the Shroud's journey from Jerusalem to Turin, Italy.

Year	Event
544	The "Image Not Made By Hands" was discovered in Edessa (southern Turkey) and became the model for all Byzantine and Orthodox icon images of Christ that followed. (see Chapter 36, "Portrait of Jesus, Ruler of All"). A sixth century text refers to the Mandylion as a "tetradiplon—doubled in four." If the Shroud of Turin were folded by being doubled four times, the viewer would see nothing but the head. The Mandylion was said to have been attached to a board so it could well be that those who viewed it would have been ignorant of the fact that they were viewing just a portion of what was actually a full-length image. Distinct crease marks have been discerned on the Shroud in the very locations suggested by the Mandylion. See "Elijah, Paul, the mantle and the cloak," following this timeline.
c. 755	Almost certainly referring to the Shroud, Pope Stephen II wrote: "Christ spread out his entire body on a linen cloth that was white as snow. On this cloth, marvelous as it is to see. . . the glorious image of the Lord's face, and the length of his entire and most noble body, has been divinely transferred."

1. John 20:6–8
2. 2 Tim 4:13.
3. *Shroud Critical Summary*, 7–46.

944	On August 14, 944, and in exchange for a great deal of money and two hundred Muslim prisoners a cloth bearing the full-length image of Christ carrying his bloodstains was received in Constantinople (Istanbul) with a great deal of fanfare and much celebration. The Emperor Constantine VII personally inspects the image and describes it as extremely faint, more like a moist secretion without paint.
1093	A list of relics in Constantinople includes "the linens found in the tomb following the resurrection."
Pre-1192	At an unknown time, the Shroud received four distinct burn marks. These are holes in the Shroud arranged in a very distinctive "L" pattern. No one knows when or how the burn holes were created (sometimes called "poker holes"). They are unique to the Shroud. The Shroud displays four sets of these four burn holes on both the rear and frontal halves of the shroud, indicating that the cloth was burned through when it was folded.
1192	1. A drawing of the entombed and enshrouded Jesus is found in an 1192 prayer book from Budapest known as the "Pray Manuscript." The illustration not only depicts the unique "L" pattern of burn holes but also the unique herringbone weave pattern of the Shroud. 2. Because of the identical positioning and "L" pattern of the burn marks, the 1192 Pray Manuscript must be depicting the Shroud of Turin. There is no other rational conclusion.
1201	The overseer of the imperial relic treasury in Constantinople states: "in this place the naked Lord rises again, and the burial sindons [shroud or cloths] can prove it." His description refers to the nudity of the man on the shroud, which flew in the fact of artistic renditions of the time which never showed a nude Christ. Thereafter the Shroud was regularly shown in Constantinople, although it was typically folded and kept in a reliquary so that only the face was visible.
1204	The knight Robert de Clari wrote that in Constantinople (Church of My Lady Saint Mary of Blachernae) there was a shroud in which the Lord was wrapped that was raised every Friday so that one could see the form of the Lord on it. In 1204 Constantinople was sacked by the Crusaders and relics disappeared. Knight de Clari states that no one ever knew what became of the shroud when the city was taken.
1205	On August 1, 1205, a nephew of one of the Byzantine Emperors, sent a letter to Pope Innocent III saying that "the linen in which our Lord Jesus Christ was wrapped after his death and before the resurrection" was in Athens.
1355	A linen shroud which is universally agreed as the Shroud is publicly displayed in Lirey, France. Large crowds of pilgrims are attracted.

ELIJAH, PAUL, THE MANTLE, AND THE CLOAK

The Old Testament foreshadows the New; what was anticipated and hidden is now revealed. A phenomenal example is the story of Elijah found in the second chapter of 2 Kings. Elijah does not die and is carried away into heaven, leaving behind for his successor, Elisha, only the priestly cloak he wore. For three days the doubters searched for Elijah, but he was not to be found.

It is amazing how Jesus elevates the hidden meaning of the Old Testament. As was the case with Elijah, Jesus leaves behind his cloak (now known as the Shroud of Turin) for his followers. For three days his enshrouded body reposed in the tomb and he was not seen. But now the stories diverge. Elijah never returned to earth except at the Transfiguration (see Chapter 24, "The Apostles Conspire") when it is made clear that he and Moses give way to Jesus. Unlike Elijah, Jesus returns to earth for forty days, leaving his cloak or mantle in the empty tomb. Elijah left his cloak for his successor and follower, Elisha. I wonder if Jesus left his cloak in the empty tomb for his followers. Elisha picks up the cloak and soon thereafter, empowered as Elijah's successor, went to a spring of water which the men of Jericho said was unwholesome and unfruitful, and through the simple act of throwing salt in the water purified it so that neither death nor miscarriage shall come from it. The simple act (relatively speaking) of Jesus dying on the cross and rising from the dead purified us and made us wholesome again just as Elisha did at Jericho's waters. Just as Elijah's mantle must have sustained Elisha, so Jesus' cloak retrieved from the empty tomb, could quite likely have sustained his followers through hard times and continues to do so. This cloak, imprinted with his photograph taken at the instant of his resurrection, is the Shroud of Turin.

Surely this was what Paul was referring to when as a prisoner in Rome he told Timothy, "When you come, bring the cloak that I left with Carpus at Troas, also the books, and above all the parchments."[4] There must have been something sacred about the cloak. With the Roman executioner closing in on him he certainly could not be concerned about retrieving a coat eight hundred miles distant to keep him warm or a mere keepsake. He was asking Timothy to bring and, by implication, protect some especially important and sacred items: the cloak, books, and parchments. He did not want them to fall into the hands of Christ's foes and likely explains the use of the non-descriptive word, "cloak," to prevent the authorities from understanding its true nature should they acquire the letter or a copy. Moreover, I wonder if he

---

4. 2 Tim 4:13.

thought that he might falter as his execution drew near and that the image of Christ on the cloak could buttress his faith.

As shown under "Pre-1355 Historical Timeline," in 544 a very sacred cloth known as the Mandylion was discovered in Edessa, Turkey. Perhaps the name given to the cloth, Mandylion, will help us uncover its origin. Paul had asked Timothy to bring him the cloak from Troas, which was a part of Troy in Turkey. Now comes an incredible coincidence or insight, depending on your orientation. First, the word used by Paul means a mantle, just the same as the one worn by Elijah. Mantle was the long white cloth worn by high priest and is known as "mandya." Second, Troy used to be known as Ilion. A reasonable conclusion is that the Mandylion discovered in Edessa means the priestly or kingly garment of the king or high priest Jesus ('mandy') that came from Ilion ('lion'), or the Mandylion. Moreover, and as described under "Pre-1355 Historical Timeline," distinct crease marks appear on the Shroud in the very places suggested by the Mandylion.

Two excellent resources discussing the relationship between the Shroud of Turin and the Mandylion are *Bible Reference to Shroud of Turin* by GoodShepherd Film Productions[5] and *Acheiropoietos Jesus Images in Constantinople: the Documentary Evidence*[6] by Daniel C. Scavone.

---

5. See Bibliography.
6. See Bibliography.

14.2

The Shroud of Turin

Facts that Compel Belief

Assume for the moment that the Shroud of Turin is a faked relic which was created around 1350, just shortly before its first universally accepted appearance. This assumption requires that an unknown artist or craftsman created an image of Christ that no one has ever been able to duplicate. In particular, and taking into consideration what we now know about the Shroud of Turin:

CREATION OF THE IMAGE

1. The forger was an artist or craftsman who surpassed the talents of all human beings to the present day, being able to produce an anatomically and photographically perfect human image in a photographic negative manner, centuries before photography.

2. Despite intense efforts from scientists, artists, skeptics, and everyone else, no one has ever been able to duplicate the image on the shroud with all its unique and inexplicable features. Although his talents exceeded that of all artisans, past or present, including Leonardo DaVinci and Michelangelo, we know of no other work he produced, either before or after.

3. No one has been able to advance any natural and theoretical explanation as to how the image was created with all its features.

4. All experts except one have concluded that the image and blood are not paintings.[1] The only scientist concluding the image and blood are paintings never examined the Shroud itself, but only the residue sticky tapes taken from the Shroud. He concluded that because there were pigment flakes and iron oxide present, they must be painted. The presence of pigment flakes and iron oxide, however, makes perfect sense. Over the centuries duplicate images were painted and they would be draped over the Shroud to be sanctified. The presence of iron oxide is uniform throughout the Shroud and reflects the way linen would have been prepared in first century Palestine.

5. Since much of what he created was invisible to the naked eye, the forger created his masterpiece without being able to see what he was creating.

    a. The image is only visible as you pull away from the shroud to a distance of three feet.

    b. For centuries only a tiny fraction of what he had created could be seen. The master forger created the image so that no one (including the forger) could see the precise details of how the man of the shroud suffered and the savagery inflicted upon him until the invention of photography. All that was ever seen until 1898 was a ghostly image and the blood.

    c. Much of what he included in his rendition could not be seen or appreciated until twentieth century biochemistry, medicine, forensic pathology and anatomy, botany, and computer analysis became available.

6. The forger would have to have produced an image which under modern equipment reveals a three-dimensional image—something that a photograph or painting or bas relief or any other artistic process cannot do.

7. There is no image under the blood. This means the forger had to first paint or transfer the bloodstains to the Shroud before he created the image, strategically placing them so he could then paint or produce an image around the bloodstains.

8. The forger created the image using lines approximately 1/100th the width of a human hair and produced the image on only the very topmost fiber threads of the shroud. The image is so superficial that if you were to shave it with a razorblade it would disappear. Blood, water, and stains soak all the way through the cloth, but not the image itself.

---

1. *Shroud Critical Summary*, 82.

Additionally, he would have to have figured a way of imparting the image without brushstrokes.

9. Then he did the same thing, but in a subtler way, on the reverse side of the portion of the cloth bearing the face of Christ because the forger created two faces—one on the front that we all see, and the other a hidden face on the reverse side of the linen. This image was first reported in 2004 and corresponds to the front image but is much fainter. And this image, like the front image, is completely superficial to the topmost crown fibers of the cloth. "Because both images are superficial (meaning there is no image or colorant of any kind between the two image layers on the extreme outer faces of the cloth) and because the images are in registry with each other, all so-far-proposed fakery proposals are moot. The images are not paintings and not some form of medieval proto-photography."[2]

THE IMAGE OF THE CRUCIFIED MAN

1. In 1350 or thereabouts, the forger knew exactly what the Roman whip, tipped with dumbbell shaped bone or metal, looked like and the wounds it would inflict when delivered alternately by two Romans. Then, he incorporated these details into the image, but in a way that no one could see until the image was photographed and the negative developed in 1898. Moreover, there are scratches in the flesh that appear in the area of the dumbbell-shaped wounds. These scratches are only visible when illuminated by ultraviolet light![3]

2. The forger also duplicated abrasion and compression marks on the scourge wounds of the shoulders so that twentieth century forensic examiners could determine that the man in the shroud had carried a heavy weight following the scourging. There could be no doubt. The artist was trying to trick scientists six hundred years in the future into believing this was Jesus.

3. The forger accurately portrayed the nails going through (or at least exiting) the wrists rather than the palms as in all other medieval representations. He also understood that the thumbs of a crucified victim

---

2. *Shroud Facts Check,* "Second Face," second paragraph.
3. *Shroud Critical Summary,* 49.

would rotate inward because of the spikes passing through the heel of the hand. Consequently, he did not show Jesus' thumbs.

4. The forger had the unheard-of ability to create images of the metacarpal bones under the skin all the way to the wrist, detectable only by ultraviolet photographs, backlit photographs, and contrast enhanced images. Edge enhanced images show the metacarpal bones quite clearly.[4]
5. The forger duplicated crucifixion blood flow patterns from the wrists, arms, and feet in perfect forensic agreement to the exact crucifixion position.
6. Against all convention of medieval artistry, the master craftsman or artist created a nude Jesus to conform to Roman crucifixion practice.

THE BLOOD

1. The forger used AB blood so that it would match the blood on the Sudarium of Oviedo, Spain (see Chapter 15, "The Sudarium Confirms the Shroud of Turin").
2. The forger knew that blood with elevated amounts of bilirubin is indicative of a violent death. He then elevated the amounts of bilirubin in the blood on the Shroud so that they could retain their reddish color and be confirmed by twentieth century science.

CREATIVE GENIUS AND ATTENTION TO DETAIL

1. The forger was clever enough to salt the linen with the pollens of plants indigenous only to the environs of Jerusalem in anticipation of twentieth century palynological analysis.
2. The forger thought of such minute details as incorporating dirt on the feet, one knee, and the nose consistent with the calcium carbonate soil around Jerusalem. The dirt on the nose and knee was a particularly nice touch because it demonstrated that Jesus fell while carrying the cross.

---

4. *Shroud Critical Summary*, 78–79.

THE LINEN SHROUD

1. "The weave and particular stitching are very distinctive and rare. Nothing comparable to the Shroud has been found that originated in medieval Europe. The late John Tyrer, a textile researcher in Manchester England studied the X-radiographs of the Shroud and stated: 'the Shroud is a very poor product by comparison (to medieval European fabrics). It is full of warp and weft weaving defects. The impression I am left with is that the cloth is a much cruder and probably earlier fabric than the backing and patches. This I think lifts the Shroud out of the Middle Ages more than anything I have seen about the textile.'"[5]

2. "The radiocarbon dating of the Shroud was done in 1988 under the project management of the British Museum. Michael Tite, the lead manager on the project for the British Museum, conducted a thorough search for a control sample from the middle ages that would reasonably match the Shroud. 'He could find nothing.' On the other hand, archaeologists have discovered ancient wool artifacts with a herringbone weave similar to the Shroud. The artifacts were found in the ruins of a Roman fort in Egypt that dated from the 1st century. Mechthild Flury-Lemberg, the textile expert who was in charge of the 2002 Shroud preservation project in Turin, has said that even though the Shroud has many weaving defects, the herringbone weaving pattern itself would have been considered very special in antiquity in Palestine."[6]

3. "The cloth is consistent with fabrics from first-century Israel, but not with medieval Europe. A forger would have had to not only forge the image, but would have had to have detailed knowledge of linen weaves of the first century and then not only reproduce it, but age it convincingly."[7] In view of the nature of the linen and the unique herringbone weave described in the above paragraphs 1–2, the forger's unsurpassed talent and genius extended to textiles. There was no room for do-overs; the image in all its staggering detail would have to have been created right the first time, with no opportunity for corrections.

---

5. *Shroud Critical Summary*, 58–59.
6. *Shroud Critical Summary*, 59.
7. Longnecker, "Latest Evidence," paragraph 7.

4. There is a full-length strip of linen sewn on the side of the Shroud. The stitching pattern of the seam is similar to that discovered in the tombs of the Jewish fortress of Masada, which date to between 40 BC and A.D. 73.[8]

This is only a partial list of the characteristics and issues the forger who lived some 150 years prior to Columbus's discovery of America would need to have overcome.

---

8. *Shroud Critical Summary*, 61.

14.3

The Shroud of Turin

Evidence against the Shroud's Authenticity

The list of reasons why the Shroud should be considered genuine is long. Surely there must be compelling evidence on the other side. Here are the ones cited.

1988 CARBON DATING TO 1260–1390

In 1988 a sample was cut from the Shroud and submitted to three laboratories (University of Oxford, ETH Zurich, and University of Arizona) for carbon dating. They concluded with 95 percent certainty that the Shroud dates between 1260 and 1390. Science had spoken and that should be the end of it. Edward Hall (now dead) was the head of the Oxford radiocarbon laboratory and in announcing the 1260–1390 range of dates said, "There was a multi-million-pound business in making forgeries during the fourteenth century. Someone just got a bit of linen, faked it up and flogged it!"[1] Spoken like a true impartial scientist.

As it turned out, however, the carbon dating process was severely flawed, and it has been conclusively shown (except for the most ardent skeptics) that the 1988 carbon dating must be incorrect. The sample tested was taken from the corner of the cloth which over the years had been repaired,

---

1. *Shroud Critical Summary*, 94.

soiled, and contaminated, and handled uncounted times. Additionally, and most damaging to the 1350 date, was the work and exhaustive research conducted by non-scientists Sue Benford and Joe Marino. They devoted untold hours of research and concluded that the part of the Shroud that was carbon dated had been repaired sometime in the Middle Ages by an invisible weaving technique called "French Weave" whereby new cotton threads are interwoven with the original threads.

In 2005 their work was confirmed. A peer reviewed scientific paper by Raymond N. Rogers, retired Fellow of the Los Alamos National Laboratory, was published in the journal *Thermochimica Acta*.[2] The paper is titled "Studies on the radiocarbon sample from the shroud of turin," and concludes that the sample used to test the age of the Shroud of Turin in 1988 was not part of the original cloth.

The abstract summarizes the paper:

> In 1988, radiocarbon laboratories at Arizona, Cambridge, and Zurich determined the age of a sample from the Shroud of Turin. They reported that the date of the cloth's production lay between a.d. 1260 and 1390 with 95% confidence. This came as a surprise in view of the technology used to produce the cloth, its chemical composition, and the lack of vanillin in its lignin. The results prompted questions about the validity of the sample.
>
> Preliminary estimates of the kinetics constants for the loss of vanillin from lignin indicate a much older age for the cloth than the radiocarbon analyses. The radiocarbon sampling area is uniquely coated with a yellow–brown plant gum containing dye lakes. Pyrolysis-mass-spectrometry results from the sample area coupled with microscopic and microchemical observations prove that the radiocarbon sample was not part of the original cloth of the Shroud of Turin. The radiocarbon date was thus not valid for determining the true age of the shroud.

When the idea of a French weave had first been proposed to Mr. Rogers, he had immediately thought this was the newest lunatic fringe theory to discredit the 1988 carbon dates. His analysis and research proved otherwise.

Then in 2013 Giulio Fanti of Padua University conducted a dating test using infra-red light and spectroscopy technology to measure the radiation intensity through wavelengths. From these measurements a date can be calculated. Fanti's method dated fibers from the Shroud to 300 BC to A.D. 400.[3]

---

2. Rogers, "Studies" 189–194.
3. Longnecker, "Latest Evidence," eighth paragraph.

The 1988 carbon dating is no longer considered reliable. A detailed examination of the improper radiocarbon dating protocol is discussed in *Shroud Critical Summary*.[4] The authors are not sure about the validity of the French Weave argument and advance their own reasons as to why the 1260–1390 date must be wrong. What we do know with absolute certainty from the 1192 Hungarian Pray Manuscript (see Chapter 14.1, "Shroud of Turin: Historical Documentation") and the Shroud's features is that the carbon date, for whatever reason, is dead wrong.

NO DOCUMENTED HISTORY PRIOR TO 1355

The facts do not support this conclusion. We have the 1192 Hungarian Pray Manuscript image as well as the number of documented indirect references to the Shroud prior to 1350. See chapter 14.1.

1389 BISHOP D'ARCIS LETTER

In 1389 Bishop Pierre d'Arcis wrote to Pope Clement VII at Avignon that his predecessor Bishop Henri of Poiters had maintained that an artist confessed to having painted the cloth. This is irrefutable contemporary evidence that the shroud is a fake.

Here's what the skeptics don't tell you:

- Nobody is sure that D'Arcis sent this letter. It is an unsigned draft.
- D'Arcis gives no evidence of either an investigation or the alleged confession supposedly given to his predecessor 30 years earlier. The name of the forger is never disclosed.
- On its face, the D'Arcis letter clearly misstates the facts. It says that the shroud was "painted," but we know that is not the case. The image was transferred to the cloth through a means that no one can identify.
- D'Arcis's successor believed the Shroud to be genuine and permitted its open veneration. Bishop d'Arcis may well have been writing about a "cunningly painted" copy of the real relic.
- But here's probably the real reason for d'Arcis's letter: The de Charney family owned the Shroud and were successfully challenging D'Arcis's authority in the diocese. D'Arcis's motivation may have been simply to undercut the authority of the de Charney's. We will never know,

---

4. *Shroud Critical Summary*, 91–98.

but we do know that he was locked in a bitter feud and was ultimately censored by Clement VII.

THE IMAGE IMPROPERLY PRESENTS CHRIST

Critics improbably try to argue that the Shroud cannot possibly be the burial cloth of Jesus because the physical characteristics are inconsistent with what a real person who was entombed would look like. The arms are too long; the fingers are too long; the hair does not lie properly; he's too tall for a first century Jew, etc. etc. In other words, the representation on the Shroud does not match the way it should be. Moreover, the resurrection as depicted on the cloth could not possibly be correct.

What incredible arrogance! God doesn't need to conform to our selective expectations. Just ask Adam and Eve—it doesn't work that way. We can't substitute our judgment of right and wrong for his, and it is the height of foolishness and arrogance for the creature to tell the Creator how he should present himself to us, his proper physical characteristics, and the resurrection protocol.

CONCLUDING THOUGHTS

As unlikely as it first appears, it is certain the radiocarbon testing results are incorrect. Almost certainly the sample (there was only one which was subsequently cut into three testing specimen) was not part of the original cloth of the Shroud of Turin. Skeptics fixate on the announced carbon testing results and refuse to give any credence to the possibility that it could be wrong and that all the other scientific evidence pointing to a much earlier date with a Mid-East origin could be correct. To do so would acknowledge the real possibility that the Shroud of Turin is indeed a photograph of Jesus taken at the instant of his resurrection. To do so would inevitably lead to the uncomfortable conclusion (uncomfortable for them) that the resurrected Jesus is in fact the resurrected Son of God, and that they are relegated to the status of mere creatures.

14.4

The Shroud of Turin

Proving the Supernatural

WHAT IF THE SHROUD IS A FAKE?

If we and millions of others are wrong and it turns out the Shroud is just a medieval fake, will that undermine our faith? The answer is no. We will be disappointed, and perhaps intensely so, because unnumbered millions sitting on the fence will say to themselves that the skeptics, agnostics, and atheists were right after all. Jesus is just a hopeful and fanciful myth. They will ignore the fundamental Christian principle that faith emerges from a simple and humble desire to know God. Our Lord does not impose himself upon us; he whispers to us and we can hear him only if we are listening. Unfortunately, I would expect that there are millions with the same mindset as Doubting Thomas and need proof to accept the Resurrection.

The Shroud will never deliver that proof. You cannot prove one supernatural event by another, and you cannot prove the Divine by science. Science can make it easier for you to believe or not believe so we look to science, including documented history, to help guide us to an understanding of what the Shroud is and its origins. If the facts supported the conclusion that it was a fake, we could accept that finding. On the other hand, and regardless of the facts, we could never prove with absolute certainty that the Shroud was the burial cloth of Jesus and that his likeness was somehow and mysteriously etched on it at the instant of the Resurrection. While the

Divine Hand cannot be proven by mortal ones, we can make it more difficult for the true seeker to escape the trail of facts which, as he learns more, leads inevitably to Jesus. Consequently, the question of whether we can rely upon the Shroud of Turin as a testimonial of Jesus' Passion, Crucifixion, and as a divinely gifted picture of Jesus when he rose from the dead is an important one.

If the Shroud were any other artifact it would have been considered conclusively proved years ago that it dated from first century Jerusalem. But because it is purported to be the burial shroud that covered Jesus at the time of his resurrection its authenticity has been subjected to unparalleled critical scrutiny and misrepresentation. If it is "proven" to be genuine then non-Christians will be sent scrambling. Consequently, it is crucial for them that the Shroud be discredited and debunked. The burden on the Shroud believer is not so intense. If it shown to be a fake, the borderline Christian who had put his faith in an image and not a living personal Jesus may sadly cease his quest for the Savior. If it is a fake, the real Christian will be disappointed and saddened, but his faith was never dependent upon a Shroud he has never personally seen and located in a faraway country. He can just shrug his shoulders and reel in his disappointment. If on the other hand the Shroud is authentic—Wow! If the Shroud is fake there could be many who will turn away from Christ's door without even trying to enter. If it is real there will be millions who, as did Thomas the Apostle, will now believe, firmly and irrevocably, and bring others to Christianity.

CONCLUSION

Realistically, and regardless of the amount of overpowering evidence, we can never prove that that the Shroud of Turin is the Resurrection linen even if we can demonstrate beyond a reasonable doubt that it wrapped the body of a crucified man wearing a crown of thorns in first century Jerusalem. Nevertheless, any fair analysis must conclude that almost certainly the Shroud of Turin is the burial cloth of Jesus, and almost certainly this is his image imprinted upon the Shroud at the instant of his resurrection. Similarly, any fair analysis must conclude that the Sudarium of Oviedo (see next chapter) is the rolled-up napkin in Jesus' tomb that John mentions in his Gospel. As is the case with the Gospel accounts of the Resurrection, the Shroud and the Sudarium together present a compelling story of God's love for us, available to anyone who seeks God with an open heart and mind.

15

The Sudarium Confirms the Shroud of Turin

THE SUDARIUM

The Sudarium of Oviedo is a 21 x 34-inch piece of cloth which tradition claims was used to cover and clean the face of Jesus before the Resurrection. There are blood and other bodily fluid stains on the cloth, but no image. The Sudarium (which means face cloth) is held in a cathedral in Oviedo, Spain. Its history is well documented, free of controversy, and is summarized in the following timeline. The evidence that this piece of cloth covered the head of the crucified Jesus and the Sudarium's relationship to the Shroud will be discussed immediately following the timeline.

HISTORICAL TIMELINE

Year	Event
30–33	John 20: 6-8 records: 6 Then Simon Peter came, following him, and went into the tomb; he saw the linen cloths lying, 7 and the napkin, which had been on his head, not lying with the linen cloths but rolled up in a place by itself. 8 Then the other disciple, who reached the tomb first, also went in, and he saw and believed;

Year	Event
570	A traveler to Palestine writes that the Sudarium was being cared for in a cave near the monastery of Saint Mark, near Jerusalem.
614	The Sudarium is in Jerusalem and is taken to Alexandria, Egypt to avoid destruction by the Persians who had attacked Jerusalem.
616	The Persians swept eastward into Alexandria and the Sudarium was carried along North Africa to Spain where it remained for many years, first in Seville and then in Toledo.
718	The invading Muslims forced the Bishop of Toledo to take the Sudarium further north. It was first kept in a cave about six miles from Oviedo and then transferred to Oviedo.
1075	The chest containing the Sudarium and other relics is opened. A list of the relics was made, which included the Sudarium.
1113	The chest in Spain is covered with silver plating, on which there is an inscription inviting all Christians to venerate this relic which contains the holy blood. The Sudarium has been kept in the cathedral in Oviedo, Spain ever since.

JOHN 20:6–8

In Jewish tradition, blood is considered the seat of life and when a person dies, all blood should be collected and buried together with the corpse. Thus, it is quite likely a cloth would have been placed over the head of Jesus immediately after his death and while he was still hanging from the cross to stop any bleeding from his mouth and nose. Covering the face was a Jewish practice of respect and compassion for the family of the dead, particularly if the face were disfigured, which would clearly have been the case for Jesus whose bloodied face was beaten and swollen.

The evidence tells us that the Sudarium of Oviedo is that cloth, and that it was the cloth rolled up in the tomb as narrated by John 20:6–8. Formal scientific testing of the Sudarium began in the early 1990s.

SCIENTIFIC CORRELATION OF THE SHROUD AND THE SUDARIUM

Correlation of the wounds. The findings indicate that the Sudarium had been placed against the face of a man who had been beaten on the front and back of the head. It presents a pattern of successive stains from perspiration, blood, and lymph which would coincide perfectly if overlaid upon the

Shroud. There are also stains from deep puncture wounds on the portion of the cloth covering the back of the head that are consistent with similar marks found on the Shroud. All of this is consistent with the Sudarium being pressed against the face of the deceased to clean the face, but not in a swiping motion.

Blood type. The blood on both the Shroud and Sudarium is relatively rare Type AB.

Pollen. Pollen samples indicate that both the Sudarium and the Shroud were at one time in Palestine. Two species of pollen unique to Palestine were found on the Sudarium which were also found on the Shroud. Pollen samples are also consistent with the fact that the Shroud and Sudarium took different routes to reach their present destinations. The Sudarium held pollen which was unique to North Africa, while the shroud does not contain the North African pollen. On the other hand, the Shroud contains pollen native to Turkey and France, which are not found on the Sudarium.

Cloth that was rolled up separately. While the blood types match, the wound marks match, the facial features and measurements coincide, and pollen studies help confirm the cloths' histories, the Sudarium does not have the "scorched" fibers present on the Shroud. There is no underlying image of a face on the Sudarium. This is consistent with the observation by John's Gospel that a separate cloth was rolled up separately from the Shroud in the tomb. It would have been placed there after the body was placed in the tomb and before the Resurrection.

FAULTY CARBON TESTING

In 2007, it was announced that samples from the Sudarium were subjected to carbon dating. They were dated to A.D. 700. This date cannot possibly be correct if for no other reason than there is clear documentary evidence tracing the Sudarium back to at least 130 years earlier, and possibly back to the beginning of the fifth century. Moreover, the laboratory conducting the tests was also given four different control cloths to date. Three of them were dated as expected. The fourth, a cloth from an Egyptian mummy, was dated to anytime in the nineteenth or twentieth centuries, and the laboratory incorrectly concluded they were fakes.[1]

Now comes the real zinger. In 2016 a study[2] confirmed that the Shroud of Turin and the Sudarium were wrapped around the head of the same corpse. In particular, "the investigation has found a number of correlations

1. Shroud website, "International Conference," 2.
2. Aleteia website, "New Study."

between the two relics that 'far exceeds the minimum number of proofs or significant points required by most judicial systems around the world to identify a person, which is between eight and 12, while our study has demonstrated more than 20.'" The author of the study concludes, "we have come to a point where it seems absurd to suggest that 'by happenstance' all of the wounds, lesions and swelling coincides on both cloths. Logic requires that we conclude that we are speaking of the same person."

SUDARIUM AND SHROUD CARBON DATINGS MUST BE INCORRECT

The carbon dating for the Shroud gives us an approximate 1350 date while the Sudarium is carbon dated at 700. Yet the 2016 investigation shows that they both covered the same person. Clearly, one or both carbon dates are incorrect. "Scientist César Barta spoke about the carbon dating process, emphasizing the fact that if carbon dating is always absolutely accurate, then we could just as well finish the congress there and then. However, there were several points to bear in mind—in specialist carbon dating magazines, about half the samples dated come up with the expected date, around 30% with an 'acceptable' date, and the other 20% is not what one would expect from archaeology. The laboratory used (via the National Museum in Madrid) said they were surprised by the result and asked if the cloth was contaminated with any oil based product, as oil is not cleaned by the laboratory processes used before carbon dating and if oil is present on a sample, the date produced by carbon dating is in fact the date of contamination."[3]

WHY DO WE HAVE THE SUDARIUM?

Let's leave this discussion with the following thought from Juan Ignacio Moreno, a magistrate in Burgos, Spain, and a leading advocate of the Sudarium's authenticity, concerning the mystery of both the Shroud and the Cloth of Oviedo: "The Sudarium is a relic rediscovered for Christians fighting a new fight. It is a love letter to our time from God: a tantalizing puzzle saved for the minds of men that have made science and knowledge their god."[4]

---

3. Shroud website, "International Conference," 2.
4. Anderson, "Other Shroud," final paragraph.

CONCLUSION

Realistically, and regardless of the amount of overpowering evidence, we can never prove that that the Shroud of Turin is the Resurrection linen even if we can demonstrate beyond a reasonable doubt that it wrapped the body of a crucified man wearing a crown of thorns in first century Jerusalem. Nevertheless, any fair analysis must conclude that almost certainly the Shroud of Turin is the burial cloth of Jesus, and his image was imprinted upon the Shroud at the instant of his resurrection. Similarly, any fair analysis must conclude that the Sudarium of Oviedo is the rolled-up napkin in Jesus' tomb that John mentions in his Gospel. As is the case with the Gospel accounts of the Resurrection, the Shroud and the Sudarium together present a compelling story of God's love for us, available to anyone who seeks God with an open heart and mind.

16

Holy House of Loreto

The Book of Luke tells us that the angel Gabriel appeared to the young virgin, Mary, and announced that with her consent she was to conceive and bear the Son of God (the Annunciation). She had been chosen by God to become the mother of Jesus, the only begotten Son of the Father ("God from God, Light from Light. . ."). This was such a phenomenal cosmic event that we sometimes wonder whether God could have left some evidence to confirm this story.

We are certain he has, and it is called the Holy House of Loreto.

The Holy House of Loreto is misnamed; it is not a house, but a brick and mortar U-shaped structure of three walls. It is approximately thirty feet long by fifteen feet wide and about fifteen feet high. In 1296 the Holy House inexplicably appeared fully constructed on the main road near Loreto, Italy, with one of its corners hanging over a ditch. There is a strong tradition and belief that this is the house in Nazareth that Mary grew up in and lived. It would have been in this house that the angel Gabriel appeared to her. It could even be the house where Jesus spent his childhood. How can this be? Loreto is located halfway up the eastern coast of Italy, about fifteen hundered miles northeast of Nazareth. Notwithstanding its location, the house has been a Catholic pilgrimage destination since the fourteenth century and several million people visit it every year. What evidence is there that this is in fact the house of Mary and how did it get to Italy?

FROM NAZARETH TO LORETO—A CHRONOLOGY

From the beginnings of Christianity, the house in which Mary lived at the time of the Annunciation and the grotto which formed one side of the Holy House was a place of pilgrimage and worship in Nazareth. In about 312 Constantine had a Basilica built over the house and the grotto, which were interred within a subterranean crypt. The House always remained protected by the original Basilica or its replacements until the Muslims invaded the Holy Land in about the year 1090. They ravaged the Christian holy places and turned churches and basilicas into mosques and destroyed other Christian sites. While the Basilica over the Holy House was destroyed, the Holy House itself and the grotto survived.

The Crusaders reclaimed the Holy Land in 1100 and built a new Basilica. In 1219 St. Francis of Assisi visited the site. Around the year 1250 St Louis IX king of France visited, prayed, and received Communion while on a Crusade to the Holy Land. But in 1263 the rebuilt Basilica was destroyed by the Muslims. As before, however, the House and the grotto remained intact.

In 1291 the Crusaders were completely driven out of the Holy Land, and with them left the last line of defense for the remaining holy Christian sites, including the Holy House. It was then that it disappeared from Palestine.

On May 10, 1291, the Holy House suddenly appeared in fields of what is now Croatia, near Trsat (sometimes called Tersatto). The day before there had been neither building nor building materials. There was nothing, but now there was a three-walled structure and inside was an ancient altar and a statue of the Virgin Mary and the infant Jesus. The local priest, who was in ill health, prayed for help. What was this building and why is it here? His hours of intense prayer were answered when the Blessed Mother appeared to him in sleep and told him that this was the Holy House of Nazareth where the Annunciation took place and it was brought here through the power of God. This was the house in which she was raised and the altar within it had been consecrated by Peter. To confirm what she was telling him, he would be restored to health.

The sudden cure of the priest convinced him and the villagers of the veracity of his vision the night before. With knowledge certain they venerated the little house accordingly.

The Governor of Dalmatia (predecessor of parts of current Croatia) sent a delegation to Palestine with the assignment of determining whether the Holy House was still there. They reported back that not only had the Holy House disappeared from Nazareth, but that the length and breadth of the walls of the dwelling found at Tersatto corresponded exactly with the foundations beneath the Basilica which had been built over the original Holy House. Moreover, the Tersatto house was built of limestone, mortar, and cedar wood, common in Nazareth, but almost unobtainable in Dalmatia.

In 1294 the Muslims continued their march northward and closed in on Croatia. On December 10, 1294, and just as suddenly as it had appeared, the Holy House vanished. Within a few years the first church was built on the site and a shrine erected. Today it is known as Our Lady of Trsat. In 1367 Pope Urban V gave the people of Trsat an oil painting of *Miraculous Mary* (also known as *Our Lady of the Graces*) in consolation for their loss of the Holy House. To this day the painting remains, in the same place where the house of Nazareth was recreated.

On the same date the Holy House disappeared from Croatia, December 10, 1294, it suddenly came to rest on a hill next to the Adriatic Sea, near the town of Recanati, Italy. Later it was moved again to a nearby forest. There it became a place of pilgrimage for a number of months, but the pilgrims became targets of bandits and the House again suddenly was moved. This time it arrived on a hill belonging to two quarreling brothers. Finally, in 1296 the House was moved again, and this time to its present location on top of an ancient public road. In total, the House had been moved five times: (1) Nazareth to Croatia; (2) Croatia to an Italian hill by the sea; (3) to a forest; (4) to the quarreling brothers' property; and (5) its present location. In each case the walls had no foundation. It finally came to rest over an ancient public road in what is now Loreto, partially dangling over a ditch.

Why would we believe this story?

There are numerous contemporaneous documents, tablets, inscriptions, churches, and other hard evidence to support this history and the traditional explanation that the House was borne from place to place by angels. There is even contemporaneous testimony from those who claimed to have seen the House in flight!

The angelic translation seems hard to believe in this day and age. Perhaps there are more rational explanations.

One explanation is that the house was disassembled, and the stones transported from Palestine by the Crusaders to its present site in Loreto, Italy. The best evidence of this tradition is that there is an Italian receipt showing the importation by the Angeles family of stones from the House of the Blessed Virgin at about the same time the House suddenly appeared.

A second tradition is that the stones were first taken to Trsat. There a delegation was sent to Nazareth to measure the dimensions of the foundation of the house for its reconstruction. The house was then rebuilt, and the local prince then gave the Holy House to the Pope and shipped it to Italy, where it was then placed in Loreto.

Among other problems, both these more "rational" traditions ignore the well-attested fact that the house first appeared (fully constructed) in Trsat, Croatia and that it then would have to have been deconstructed and moved three more times and then moved to its present location. The House would have to have been reconstructed five times. But the real question is whether this is the house of Mary.

EVIDENCE THAT THIS IS THE NAZARENE HOUSE OF MARY

There is powerful, but not conclusive, evidence that this is the site of the Annunciation. In particular:

1. In 1296 the fully constructed House (the three walls, altar, and the statue of Mary) suddenly appeared overnight at its present location. There was no planning, drawings, materials, workers—the House simply showed up and claimed its spot.
2. It appeared on the area's principal public road. There can be no rational explanation for building a house on the region's principal public road in the 1290's. It is as though the House proclaims that this is not its real home.
3. Unlike all other houses in the region it had no foundation.
4. A corner of the House was incomprehensibly hanging in the air over a ditch. (Because the House had no foundation, was partially "built" hanging over a ditch, and the nature of the soil, supporting arches were later added.)
5. The House originally had one door which faced north. Locals never built their house with doors facing north because of the prevailing northern winds. The original northern door was later filled in and two other doors were opened to accommodate the pilgrims.
6. The position of the original door was on the longer side of the house and not on the shorter side, which would have been more usual.
7. In Nazareth at the time of Jesus, the three walls would have been snugged against the opening to a grotto (a shallow cave or recess). The area enclosed by the three walls and the grotto itself would have constituted the living area. The part where the altar now stands would have been the opening to the grotto. Over the altar stands a replica of a wooden statue of the Madonna. The original one, made of cedar of

Lebanon, arrived in the Loreto region together with the house in 1294, but was destroyed by fire in 1921.

8. The dimensions are such that if we were to transfer these three walls to the grotto at Nazareth every dimension, every size and every proportion matches perfectly. This had been confirmed as far back as 1292, and later in 1296 and 1524. This is a typical house from Palestine in the first century.

9. In the original part of the house the walls from ground level up to about nine feet are built with stones identical to those used in Palestine at the time of Jesus, but quite different from stones in the Loreto region. The working and finishing of the stones and patterns were well-known in the Nazarene area.

10. The mortar used in the walls is of Palestinian origin, and precisely in the area around Nazareth. This mortar was not used in Italy. It does not seem realistic for the crusaders to bring the makings of mortar with them from Palestine.

11. The stones used in the altar are of Palestinian origin and of the same style of finishing as the walls. The altar would be consistent with the conclusion that after the Resurrection the first disciples transformed the House of the Lord's mother into a place of worship. This could very well be the most ancient altar in all of Christianity and we can easily envision Peter standing and kneeling before it, offering the Eucharist.

12. There are about sixty graffiti in the form of engraved markings which are dated between the first and third centuries after Christ. Some are the initials of Jesus in Hebrew. The graffiti were typical Judeo Christian. One is written in Greek with two letters in Hebrew and it says in Greek, "Oh Jesus Christ Son of God."

13. The remains of an ostrich egg were found which was totally inappropriate in Italy while they were frequent in mid-east Christian churches. It is hard to fathom why the Crusaders would return with the remains of an ostrich egg.

14. In the thirteenth century the settlement and, later, city that we now know as Loreto, Italy did not exist. Suddenly something of such importance occurred to mandate the building of a basilica and the building of a town. There was nothing. Then, and quite suddenly, the location became a site of pilgrimage and miracles and immediately endowed with a rich tradition explaining the sudden appearance of these three walls, altar, and statue on the major public road of the time.

FACING THE FACTS

Clearly, there can be a lot of confusion surrounding events which occurred more than 700 years ago in medieval Europe. Nevertheless, regardless of which transportation tradition we believe, we need to account for a number of inexplicable facts, including the fact that the House was constructed five different times in five different locations overnight and with no knowledge of anyone that it was being constructed.

While we can never prove the mode of removal from Palestine and the history of its journey, nearly all evidence points to a divine intervention and angelic transportation according to the 700-year-old tradition. The one countervailing piece of evidence of the document dated in September or October 1294 stating that the stones from the House of Mary were being imported. But even this documentation does not mention how many stones, what the circumstances were or give any detail.

Whatever tradition we consider the most likely, they all point to one undeniable conclusion: these walls and the altar originated in first century Palestine and were considered a holy site by the earliest Christians, all consistent with the continuing belief that these were the walls of the Holy House of Mary where the Annunciation occurred. Whether they arrived in Loreto by angelic flight or by multiple deconstructions, shipments by land and sea, and the multiple reconstructions, we know this House is a gift from God to us to help us in our faith.

Today the Holy House stands as one of the most sacred and important of all Catholic shrines. Written at the door of the basilica are these words: "The whole world has no place more sacred... For here was the Word made Flesh, and here was born the Virgin Mother..."

There are numerous internet sites describing the Holy House of Loreto. I would suggest the article by Servants of the Pierced Hearts of Jesus and Mary.[1]

---

1. See Bibliography.

17

Science and Evolution

RES IPSA LOQUITUR

In the 1860's England a Mr. Byrne was walking along a street when a barrel of flour rolled out of the defendant's second-floor window and landed on him. He sustained serious injuries and sued. To collect damages, however, he had to prove defendant's negligence. He could not; there were no witnesses as to why the flour barrel rolled out the window and he could not put forward anything to show that the defendant was negligent. The English court, nevertheless, invoked the doctrine of *res ipsa loquitur* and found for the plaintiff. Sometimes the causes for events are so obvious that there is no need to find supporting evidence. The thing speaks for itself—*res ipsa loquitur.*

When it comes to the human body and its complexity, it is impossible to conclude anything but a divine Creator. *Res ipsa loquitur.*

LIFE: GOD'S CREATION

Just for a moment think about the complexity and wonder of human life, or any life form. From a speck of cells, each with incredible complexity and the size of a pinhead, a human being grows and develops into a living organism with eyes, ears, a liver, a staggeringly complex reproductive system (two independent and complementary variations, requiring both working together to function), a digestive system, lungs, bones, an interlocking highway of nerves and blood vessels, a brain, a heart, etc., etc., each of which is in turn supported and built by a complex assemblage of cells and their equally complex component parts. These complementary cells and organs have no meaning or use except as part of an unimaginably complex human which grows from a speck to a complex intra-active adapting structure of diverse parts mostly kept in by the skin. None of these human operational systems could ever create themselves, develop or survive for even an instant without a pre-determined target of what the end product was going to be and the simultaneous development of other systems. To illustrate, consider this image of the human ear and brief discussion of how we hear:[1]

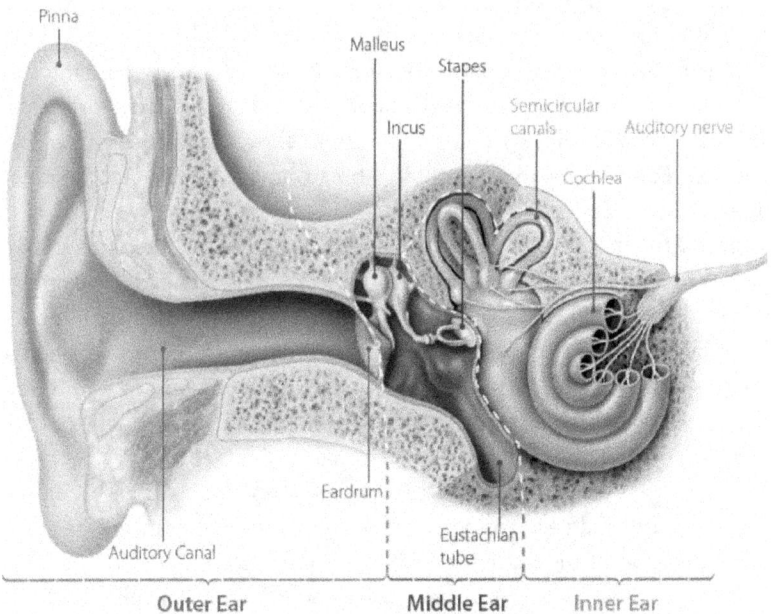

Both ears collect acoustic signals from multiple directions. The complex structure of our ears then process this information and passes it to the brain for interpretation.

1. Our outer ear collects the sound vibrations and funnels them through the ear canal to the eardrum.

---

1. Digisound website, "How does our ear work?"

2. These sounds make your eardrum vibrate and passes soundwaves to the middle ear.
3. The middle ear consists of three bones (the hammer, the anvil and the stirrup), one of which is the hardest and smallest bone in your body. The vibrations are then transmitted and amplified to the oval window of the inner ear.
4. Fluid in the inner ear stimulates the hair cells. The outermost hair cells are responsible for the high frequencies, whilst the inner hair cells are responsible for the mid and low frequencies. When these hair cells are damaged it affects your ability to hear.
5. Electrical impulses are then sent from the hair cells along the auditory nerve to the brain for interpretation.

Still, this part of the hearing system is of no consequence unless a pre-existing communication system transferred data to the brain, which in turn must have been developed earlier or simultaneously to receive and interpret the messages. None of these systems or parts make any sense or create a survival advantage unless all three came into existence at once and worked together. For example, there would be no advantage having a communication channel unless there were something to communicate. We could go on forever. And this is just the ear. Consider the *multitude* of other human body parts and systems which require an ever increasingly complex development alongside other independent and synergistic operating systems to function.

Take the time to google human anatomy or specific parts of the human body (shoulder, foot, eye, etc.). The intricacy and complexity of our bodies defy an explanation of simple chemicals becoming increasingly complex and working together to produce the human body.

Mere words cannot adequately explain the complexity of the human organism. I would urge you to watch some film showing the truly miraculous operation of the human body's ten major systems.[2] As you do so try to imagine how these complex systems could have gradually developed, considering their complexities, integration, the complex sub-systems within each, how they could have evolved one step at a time before they developed a useful function, and how the components could grow and assemble themselves from the union of the head of a sperm (microscopic in size) and an ovum (size of a pinhead) . Both the sperm and ovum are staggeringly complex, each consisting of still other operating microscopic biological

---

2. See in particular the National Geographic presentation at https://www.youtube.com/watch?v=Ae4MadKPJCo (YouTube search words: human body 101 national).

machines (where did these come from?). As you view these videos,[3,4] marvel at the complexity and numerous component parts of the sperm and ovum and ask yourself whether it is even remotely reasonable for these microscopic reproductive machines to have randomly developed on their own.

Res ipsa loquitur.

Here are some YouTube presentations for our various systems; there are many more.

- **Respiratory.** https://www.youtube.com/watch?v=kacMYexDgHg
- **Nervous.** https://www.youtube.com/results?search_query=science+nervous+system
- **Skeletal.** https://www.youtube.com/watch?v=UPrxQkjjExI
- **Muscular.** https://www.youtube.com/watch?v=rMcg9YzNSEs
- **Cardiovascular/Circulatory.** https://www.youtube.com/watch?v=_lgd03h3te8
- **Endocrine.** https://www.youtube.com/watch?v=ER49EweKwW8
- **Lymphatic.** https://www.youtube.com/watch?v=cCPyWFK0IKs
- **Urinary.** https://www.youtube.com/watch?v=CkGqp5tr-Qk
- **Digestive.** https://www.youtube.com/watch?v=Og5xAdC8EUI
- **Reproductive.** https://www.youtube.com/watch?v=_5OvgQW6FG4&ab_channel=NucleusMedicalMedia
- **Skin.** https://www.youtube.com/watch?v=uH_uzjY2bEE

Now, I refer you to the intricate structure and operation of the human cell,[5] and the diverse biological machines within. These separate microscopic entities work together to maintain and divide the cells. Each cell within the body (and there are trillions of them) has its own complex infrastructure with its various components each having a specific role and purpose. The twisting DNA defies explanation. And this is just for one human body. Now consider the billions of such human individuals. Consider also that there are literally a million different species, each with its own individual

---

3. https://www.youtube.com/watch?v=_Mum9z-8kks (YouTube search words: structure sperm cell).

4. https://www.youtube.com/watch?v=q5aO62pTAiA (YouTube search words: structure ovum).

5. An excellent video (there are others as well) can be found at https://www.youtube.com/watch?v=URUJD5NEXC8 (YouTube search words: biology cell structure nucleus).

DNA composition and each again containing a message of complexity and impossibility.

These *billions and trillions (and trillions beyond)* of min-universes of unfathomable diversity and wonder cannot be explained by the use of one word, "evolution." Evolution does not explain anything about the process of life creation and development; it can't. When you strip away all the adornments it is merely a word which states that different life forms exist at different places and at different times. It does not and cannot explain how the astronomical improbabilities inherent in this belief system were overcome.

For example, consider our visual system which includes the eye, the optic nerve and brain. The eye itself functions through a number of independent and inter-related systems. Here is how www.webmd.com describes the process:

> Light reflects off an object, and if that object is in your field of vision, it enters the eye.
>
> The first thing it touches is a thin veil of tears in the front. Behind this is your eye's front window, the cornea. This clear layer helps focus the light.
>
> On the other side is liquid called the aqueous humor. It circulates throughout the front part of your eye and keeps pressure inside constant.
>
> After the aqueous humor, light passes through the pupil. This is the central round opening in your iris, the colored part of your eye. It changes size to control how much light gets in farther back. Next up is the lens. It works just like a camera to focus light. It adjusts shape depending on whether the light reflects off something near to you or far away.
>
> This light now pierces the center of the eye. It's bathed in moisture from a clear jelly known as the vitreous.
>
> Its final destination is the retina, which lines the back of your eye. It's like the screen in a movie theater or the film in a camera. The focused light hits cells called photoreceptors.
>
> Unlike a movie screen, the retina has many parts:
>
> **Blood vessels** bring nutrients to your nerve cells.
>
> The **macula** is the bull's-eye at the center of your retina. The dead center is called the fovea. Because it's the focal point of your eye, it has more special, light-sensitive nerve endings, called photoreceptors, than any other part.
>
> **Photoreceptors** come in two kinds: rods and cones. They're special nerve endings that convert the light into electrochemical signals.

Retinal pigment epithelium (RPE) is a layer of dark tissue beneath the photoreceptors. These cells absorb excess light so the photoreceptors can give a clearer signal. They also move nutrients to (and waste from) the photoreceptors to the choroid.

The **choroid** is separate from the RPE. It lies behind the retina and is made up of many fine blood vessels that supply nutrition to the retina and the RPE.

Sclera is the tough, white, fibrous outside wall of your eye. It's connected to the clear cornea in front. It protects the delicate structures inside the eye.

Signals from the photoreceptors travel along nerve fibers to the optic nerve. It sends the signals to the visual center in the back of the brain.

And that's how you see: Light, reflected from an object, enters the eye, gets focused, is converted into electrochemical signals, delivered to the brain, and is interpreted, or 'seen,' as an image.[6]

Vision is but one of the numerous complex systems which grace our bodies. Ask yourself how a clump of inorganic material could self-assemble into diverse and completely different parts to enable vision. The construction would have to be immediate and simultaneous. The retina cannot function without the cornea; nothing works without the optic nerve; the brain would have to be functioning to interpret the data, etc., etc. There can be no rational explanation other than a Creator.

As you view the videos and consider the complexity of the human operating systems and the underlying trillions of cells, it should be apparent that these wonderous machines could not self-assemble.

Res ipsa loquitur.

---

6. https://www.webmd.com/eye-health/amazing-human-eye (YouTube search words: Vision Basics: How Does Your Eye Work?)

18

Miraculous Healings

What better proof is there of God's existence, omnipotence, and powerful love than a miraculous healing? The instant and clearly perceived reversal of a debilitating illness, physical handicap, or the gift of sight where minutes earlier there was blindness is but a reflection of God's grace, given so that we might believe. Such a miracle is a sudden loving event that defies rational or scientific explanation. Nevertheless, we often forget that the glorification of God and the calling of people to the Lord's table is always the miracle's primary purpose. The grace of restored health is but a secondary purpose. A miracle always provides a clear sign of God's intercession and is a supernatural phenomenon; it is much more than an event which is merely remarkable or improbable.

We will examine five claimed miraculous healings.

- Marie Bailly and Nobel Laureate Alexis Carrel (1902, 1944)
- Jack Traynor (1923—Lourdes)
- Gabriel Gargam (1901—Lourdes)
- Marion Carroll (1989—Knock, Ireland)
- Francis Pascal (1938—Lourdes)

You will note that four of the above miraculous healings took place at Lourdes. St. Bernadette's home is over-represented simply because its miraculous healings are so well documented that they preclude fraudulent or erroneous claims.

An internet search will reveal hundreds and thousands of reported miraculous cures. It is hard to separate the real from the fraudulent or from the natural course of events. Nevertheless, they are out there, and it is up to you separate the wheat from the chaff. For example, you may wish to begin with Father Atwell's miraculous cure[1] at the age of sixteen (1974—Montana).

---

1. Armstrong, "Miraculous Healing."

18.1

Jack Traynor

Here is an instantaneous and scientifically inexplicable Lourdes healing not included in the list of seventy officially recognized Lourdes miracles—the case of Jack Traynor. Here is his story.

BACKGROUND

Jack Traynor was an Irishman living in Liverpool, England who fought in World War I. On May 8, 1915, he was wounded in the head and chest by machine gun fire. A bullet ripped through the inner side of his upper right arm and lodged under the collarbone, paralyzing his right arm. Three times he was operated on in an attempt to sew together the severed nerves in the upper arm. All three operations failed. While on a hospital ship Traynor suffered his first epileptic attack, and they became more frequent as time went on.

Amputation of his right arm was advised since it appeared the torn and shrunken nerves could never be repaired. Traynor would not consent.

In November 1916, another doctor tried unsuccessfully to suture the nerves. Traynor was discharged from the service and determined to be 100 percent permanently disabled. He spent months in various hospitals as an epileptic patient. In April 1920, a doctor concluded that the epilepsy was probably the result of head wounds suffered in the war and operated on the skull. The operation left Traynor with an open hole about an inch wide in his skull, exposing his brain. A silver plate was inserted to shield the brain, but the epileptic condition was no better after the operation, with seizures occurring as often as three times daily.

"Both legs were partly paralyzed, and nearly every organ in Traynor's body was impaired." For eight years he had been confined to a wheelchair, living with his wife and children in a house on a disability pension. He would sit for hours outside the house and had to be lifted from his bed into the chair and back again.

LOURDES

It was then that he made the decision, against the advice of his doctor and priest, to journey to Lourdes with a 1,200-person pilgrimage from Liverpool. His doctor and priest were afraid the trip would be too difficult and that he would die on the journey. He ignored their pleadings.

> The year 1923— the eighth after he became a casualty in Gallipoli [Turkey]—found him leading this helpless existence. I have counted the names of ten doctors through whose hands he had passed up to then. The result of all their efforts and examinations was to prove that he was completely and incurably incapacitated. Unable to stand or walk, subject to frequent epileptic fits, with three open wounds, one of them in his head, without the power of feeling or movement in his torn and shrivelled [sic] right arm, he was indeed a human wreck. Somebody arranged to have him admitted to the Mossley Hill Hospital for Incurables on July 24th, 1923. But by that date Jack Traynor was to be in Lourdes.

As he arrived to board the train from Liverpool he was joined by other pilgrims and, because of the publicity he had received in the local newspapers, people mulled about him and he missed the first train. He boarded the second.

Traynor later recalled:

> I remember practically nothing of the journey, except seeing a number of sick people on stretchers beside me on platforms and docks, some of them bleeding, all of them suffering. I believe that I was very sick on the way. Three times they tried to take me off the train in France to bring me to a hospital, as I seemed to be dying. Each time there was no hospital where they stopped,

and the only thing to do was to go on again, with me still on board.

At Lourdes he was cared for by two Protestant young ladies from Liverpool who happened to be in Lourdes just by chance. They had recognized him as the person sitting outside his house all the time. On July 24, 1923, he was examined by three doctors who had accompanied him and the other Liverpool pilgrims. Their signed statement is on record and they found him to be suffering from:

1. Epilepsy ["We ourselves saw several attacks during his journey to Lourdes"];
2. Paralysis of the radial, median and ulnar nerves of the right arm;
3. Atrophy of the shoulder and pectoral muscles;
4. A trephine opening in the right parietal region of the skull; in this opening, about 2.5 cm. [one inch], there is a metal plate for protection;
5. Absence of voluntary movement in the legs and loss of feeling;
6. Lack of bodily control.

While at Lourdes he suffered more epileptic seizures and hemorrhages. One of the pilgrims even wrote Traynor's wife that there was no hope for him and that he was expected to die in Lourdes.

HEALING

On July 25 it happened. The following quotations are directly from Jack Traynor.

> I was wheeled down [to the baths] to wait my turn. There were many to be bathed and we all wanted to be finished before the afternoon procession of the Blessed Sacrament, which began at four o'clock. My turn came, and when I was in the bath, my paralysed legs became violently agitated. The brancardiers [volunteers at Lourdes who assist the sick in their journey] became alarmed once more, thinking that I was in another fit. I struggled to get on my feet, feeling that I could easily do so, and wondered why everybody seemed to be against me. When I was taken out of the bath, I cried from sheer weakness and exhaustion.
>
> The brancardiers threw my clothes on hurriedly, put me back on the stretcher and rushed me down to the square in front of the Rosary Church to await the procession. Practically all the

other sick were already lined up. I was the third last on the outside, to the right as you face the church.

The procession came winding its way back, as usual, to the church, and at the end walked the Archbishop of Rheims, carrying the Blessed Sacrament. He blessed the two ahead of me, came to me, made the sign of the cross with the monstrance and moved on to the next. He had just passed by when I realized that a great change had taken place in me. My right arm, which had been dead since 1915, was violently agitated. I burst its bandages and blessed myself—for the first time in years.

I had no sudden pain that I can recall and certainly had no vision. I simply realized that something momentous had happened.

Traynor was taken back to the hospital. There the three doctors who had examined him the day before examined him again. They reported, "We find that he had recovered the voluntary use of his legs; the reflexes exist. There is intense venous congestion of both feet, which are very painful. The patient can walk with difficulty."

Traynor continues:

The chimes in the basilica above the Rosary rang the hours and half-hours as usual through the night, playing the air of the Lourdes 'Ave Maria.' Early in the morning I heard them ringing, and it seemed to me that I fell asleep at the beginning of the 'Ave.' It could have been a matter of only a few seconds, but at the last stroke I opened my eyes and jumped out of bed. First, I knelt on the floor to finish the rosary I been saying, then I dashed for the door, pushed aside the two brancardiers and ran out into the passage and the open air. Previously I had been watching the brancardiers and planning to evade them. I may say here that I had not walked since 1915 and my weight was down to eight stone [112 lbs].

Dr Marley was outside the door. When he saw the man over whom he had been watching during the pilgrimage, and whose death he had expected, push two brancardiers aside and run out of the ward, he fell back in amazement. Out in the open now, I ran towards the Grotto, which is about two or three hundred yards from the 'Asile.' [the hospital] This stretch of ground was gravelled then, not paved, and I was barefoot. I ran the whole way to the Grotto without getting the least mark or cut on my bare feet. The brancardiers were running after me but they could not catch up with me. When they reached the Grotto, there I was on my knees, still in my night clothes, praying to Our Lady and thanking her. All I knew was that I should thank her and the Grotto was the place to do it. The brancardiers stood back, afraid to touch me.

When Traynor took off the last of his bandages on returning from the Grotto on the morning of July 26, he found every one of his sores healed.

Early in the morning of July 27th the three [same] doctors examined Traynor before the pilgrimage left Lourdes. Their statement says that:

1. He can walk perfectly;
2. He has recovered the use and function of his right arm;
3. He has recovered sensation in his legs;
4. The opening in his skull has diminished considerably.
5. There have been no more epileptic crises.

RETURNING TO LIVERPOOL

The news of Traynor's instant cure was telegraphed to the Liverpool newspapers.

Traynor continues:

My wife went down to the station with her friend, Mrs Reitdyk. It seemed as if all Liverpool had gathered there. The people had seen the news of the miracle in the evening papers and had come down to see me. There were extra police on duty to handle the crowd, while railway officials stood at the entrance to the platform to keep the people from rushing the train.

With difficulty my wife and her friend reached the platform gate, where she told the official that she was Mrs Traynor and asked to be allowed through.

"Well," replied the man, "all I can say is that Mr Traynor must be a Mohammedan, because there are seventy or eighty Mrs Traynors on the platform already!"

A PERMANENT CURE

Traynor concludes his testimony:

I am in the coal and haulage business now [1937]. I have four lorries or trucks and about a dozen men working for me. I work with them. I lift sacks of coal weighing around 200 pounds with the best of them and I can do any other work that an able-bodied man can do. But officially I am still classified as 100 per cent disabled and permanently incapacitated!

I never accepted a penny from anybody at the time of my cure or after it. I came back from Lourdes penniless, except for my way pension. I have never permitted any money to come to my family in connection with my cure or the publicity that has followed it. Nevertheless, Our Lady has improved my temporal affairs, too, and thanks be to God and to her, I am now comfortably situated, and my children are all well provided for. Three of them have been born since my cure, one a girl whom I have named Bernadette.

The two non-Catholic girls who looked after me when I came to Lourdes joined the Church as the result of my cure. Their family at home in Liverpool followed their example, and so did the Anglican minister of the church they had been attending. I know of another parson who would like to follow suit, only that he is a marred [sic] man with a family. A large number of conversions in Liverpool have resulted from the miracle.

I go to Lourdes now every year and work as a brancardier there. I have gone twice and three times in one season.

John Traynor (center) when he was helping with the sick at Lourdes, June 1940.

EPILOGUE

This account was compiled and written by the Reverend Patrick O'Connor, Missionary of St. Columban, who met Traynor in 1938. Traynor was then a robust 224 lbs and in perfect health. All quotations are from Father O'Connor. He concludes his narrative:

> The official report, issued by the Medical Bureau at Lourdes on October 2nd, 1926, declared that "this extraordinary cure is absolutely beyond and above the powers of nature."
>
> "The most striking part of this multiple miracle is probably the instantaneous cure of the right arm. The nerves had been severed for eight years. Four surgical operations had revealed that they were truly severed and had failed to reunite them. More than mere suture would be necessary before the arm could feel and move again; the shrunken nerves would need to go through a long process of regeneration A feat that expert surgery had failed four times to do and a process that requires months of gradual restoration were achieved instantaneously as the Blessed Sacrament was raised over John Traynor."
>
> Another group of experts testified—though unconsciously—to the miracle. These were the doctors and officials of the War Pensions Ministry. These gentlemen, after years of examination, treatment and inspection, certified that John Traynor was incurable, and they showed the strength of their conviction by awarding him full disability pension for life. They have never revoked that decision.
>
> As I was about to publish this account, news has come that John Traynor died on the eve of the feast of the Immaculate Conception, 1943. The cause of his death was hernia, in no way related to the illness and wounds of which he was cured in Lourdes. For more than twenty years he lived a vigorous life, every moment of which he owed to the miracle of July, 1923. For more than twenty years he was a standing, stalwart testimony to the power of Almighty God and the efficacy of the intercession of Mary Immaculate. In his rugged person he presented a tangible argument with which unbelief could not wrestle without being overthrown. For some this miracle has brought the surrender which is a gain and a victory. Others—it has happened from the beginning and will happen to the end—have taken flight from the facts, in one direction or another.
>
> Miracles such as the cure of John Traynor are, of course, rare, while they are real. They point the way not to a wide-open

exit from all physical suffering but rather to the spiritual recoveries and triumphs that are certain to come from unhesitating faith and a childlike approach to Jesus Christ, through Mary, His Mother and ours.

All quotations are from Father O'Connor's account entitled *I Met a Miracle — The story of Jack Traynor*[1], by the Reverend Patrick O'Connor, missionary of St. Columban.

Why are so many not miraculously cured, but others are? We cannot possibly answer that question, but perhaps Jack Traynor was cured just to help you believe.

---

1. Available online at http://www.faithandfamily.org.uk/publications/jack_traynor.htm.

18.2

Marie Bailly and Nobel Laureate Alexis Carrel

MIRACULOUS CURE OF MARIE BAILLY

The case of Marie Bailly is but one example of an inexplicable instantaneous healing not included in the list of seventy officially recognized miracles. I will discuss this cure and the surrounding circumstances for two reasons. First, it includes a detailed description of the instantaneous cure of Marie Bailly as it happened and as recorded by the attending physicians. Second, the healing was also witnessed by an agnostic doctor and researcher, Alexis Carrel, who in 1912 received the Nobel Prize in medicine.

The following extensive narrative relating to the illness and 1902 cure of Marie Bailly are given to us by Dr. Boissaire, the head of the Lourdes Medical Bureau from 1892 to 1914.[1]

> Marie Bailly's cure is one of the most interesting we have witnessed. It is interesting especially from a scientific view-point. It is impossible to come across an investigation done with a surer and a more rigorous method. For the last three years that girl was under treatment at the Lyons and Sainte-Foy Hospitals; eight doctors waited upon her and brought us their testimony.

---

1. Boissaire, *Miracles of Lourdes*, 93–109.

One whose talent and whose impartiality are above suspicion entered the pilgrims' train, always kept his eye upon that sick girl, and at Lourdes followed her to the hospital, to the grotto, to the baths, everywhere.

He witnesses her cure, he notices hour by hour, minute by minute, the changes that take place under his eyes. It is a kind of resurrection he describes as a man of science, discarding from his mind and from his pen all comments, marking one by one all the symptoms he observes: that interrupted breathing which gradually becomes regular, that agonizing heart which begins to beat rhythmically, those blue cheeks which assume a rosy color. It is a photograph which brings under our eyes a most touching drama; science alone could thus give with precision all the details of a cure too important to be left to the judgment and the impressions of the vulgar herd.

Her Youth—Her Illness

Marie Bailly's father and mother died of pulmonary tuberculosis; one of her brothers died of the same disease; and another has been declared consumptive by an examination board. How could Marie Bailly escape that hereditary influence. "Since I was thirteen," she said, "our family physician, Dr. Terver, advised me to live in the country, and forbade me all mental labor. I had a very disquieting cough, frequent hemorrhages, and endless bronchial troubles during winter. After various alternatives, at seventeen, in February, 1896, I took ill with a double pleurisy with considerable bleeding; I had to go to St. Joseph's Hospital to be operated on; my condition was so critical that Dr. Chabalier refused to make the puncture, saying that I should not live through the night. They gave me the last Sacraments, and the Sister put around my neck a miraculous medal.

"Against all expectations I was better on the morrow and the doctors found me capable of undergoing the operation. By two successive punctures they drew from me three quarts of liquid. I stayed in bed five months; and after leaving the hospital, I improved enough to live an ordinary life for two years.

"My mother's death, which occurred in December, 1898, called forth new accidents: swollen from my feet to my head, I choked; I was placed again at St. Joseph's Hospital under Dr. Clement's treatment. The note at my bed bore *nervous dyspnoea;* within two months they put seven plasters on me; I took calming drinks, and also phosphate of lime and cacodylate. As I did not recover, they sent me on April 7, 1899, to the Sainte-Foy Hospital.

"Dr. Roy, hospital doctor, wrote on his tablet: *pulmonary tuberculosis, laryngitis*. He kept on giving me arsenic in pills and through injections, gave me creosote, and tried the reclining chair in the open air. I lost my voice; the disease seems to attack the larynx, and they apply lactic acid to my vocal chords. Dr. Fondet notices an infiltration in the cartilages." Hoping some benefit from purer air, Marie Bailly starts for Chabannes, near Le Puy, in May, 1901.

It was at that time that she felt violent pains in the intestines, and that tuberculosis seemed to spread its ravages in that region. All summer she is in a bad condition; a general decline is noticeable, and she loses flesh and her appetite as well. Her abdomen grows larger, and becomes very sensitive. On November 7, 1901, she returns to the Sainte-Foy Hospital. Dr. Roy diagnoses, *tubercular peritonitis*. She took to bed in the beginning of December, not to rise again until May 28, 1902, at the Lourdes bath. In January, 1902, she had violent headaches, stiffness of the neck, and of the limbs, and delirium. Dr. Roy recognizes *tubercular meningitis;* the prognosis seems fatal to him. It appears that on a certain day he even signed her death certificate.

Towards the end of February she got over the meningitis, but peritonitis kept running its course. In March Dr. Roy sent her back to St. Joseph's Hospital to be operated on—a last attempt to stop the progress of peritonitis.

Marie Bailly was placed under treatment of the hospital surgeon, Dr. Goulioud. He examines her and has her auscultated, and his observations are recorded by his assistant. He recalls the previous bad condition; her abdomen is swollen, is sore, and there is no liquid. In the lung a hollow sound on a level with the spine and the right shoulder blade; her temperature was very unsteady; no albumin. Dr. Goulioud diagnoses *tubercular peritonitis*, and in her critical state the operation should, he thinks, not be performed.

He turns the sick lady over to Dr. Clement. We heard he made the same diagnosis: *tubercular peritonitis*. Marie Bailly remained a few days under his care, and was sent back again to Sainte- Foy. She keeps on declining. Her emaciation is extreme, her abdomen very sore, and Dr. Roy considers her doomed. He lets her start for Lourdes with a certificate in which he affirms the existence of *tubercular peritonitis*

Up to this, everything seems to justify that diagnosis: the antecedents, the pleurisy, the tubercular pains on the side of the chest, the meningitis, Dr. Goulioud's statements, as well as the certificate of Dr. Roy, who kept her two years and a half in the hospital wards; the verdict seems unanimous.

The Pilgrimage—The Cure

"To what cause must I attribute my going to Lourdes? Doubtless to a secret design of Divine Providence," so speaks Miss Bailly. "Long since I had quit asking for my cure. One day while at the hospital, I heard the doctor say that I had consumption. This grieved me deeply; I was scarcely twenty, and it was hard for me to realize that I was hopelessly doomed. One is resigned to sickness and suffering, as long as there is a little gleam on the horizon; but when the future closes abruptly, it is death and the grave. Still gradually I braced up, and I offered my life as a sacrifice, and awaited the end submissively and resignedly, and I can't explain how the thought of repairing to Lourdes occurred to me. One night during March, in a moment of bitter suffering, the thought of Lourdes flashed through my mind. I understood that there I should be healed. Notwithstanding the opposition of the members of my family, of nuns even, who strove to put the idea out of my mind, as I was not able to stand the journey, I got myself inscribed, and I started with the pilgrimage. They carried me on a stretcher to the train, where I lay on a mattress completely doubled up—the car compartment being too narrow to let me stretch out.

"The journey was very hard; the pains in my intestines were horrible. I feared I should not reach Lourdes alive. The physician who stayed a long time in my car must have been astonished to see me hold out. He asked if I expected to be cured, if I had faith, adding: 'All the sick have'. And I thought the Blessed Virgin would heal me, but I said: 'Let her hasten, for I am going'. During the whole journey I took nothing, not even a spoonful of tea."

Here follows the physician's diary:

"*Monday, May 26th. On train.*—Girl of twenty-two, pale, emaciated, with drawn features, lying on her back, dressed in black. Her much swollen abdomen attracts attention. There is on the left side a more marked protuberance; there is a more resisting mass; no liquid, a dull sound.

"The abdomen, it appears, contains hard masses separated by a more depressible part; it is the symptom of peritonitis in its last stages. These symptoms, the hereditary and personal antecedents, the diagnosis of such a competent surgeon as Dr.

Goulioud, make me pronounce her affected with *tubercular peritonitis.* I could not reasonably make another diagnosis.

"Pressing on the left side of the abdomen causes much pain; the breathing is rapid and broken; pulse 120, oedema (dropsy) of the legs. At certain moments her body stiffens, yet the patient is calm without any mystic exaltation.

"*Tuesday, May 27th. Lourdes.*—At two o'clock the patient was taken from the train to the hospital Immaculate Conception ward. She is put to bed and made to rest till morning. The journey made her worse. Vomitings, much severer pains, quicker breathing, pulse 120.

"*Wednesday, May 28th.* —The rest failed to help the patient. At her request she is put upon a stretcher, and carried to the grotto and bathing place; they don't bathe her, but merely sponge her chest and abdomen with cold water. At her return to the hospital at ten o'clock a.m., her condition is very critical. Pale, with-drawn features, and very fast breathing. The heart very weak, its pulsations 150 a minute, the face slightly blue. Caffeine injection, hot cloths, ice on the abdomen.

"*May 28th, 1:15 P.M.*—Very bad state. The patient can scarcely answer the questions put her. She raves. Abdomen very sore, very tight. Irregular pulse, low, scarcely countable, 160; broken breathing 90 a minute, contracted face, very pale, and slightly purple. Nose, ears, extremities cold. Just now arrives Dr. Geoffray, of Rive-de-Gier; he looks at the patient, feels, strikes, and auscultates the heart and the lungs. He tells us that she is dying. As she can take nothing, and wants to return to the grotto, they carry her thither on a stretcher.

"*1:50 P.M.*—The patient is at the bathing place, motionless, lying on her back, her head thrown backwards, discolored, with a purple hue on the cheek bones, breathing very fast; the protuberance of the abdomen is noticeable through the cover."

She enters the bath. Marie Bailly will now complete the doctor's diary: "In the extremity in which I was, everybody wondered that I wanted to be taken back to the bathing place. Yet I demanded it, and thanks to my nurse's devotedness, I at last got there, followed by a person who carried my shroud. The carriers thought of praying for my last moments. The doctor declared that moving me would hasten my death, and that after a few steps I should be a corpse.

"I could pray no longer, yet I thought of the loving Virgin, and I was convinced that I was dying while being carried out, but that I should return healed. On arriving at the piscina, they would not put me in the water, but simply sponged me. At first

I suffered horribly; the ladies insisted on stopping, but they proceeded however, as I begged them to continue. Just then I said interiorly to Our Lady of Lourdes, 'If you wish it, you can cure me just as well through the ablutions as through the bath.'"

They sponged her again upon the stretcher. They are afraid to move her; as the water touches her, she experiences unprecedented throes, then suddenly she is calm, she rises: "I am cured," she said. "She's losing her senses," interposed the nurse. Meanwhile her cheeks color up, her look becomes lively, and as they take her from the watering place, she chimes in the *Magnificat*.

2:20 P. M.—Here we resume the doctor's recital: "Upon leaving the piscina they carry her before the grotto, the stretcher is set on the ground; few people as yet; the religious ceremonies have not begun. The sick girl is in the broad daylight; it is easy to examine her.

"*2:30 until 2:40 P. M.*—The breathing slackens, and becomes more regular. The look of her face is changing; a very slight rosy hue is spreading over her countenance. She seems to feel better, and she smiles at the nurse bent over her.

"*2:55 P. M.*—The profile of her body visible under the cover is changing, and the protuberance of the abdomen is lowering. A general improvement becomes evident.

"*3:10 P. M.*—The hands, the ears, and the nose are warm. Her breathing has slackened to forty a minute; the heart is stronger, more regular, but fast at 140. She tells us that she is feeling better. They make her take some more milk, and there is no more vomiting.

"*3:20 P. M.*—She rises and looks around her. The cover has sunk over the abdomen. Her limbs move, and she turns her body to the right side. Her face has become calm and rosy.

"*3:45 P. M.*—The stretcher is brought close to Holy Rosary Church.

"*4:15 P. M.*—The improvement is marked. The breathing is easy, and the face rosy. She tells us that she is feeling quite well, and that if she dared she could get up. Everybody can tell the change in her. They carry her to the Verification Bureau on a mattress. She leaves in a little cart. The doctor's statements are inscribed on our registers. Our report tallies with the impressions of our colleagues.

"*7:30 P. M.*—Examined at the hospital. General aspect excellent; much emaciated face, but calm and rosy; very regular breathing. Her abdomen has now the soft, elastic and depressed wall of a healthy, but very thin girl of twenty. That extremely thin wall allows a very easy and clear exploration of the organs;

the aorta beats under the finger; way down on the right side a hard mass going up to the loins. Between one's hands one can feel a very hard cake which is not sore, as big as the forearm, adhering solidly to the rear wall of the abdomen. That tumor does not move during the movements of breathing.

"*8:00 P. M.*—The improvement continues; stronger voice; breathing 30, pulse 100, regular and full.

"*May 29th, 6:30 A. M.*—General condition perfect. She gets up and eats; breathing 18; pulse 88; abdomen absolutely normal. The hard mass noticed in the region of the loins yesterday has well-nigh disappeared. There remains a little tumor which is not painful, deep seated, and very hard.

"*Friday, May 30th.*—The patient has dressed and walks around. She can climb a staircase. Her strength is rapidly coming back. Almost unassisted she steps into the cars, and travels twenty-four hours seated on the bench of a third class compartment. She is very calm; no mystic excitement; she strives to hide herself from the gaze of the people who surround her. She reenters the Sainte-Foy Hospital."

After the Cure

"*Wednesday, June 4th.*—Marie Bailly looks like a healthy girl; good appetite; speedy increase in weight, almost a pound. Absolutely flexible abdomen; every tumor gone.

"*August 8th.*—Leaves the hospital. Is accepted as novice by the Sisters of St. Vincent de Paul. The doctors since that time took twice or three times a specimen of her blood to make the sero-diagnosis of tuberculosis. That reaction has been positive; which proves that Marie Bailly had tuberculosis.

"Practically she must be considered as cured. It is hard to conceive what that girl was on May 28th at 2:00 p.m. She was a corpse carried to the piscina. For several years people had watched the evolution of her tuberculosis on the lungs, the brain, and the peritoneum. It was not an accidental consumption, but a hereditary one; her father and mother having died of that disease. Ever since she was thirteen, she had been fighting against the grip of that fell destroyer. Her system was broken-down; all the springs were worn—she was dying. The doctors who were in Lourdes then have been pleased to record their impressions on our registers, and we read in our report:

"*May 28th, 7 P.M.*—We have been deeply amazed to behold the girl who was so ill this morning, sitting on her bed, chatting with the nurses, smilingly answering our questions, and to see the enormous swelling of the abdomen completely gone. The tumors which troubled her melted under our eyes; the breathing and the heart had resumed their normal play. It is a sudden, a marvelous cure, a real resurrection."

Dr. Geoffray, of Rive de Gier, adds with his own hand:

"This medical report which I sign is the plain truth; such a serious trouble has never been cured in a few hours as they came to pass here.

Dr. Geoffray.

Lourdes, May 29, 1902"

Marie Bailly at the Novitiate of the Sisters of St. Vincent de Paul

Marie Bailly has been at the novitiate Rue du Bac, Paris, since November, 1902. We saw her there in the middle of the following February. We should never have recognized our patient of the Lyons pilgrimage. Upon leaving Lourdes, she was cured, but she was still pale, weak and staggering. She wore on her countenance the trace of her long suffering. At Paris I found the girl completely transformed. She had gained thirty-six pounds; from seventy-eight pounds she had increased to one hundred and fourteen pounds. Everything in her looks, and her face breathed life and health. In her eyes one could read the brightness of her soul, the novitiate having added that touch of perfection which is the work of grace. With a very sweet voice she gave slow but clear cut answers, striving to overcome her bashfulness, very chary of details, she waited for my questions.

The story of her life is summed up in one word: suffering. She had been sick ever since she was thirteen. It is suffering undoubtedly that merited for her the exceptional grace with which she has been favored. Raised in the shadow of Our Lady of Fourvieres, she had a great devotion to the Blessed Virgin, and the *Memorare* was her prayer of predilection.

Marie Bailly remained a nun for the rest of her life. She died in 1937 at the age of fifty eight.

DR. ALEXIS CARREL

In 1912 Alexis Carrel received the Nobel Prize in medicine. He was one of the attending physicians on the train that took Bailly to Lourdes. He remained with her as she spontaneously healed. Carrel was a firm agnostic and went to Lourdes simply to see close-up the rapid healing of wounds reported at Lourdes. He did not believe in miracles, then or even after the Bailly healing which he personally witnessed. He was convinced that natural forces were responsible for Bailly's sudden cure and kept returning to Lourdes to understand how this process could work. In 1910 he again witnessed another miraculous healing when he saw the sudden restoration of sight to an eighteen-month-old boy who was born blind.

Despite witnessing these two miracles Carrel remained an agnostic. Then, two years after Bailly's death Carrel met a Trappist monk, Alexis Presse. Father Alexis had devoted ten years restoring and reopening abbys throughout France. In 1939 he started working on an abbey close to Carrel's summer residence, and it was there that the two met. Father Alexis had devoted years to repairing abbys, and now he was given the task of repairing Carrel's soul. Not an easy project, but four years later in 1944 Carrel was on his death bed in Paris. Father Alexis received word and rushed to be by Carrel's side. There, Carrel was converted to Catholicism and received the final sacraments. He had returned to the faith of his parents and his childhood.

MIRACLES AT LOURDES

There have been literally thousands of cures at Lourdes which can only be described as scientifically and medically inexplicable, but only seventy have been declared miraculous by the Church. Marie Bailly's instant is not one of them. We do not know how many cures can be considered "miraculous," but all it takes is just one to demonstrate the loving hand of God. And we do not know how many spiritual cures flowed from Lourdes waters. Carrel's was certainly one; maybe yours or that of one of your loved ones will be another.

Jesus told some of the Jews that even though they heard him and saw his works, they still would not believe he was the Messiah, and they kept asking for more proof. Jesus responded by telling them that "You refuse to believe because you are not my sheep."[2]

I wonder how many good people refuse to believe because, quite simply, they don't want to. They are not his sheep. The gospel tells us that it is hidden from those who put their trust in other gods [think self, money, power, etc.] and don't want to believe.

2. John 10:26.

OUR LADY OF LOURDES

God always seems to reveal himself most effectively and most often to the most innocent, and that's what he did in 1858 when Mary, the mother of Jesus, appeared to Bernadette in rural France and told her to scratch out a spring, ask the parish priest to build a church, and requested processions. Bernadette did all this, the priest complied, and the processions began. They continue to this day—as do the miraculous cures.

18.3

Gabriel Gargam

Miracles, and particularly miraculous healings, bring home the point that every now and then God opens a portal to heaven. Still, many walk by and scoff. They say there is no portal and that the so-called miraculous event never happened. When that's shown to be wrong they maintain that what appears to be a miraculous healing is sheer trickery or a cure that would have happened anyway. Perhaps it's merely a manifestation of the innate ability of the body to cure itself through the power of suggestion. Finally, it will be argued that at the present time we just don't know why something occurred but are certain that someday we will. When all these objections fail, the event is simply ignored—much like Fatima and Lourdes.

Here is another documented cure that has no explanation other than the intervening hand of God— the story of Gabriel Gargam.

Gabriel Gargam was born in 1870. In 1899 he was severely injured in a train accident which left him paralyzed from the waist down. After eight months he had wasted away to 78 lbs and reduced to a mere skeleton. He could not take any solid food and could only be tube-fed. He sued the railroad and it vigorously defended. Doctors unanimously testified that he would be a hopeless cripple for the rest of his life. There could be no deception. Gargam won his case and received monetary payment from the railroad for the rest of his life.

For two years he was essentially bed-ridden and two nurses were required to attend him daily. There was no doubt about his condition. He was paralyzed from the waist down and could not help himself in even the most trifling affairs. Finally, and even though he had not been to church for seventeen years, he acceded to the pleas of his mother and his aunt (a nun) to go to Lourdes.

> Previous to the accident Gargam had not been to Church for fifteen years. His aunt, who was a nun of the Order of the Sacred Heart, begged him to go to Lourdes. He refused. She continued her appeals to him to place himself in the hands of Our Lady of Lourdes. He was deaf to all her prayers. After continuous pleading of his mother he consented to go to Lourdes. It was now two years since the accident, and not for a moment had he left his bed all that time. He was carried on a stretcher to the train. The exertion caused him to faint, and for a full hour he was unconscious. They were on the point of abandoning the pilgrimage, as it looked as if he would die on the way, but the mother insisted, and the journey was made.
>
> Arrived at Lourdes, he went to confession and received Holy Communion. There was no change in his condition. Later he was carried to the miraculous pool and tenderly placed in its waters— no effect. Rather a bad effect resulted, for the exertion threw him into a swoon and he lay apparently dead. After a time, as he did not revive, they thought him dead. Sorrowfully they wheeled the carriage back to the hotel. On the way back they saw the procession of the Blessed Sacrament approaching. They stood aside to let it pass, having placed a cloth over the face of the man whom they supposed to be dead.
>
> As the priest passed carrying the Sacred Host, he pronounced Benediction over the sorrowful group around the covered body. Soon there was a movement from under the covering. To the amazement of the bystanders, the body raised itself to a sitting posture. While the family were looking on dumbfounded and the spectators gazed in amazement, Gargam said in a full, strong voice that he wanted to get up. They thought that it was a delirium before death, and tried to soothe him, but he was not to be restrained. He got up and stood erect, walked a few paces and said that he was cured. The multitude looked in wonder, and then fell on their knees and thanked God for this new sign of His power at the Shrine of His Blessed Mother. As Gargam had on him only invalid's clothes, he returned to the carriage and was wheeled back to the hotel. There he was soon dressed, and proceeded to walk about as if nothing had ever ailed him.

For two years hardly any food had passed his lips but now he sat down to the table and ate a hearty meal.

On August 20th, 1901, sixty prominent doctors examined Gargam. Without stating the nature of the cure, they pronounced him entirely cured. Gargam, out of gratitude to God in the Holy Eucharist and His Blessed Mother, consecrated himself to the service of the invalids at Lourdes.[1]

For fifty years Gargam returned annually to Lourdes and worked as a brancardier (a volunteer at Lourdes who assist the sick in their journey). He died in 1953 at the age of eighty three. Gargam's cure is not included among the seventy officially recognized miracles.

Lourdes doesn't have a monopoly of miraculous cures. Just a little bit of research will reveal unexplained and instantaneous cures all along the Christian spectrum. Thousands upon thousands have occurred and they all have one thing in common—a turning over to God and the acceptance of his will. We know they are granted to Catholics and other Christians alike. Confirmable miracles may also be granted to non-Christians, but if they are, they're kept under wraps.

The lesson is that when you suffer and are in a horrible situation please pray for a miracle. God may grant it, and that miracle may be even more impressive and permanent than a physical cure. It may be the miracle of a renewed spiritual birth of your faith.

---

1. Our Lady of the Rosary Library website, "Miracles of Lourdes—The Story of Gabriel Gargam."

18.4

Marion Carroll

As discussed in chapter 11, Our Lady of Knock demands our attention. Well, one may ask—what about miracles. Aren't these Marian apparitions supposed to be accompanied by miracles? In truth, the parish priest recorded a number of unexplained healings, but there was no scientific documentation. Unlike Lourdes, Knock is not generally known as a place of inexplicable healings. Yet they occur.

Here's one—the case of Marion Carroll.[1]

Before she went to Knock in 1989 Marion Carroll's health had deteriorated steadily for 15 years. She suffered from multiple sclerosis and for the last few years was completely bedridden or confined to a wheelchair. She had no power in her legs or right arm. Her left side was very weak with limited power. She was blind in her left eye and limited vision in her right eye. She was essentially blind. Her speech was so slurred few could understand her. Her food had to be liquefied because she could no longer swallow solids. She had no control over her bowel and bladder. She suffered from epilepsy, had thyroid problems and a kidney infection. There was no cure.

What she did have was a loving and completely unselfish husband and two children. They took care of her. They fed her, washed her, and changed her. She was dying. She lived in Athlone, Ireland (about 50 miles southeast

1. The story of Marion (sometimes spelled Marian) is readily accessible on the internet, including YouTube.

of Knock) and was ready for death. Although she was a devout Catholic, she had no desire to visit Knock. Twenty years earlier she had visited the shrine shortly after a gale and it was completely deserted. She thought it a "miserable place." Nevertheless, in 1989 she was persuaded to go.

At the basilica she was strapped on a stretcher under a statue of Our Lady of Knock. She didn't pray for herself, but for her husband. She told Mary that since she was a wife and mother, the Blessed Virgin would know how she felt. Later, Marion learned that for all these years of infirmity her husband had been praying for her. He had prayed that the Lord take him and cure her.

When she received Holy Communion from her bishop, she got a very bad pain in both her heels, which was very unusual. A short time later her bishop came with the Blessed Sacrament in the monstrance to bless the sick. He came to the stretcher and held it up. It was then the pain disappeared. She sensed a "beautiful feeling, like a whispery breeze" telling her that she could get up and walk.

After Mass, she told a friend and the stretcher straps were undone. Her legs swung out and she got up. She wasn't sore or stiff, even after three years being confined to a bed and wheelchair. Her speech was suddenly perfect. She was able to hold her head up without the supporting collar she had used for years. She was using her hands and legs. But what she remembers most about Knock had nothing to do with walking or moving. What she remembers is that right in front of her she saw her own heart and it was "so full of joy and peace and I looked, and it was like looking directly into the sun and the rays that came back towards me and gave all those gifts of peace and joy and great love."

Thirty plus years later Marion remains in health. She leads a ministry of healing and travels throughout the world. She said that whatever healings take place are a gift from Jesus. When she prays for others she's just "giving out the prescription and He's the doctor." Her cure at Knock does "not belong to me. This is a special gift to you and to the people of the world to let you know that they are there. But life gets pretty hard at times and we're so human at times that we need to see, feel and touch God's love."

In 2019 the Irish Catholic Church formally recognized Marion's cure as medically inexplicable.

18.5

Francis Pascal

We could go on endlessly describing events that have no explanation other than the intervening hand of God. Miraculous instant healings are but one example. Still, the skeptic argues that even the medically inexplicable healings are inexplicable simply because we do not understand the power of the body to heal itself through the power of suggestion.

Consider the case of the blind three-year-old Francis Pascal. Did he heal himself?

Faith may move mountains, religious fervor may unleash bodily mechanisms to destroy illness, but is it possible that a little boy, age three, blind and paralyzed could instantly be cured in the waters of Lourdes? The answer is yes, and the cure of Francis Pascal is included among the seventy officially recognized cures.

In December 1937 Francis Pascal contracted meningitis and was rendered completely blind and paralyzed. Five doctors and specialists examined him before he traveled to Lourdes in August 1938 and confirmed that he could not distinguish night from day and was paralyzed in arms and legs. In 1957 his mother was interviewed, and tells us:

> I was in despair. My only baby was blind and stiff as a board, and all the doctors said nothing could be done. I took him to

Lourdes as a last hope. I had faith, but not much. I told Our Lady I wanted Francis to die if she wasn't going to cure him.

I carried him to the baths myself. He screamed when the attendants lowered him in the water. I thought he was having a fit. He certainly wasn't cured, and I hesitated to take him again. But two days later I did. This time he made no fuss, and as I carried him back to the hospice where they care for the sick pilgrims he suddenly pointed to one of the other pilgrim wheel-beds.

"Look, Mamam [Pascal is French]," he cried, "the lady's wheeling a little carriage."

I was so excited I nearly fainted. My little Francis could see and move. He wobbled a bit when he first tried to walk, but soon he walked normally.

All quotations are from a newspaper article[1] authored by Rhona Churchill which appeared in the *Ottawa Citizen* on June 19, 1957. Ms. Churchill also interviewed the family doctor who had taken care of little Francis. Dr. Darde confirmed everything that Francis's mother had said.

When Mme. Pascal brought him back to me walking and seeing perfectly, I cried: "Mon Dieu [My God], but it's a miracle."

I took him into the street and pointed to my car. I said: "What is it?" He said, "It's a car, Monsieur." I said: "What color is it?" He said: "It is red."

I was just as excited as Mme. Pascal. I wept. I have kept in touch with the family ever since. Francis is a good, quiet lad, hardworking and homeloving. Not one for drinking with the boys or chasing the girls. I think he deserved his miracle.

Francis's case was carefully documented. In 1946 eleven doctors examined him and reported:

That the medical records proved that Francis had suffered from meningomyelitis with choked disc, flaccid paralysis of the lower limbs, stiffness of the upper limbs, cerebellar disturbance and total blindness;

That the symptoms of paralysis and blindness disappeared abruptly at a time when the development of the disease left no hope that they would even improve;

That the cure was definite, instantaneous and complete;

That there was no medical explanation for it.

In July 1947 Francis was examined again, this time by fifteen doctors, including four specialists. A year later he was examined by twenty doctors.

1. Churchill, "Blind Cured."

Their conclusion was that "The cure of Francis Pascal is humanly inexplicable, took place without medical aid, has lasted 10 years, is beyond the realm of natural law."

Francis Pascal became an official Lourdes miracle cure in May 1949.

There can be no doubt. This was a miraculous cure. Who benefitted? Clearly, Francis Pascal did, his mother and family, and so did the other members of the Body of Christ. That would, or should, include you.

19

Miraculous Events

Miraculous events are occurrences which we know with 100 percent certainty took place and that have no explanation, not even as spectacular coincidences, other than divine intervention. They reveal God's love and presence. In the next four chapters we will consider some of these.

- Jerusalem every Easter Saturday: Miracle of the Holy Fire. Chapter 19.1.
- Wisconsin 1871: Great Peshtigo Fire. Chapter 19.2.
- China 1900 and confirmed in 1995: Our Lady of China. Chapter 19.3.
- Wyoming 1986: Cokeville. Chapter 19.4.

The beneficiaries of God's intervention in the Great Peshtigo Fire were Catholics and others of unknown faith. The Miracle of the Holy Fire can rightfully be said to belong to the Eastern Orthodox faith, but witnesses come from all Christian traditions. While Our Lady of China's beneficiaries in 1900 were primarily Catholic, the direct witnesses were trying to eradicate Christianity; in 1995 the witnesses were primarily Catholic but other witnesses were both Christian and non-Christian. In Cokeville the beneficiaries were mostly Mormon children and other children of unidentified Christian churches.

No Christian sub-faith has a monopoly on God's saving grace.

As is the case of miraculous healings, a miraculous event always provides a clear sign of God's intercession; it is much more than an event which is merely remarkable or improbable.

19.1

Miracle of the Holy Fire

Most of the miracles we describe have a Catholic orientation in that they are either Marian appearances to faithful Catholics or miracles associated with those apparitions. Our focus has been on these quite simply because they can be verified by empirical evidence, including testimony of multiple witnesses. Miracles, however, are not confined to those of the Catholic faith, and the Miracle of the Holy Fire is but one example. Until recently there has been little or no physical evidence to confirm this annual Easter event. Now, however, because of the rapidly increasing availability of tape and digital recordings, what was once supported only by testimony now lends itself to filmed verification.

THE CHURCH OF THE HOLY SEPULCHRE

The Church of the Holy Sepulchre encloses the places where it is generally believed Christ was crucified, entombed, and rose from the dead. It is time to visit this most holy Christian site and witness a miracle that recurs every year on Holy Saturday (that is, the Saturday between Good Friday and Easter as celebrated by the Eastern Orthodox), and has faithfully done so since the fourth century, and possibly before. The miracle is called the Miracle of the Holy Fire and is given to us through the Eastern Orthodox Church.

The tomb of Christ is enclosed by a chapel within the Church of the Sepulchre, and it is there that the Holy Fire reveals its divine origin by spontaneously emerging, first as a mist-like light, from the stone upon which they placed Jesus' crucified body. The light rises and transforms into a fire which in turn ignites the candles held by the Greek Orthodox Patriarch of Jerusalem as he prays alone in the tomb of Christ. Since the Patriarch is there alone in the tomb of Jesus it seems difficult to objectively verify the miraculous nature of the event. In fact, it doesn't seem miraculous at all because one person going into the tomb without a fire, being there alone, and then coming out holding a lit candle sounds like material for a good yawn. There must be more. There is.

TIMELINE FOR THE ANNUAL OCCURRENCE

Here is a condensed description of this annual miracle from the official website.

Ceremony of Holy Light

In order to be as close to the Sepulchre as possible, pilgrims camp next to it. The Sepulchre is located in the small chapel called Holy Ciborium, which is inside the Church of the Resurrection [Sepulchre]. Typically they wait from the afternoon of Holy Friday in anticipation of the miracle on Holy Saturday. Beginning at around 11:00 in the morning the Christian Arabs chant traditional hymns in a loud voice. . . . But at 1:00 pm the chants fade out, and then there is a silence. A tense silence, charged from the anticipation of the great demonstration of God's power for all to witness.

Shortly thereafter, a delegation from the local authorities elbows its way through the crowd. At the time of the Turkish occupation of Palestine they were Muslim Turks; today they are Israelis. Their function is to represent the Romans at the time of Jesus. The Gospels speak of the Romans that went to seal the tomb of Jesus, so that his disciples would not steal his body and claim he had risen. In the same way the Israeli authorities on this Holy Saturday come and seal the tomb with wax. Before they seal the door, they follow a custom to enter the tomb, and to check for any hidden source of fire, which would make a fraud of the miracle.

How the miracle occurs

[Orthodox Patriarch Diodor tells us what transpires when he enters the tomb:]

"I enter the tomb and kneel in holy fear in front of the place where Christ lay after His death and where He rose again from the dead. I find my way through the darkness towards the inner chamber in which I fall on my knees. Here I say certain prayers that have been handed down to us through the centuries and, having said them, I wait. Sometimes I may wait a few minutes, but normally the miracle happens immediately after I have said the prayers. From the core of the very stone on which Jesus lay an indefinable light pours forth. It usually has a blue tint, but the colour may change and take many different hues. It cannot be described in human terms. The light rises out of the stone as mist may rise out of a lake — it almost looks as if the stone is covered by a moist cloud, but it is light. This light each year behaves differently. Sometimes it covers just the stone, while other times it gives light to the whole sepulchre, so that people who stand outside the tomb and look into it will see it filled with light. The light does not burn — I have never had my beard burnt in all the sixteen years I have been Patriarch in Jerusalem and have received the Holy Fire. The light is of a different consistency than normal fire that burns in an oil lamp. . . At a certain point the light rises and forms a column in which the fire is of a different nature, so that I am able to light my candles from it. When I thus have received the flame on my candles, I go out and give the fire first to the Armenian Patriarch and then to the Coptic. Hereafter I give the flame to all people present in the Church."

While the patriarch is inside the chapel kneeling in front of the stone, there is darkness but far from silence outside. One hears a rather loud mumbling, and the atmosphere is very tense. When the Patriarch comes out with the two candles lit and shining brightly in the darkness, a roar of jubilee resounds in the Church.

The Holy Light is not only distributed by the Archbishop, but operates also by itself. It is emitted from the Holy Sepulchre with a hue completely different from that of natural light. It sparkles, it flashes like lightning, it flies like a dove around the tabernacle of the Holy Sepulchre, and lights up the unlit lamps of olive oil hanging in front of it. It whirls from one side of the church to the other. It enters some of the chapels inside the church, as for instance the chapel of the Calvery [sic] (at a higher level than the Holy Sepulchre) and lights up the little lamps. It lights up also the candles of certain pilgrims. In fact there are some very pious pilgrims who, every time they attended this ceremony, noticed that their candles lit up on their own accord! [T]his divine light also presents some peculiarities: As soon as it appears it has a bluish hue and does not burn. At the first moments of its appearance, if it touches the face, or the mouth, or the hands, it does not burn. This is proof of its divine and supernatural origin. We must also take into consideration that the Holy Light appears only by the invocation of an Orthodox Archbishop.

"The miracle is not confined to what actually happens inside the little tomb, where the Patriarch prays. What may be even more significant, is that the blue light is reported to appear and be active outside the tomb. Every year many believers claim that this miraculous light ignites candles, which they hold in their hands, of its own initiative. All in the church wait with candles in the hope that they may ignite spontaneously. Often unlit oil lamps catch light by themselves before the eyes of the pilgrims. The blue flame is seen to move in different places in the Church. A number of signed testimonies by pilgrims, whose candles lit spontaneously, attest to the validity of these ignitions. The person who experiences the miracle from close up by having the fire on the candle or seeing the blue light usually leaves Jerusalem changed, and for everyone having attended the ceremony, there is always a "before and after" the miracle of the Holy Fire in Jerusalem.[1]

I urge you to view some videos of the Miracle of the Holy Fire, easily accessible on the official website or through a YouTube search. As you will see, the miracle isn't just that the Patriarch emerges with a lit candle. For more than fifteen hundred years (before flash bulbs and other electronic and electrical devices) his emergence from the tomb was, and continues to be, often preceded or followed by spectacular displays of light, as of lightning.

Who says God hides? For more than fifteen hundred years God has revealed himself in this annual miracle. You are hereby invited to Jerusalem for the next Paschal Holy Saturday, and you too will be able to witness and participate in the Miracle of the Holy Fire.

---

1. Holy Fire website, "Holy Fire Description."

A FRAUDULENT CLAIM?

How many witnesses does it take to prove conclusively an event? At Fatima there were seventy thousand on that October 13, 1917. Over the centuries the number of witnesses to the Holy Fire led by the Jerusalem Patriarch of the Eastern Orthodox far exceeds that number. If this were a fraud the testimony of the Patriarch quoted above, which substantially tracks the testimony of all his predecessors for the past one thousand six hundred years, would have to be a lie. The smoke of Satan certainly would have to have penetrated the very core of the Orthodox.

It hasn't. Any objective analysis must conclude that something spectacularly divine occurs every year in Jerusalem, just as the spectacularly divine Jesus appeared, died, was entombed, and resurrected two thousand years ago.

HIDDEN TREASURE

Why haven't you heard about this event? I think part of the reason for the lack of publicity in the West is that Protestants generally are wary about claimed miracles unless they originate within their own culture (that's just my opinion) and tend to disassociate themselves from them. Catholics, to the extent they even think about them, tend to focus on Marian apparitions. Their plate is full, so to speak. The Catholic hierarchy tends to ignore the annual Holy Fire (at least publicly), either deliberately or subconsciously, perhaps because the Catholic clergy is not involved (that's just a guess). It's not a conspiracy, but a lack of attention in much the same way that non-Catholics ignore Fatima, Lourdes, etc.

The Eastern Orthodox tradition is somewhat foreign to our Western Christianity culture. When given a choice, it is always easier to opt for the familiar. There are plenty of miracles to go around and it is understandable that in our Western Christian heritage we would focus on the familiar. We need to stop being so provincial. Rain and sun fall upon everyone, as do God's miracles and grace.

19.2

Hell's Fire Restrained

The Great Peshtigo Fire

ST. POLYCARP

In the first century Smyrna was a major port city on the east coast of Turkey and a Christian center when Polycarp (A.D. 69–155) was bishop. Polycarp was a disciple of the Apostle John and, along with Clement of Rome and Ignatius of Antioch, is considered one of the principle Fathers of the Church. In addition to learning from John, Polycarp was also in communion with others who had seen and heard Jesus. During his time as bishop he endured persecutions, culminating in his martyrdom at the age of eighty-six.

St. Polycarp's death was described in a letter from the Church at Smyrna to the Church at Philomelium. The letter describes how Polycarp, who knew that he would be burned alive, endured his martyrdom. First, he was pressed to deny Christ, and promised that if he did so he would be saved. He refused and said, "How then can I blaspheme my King and my Savior?" The Romans then said they would set wild beasts upon him and when that threat didn't produce the desired effect, they proclaimed that he would be burned alive. Polycarp responded, "You threaten me with fire which burns for an hour, and after a little is extinguished, but are ignorant of the fire of the coming judgment and of eternal punishment, reserved for the ungodly. But why do you tarry? Bring forth what you will."[1]

The letter describes what happened next:

> Those who were appointed for the purpose kindled the fire. And as the flame blazed forth in great fury, we, to whom it was given to witness it, beheld a great miracle, and have been preserved that we might report to others what then took place. For the fire, shaping itself into the form of an arch, like the sail of a ship when filled with the wind, encompassed as by a circle the body of the martyr. And he appeared within not like flesh which is burnt, but as bread that is baked, or as gold and silver glowing in a furnace. Moreover, we perceived such a sweet odor [coming from the pile], as if frankincense or some such precious spices had been smoking there.[2]

Finally, they pierced him with a dagger and Polycarp died.

In 1871 the miracle of an encircling but non-consuming fire was repeated in the USA when the saving hand of God dramatically revealed itself in a five-acre area about ten miles northeast of Green Bay, Wisconsin. This miracle is commemorated as the National Shrine of Our Lady of Good Help, but had its genesis some years earlier in Belgium, Adele Brise's country of birth.

ADELE BRISE—1859

Adele Brise was born in 1831 and because of a childhood accident was blind in one eye. Although she had no formal education, Adele made a commitment with several of her girlfriends to enter a religious missionary order. Her friends kept their commitment, but in obedience to her parents Adele immigrated to the USA with them and her three siblings in 1855. They settled on 240 acres about fifteen miles northeast of present-day Green Bay.

On October 8, 1859 Adele was going to a grist mill when she saw a lady all in white standing between two trees, one a maple and other a hemlock. Nothing was said and the vision slowly disappeared.

The closest Catholic Church was eleven miles away and on October 9, on her way to Mass, and accompanied by her sister and a neighbor, the Lady appeared again at the same place. The other two could not see anything, but

---

1. Knight, "Martyrdom," chapter 11.
2. Knight, "Martyrdom," chapter 15.

they could tell by Adele's look that she was frightened. After a few minutes the vision disappeared, just as it had the day before.

After Mass, Adele told the priest about her vision and how frightened she had been. He told her that if it were a heavenly messenger, she would see it again, not be frightened, and ask in God's name who it was and what it desired of her.

On her return home after Mass she was again accompanied by her sister and a neighbor, and this this time they were joined by a laborer who was working for the church. For the third time Adele saw the apparition. Adele fell to her knees and the apparition identified herself as the Queen of Heaven, who prays for the conversion of sinners. She wished Adele to do the same and to teach the children in "this wild country" what they should know for salvation. Despite Adele's protestations of being unworthy, the Queen of Heaven told her to teach them "their catechism, how to sign themselves with the sign of the Cross, and how to approach the sacraments; that is what I wish you to do. Go and fear nothing. I will help you."[3]

And that was it. No more appearances, but for the remainder of her life until she died in 1896 Sister Adele Brise was faithful to this mission. She was faithful to her commitment made years earlier in Belgium. She started to visit homes within a fifty-mile radius and began instructing children in the faith.

Several single women offered to assist Adele and, before long they formed a religious community called the Sisters of Good Help. With their assistance and the help of a devoted priest, Adelle raised sufficient funds so that by 1867 they were able to open a school. The sisters also had a tiny shrine chapel, ten feet by twelve, that had been built by Adele's father on the site of the apparitions. A larger one was completed before the opening of the school. The last thing the sister had constructed was a convent. By 1871, the school, St. Mary's Academy, had ninety-five boarding students, many of whom were orphans.

THE GREAT PESHTIGO FIRE

On October 8, 1871, the twelfth anniversary of the first visitation by the Blessed Virgin to Adele, the worst fire disaster in United States history occurred. An area twice the size of Rhode Island was destroyed by raging infernos. About one-half of the two thousand inhabitants of Peshtigo, Wisconsin died. The number of casualties in the affected areas was estimated to be between 1,400 and 2,500.

3. Kelly, "Marian Wisconsin Apparition."

A wall of fire, a mile high and five miles wide, leveled forests and towns as it raced along, sucking in the fueling oxygen from an incoming cold front, and causing what is called a "firestorm" with hurricane-force winds of 90–100 miles per hour. Survivors describe people dying even in the Peshtigo River who were stuck in the burning marsh too close to shore. Others died of hypothermia from the frigid waters. Eye-witness accounts of the fire are shuddering to read. By evening, the settlers in the village of Robinsonville, not too far away, could see the fire in the east and it was heading their way, rapidly. There was no outrunning it, no escape. Terrified, they ran to the shrine where they prayed with Sister Adele to the Queen of Heaven for a miracle. All during the night they processed around the grounds with Sister Adele carrying a statue of Mary. The air grew hotter and hotter as they prayed and prayed into the ghastly-lit night. Suddenly, the sky grew less brilliant and a cooler wind rushed in from the west. With the rising of the sun it began to rain and the rain became a downpour. They were all saved. The fire was extinguished from heaven. Every year there is a procession at the shrine in commemoration of this event.[4]

The worst firestorm in USA history left a scene of total devastation—nothing but charred remains and ashes. In the middle of this total destruction was the green oasis of Our Lady of Good Help and her protected five acres. The surrounding land was destroyed by the fire, but the chapel and the five acres proved to be a sanctuary from hell's fury. They alone remained untouched. All the people and their livestock that had taken refuge were unharmed. Theirs was the only patch of safety in the encircling fire. Just as God reached down and saved Polycarp from the encircling flames some seventeen hundred years earlier, he did it once again—this time just a few miles from the future home of the Green Bay Packers.[5]

---

4. Kelly, "Marian Wisconsin Apparition."

5. A first person account is given by Reverend Peter Pernin, who was the parish priest for Peshtigo and nearby Marinette, whose churches burned to the ground. He published his account of the fire in 1874, republished in 1999 as *The Great Peshtigo Fire: An Eyewitness Account (Wisconsin)*. See the website for The American Society for the Defense of Tradition, Family and Property. http://www.tfp.org/stop-wildfires-human-efforts-fail-lesson-peshtigo-fire-miracle/.

FIRST APPROVED MARIAN APPARITION IN THE USA

The appearances by the Blessed Virgin to Adele Brise in 1859 was approved by the Catholic Church on December 8, 2010 as the first approved Marian apparition in the United States when the bishop of Green Bay, affirmed:[6]

> I declare with moral certainty and in accord with the norms of the Church that the events, apparitions and locutions given to Adele Brise in October of 1859 do exhibit the substance of supernatural character, and I do hereby approve these apparitions as worthy of belief (although not obligatory) by the Christian faithful. I encourage the faithful to frequent this holy place as a place of solace and answered prayer.

Lourdes is unique in that its reported miracles reported are exhaustively studied over a number of years and sometimes decades. Most remain unexamined, as do all the reported miracles associated with Our Lady of Good Help. Nevertheless, there have been numerous miraculous cures reported.

THE GREAT CHICAGO FIRE

The Great Chicago Fire provides an interesting, but somewhat unrelated, footnote to The Great Peshtigo Fire.

The fire that history records as being important on that October 8 occurred not in Wisconsin, but in Chicago, some two hundred miles south. It destroyed four squares miles, killing 250 people. Ninety thousand were left homeless. Father Arnold Damen was the pastor of Holy Name Church on Chicago's north side. At the time of the fire he was in Brooklyn, New York. When he was informed of the Chicago fire and that his parish and church were in the projected path. Father Damen knelt before the altar and begged the Lord to spare his parish. As he was praying the winds shifted, sending the flames in another direction.

Was this the intervening hand of God to help his faithful? Are the inexplicable healings reported at Our Lady of Good Hope miraculous gifts from God? We can't know, but the coincidence is noteworthy. If we are doubters, these inexplicable cures and the story of Father Damen's intercession will not persuade; if we believe, they only confirm what we already knew.

Believe to understand.

---

6. Kelly, "Marian Wisconsin Apparition."

19.3

Our Lady of China

Some events can only be explained as divine intervention. Our Lady of China is one such event, witnessed by a multitude of hostiles in 1900 who acted contrary to their own best interests because of such intervention. This event was confirmed by another in 1995.

The Boxer Rebellion was a violent internal uprising that took place in China between 1899 and 1901. The Boxer's mission was to exterminate and drive out foreign powers and Christians. In 1900, ten thousand Boxer soldiers surrounded the village of Dong Lu, located about ninety miles southwest of Beijing and vowed to kill all the village Catholics, believed to have numbered between 700 and 1,000. The village priest invoked the Blessed Virgin to save his people. With only a few guns and one cannon the villagers were able to fight off the attackers four times.

THE 1900 MIRACLE

Suddenly, the attacking soldiers started to shoot senselessly into the sky and fled. They never came back. Later, some Boxers who had converted said that a woman in white had appeared above Dong Lu and in their fear fired at her, but without effect. The Lady did not leave and a strange horseman, many believe to be St. Michael the Archangel, put them to flight. In gratitude to the Blessed Mother for her protection a large gothic church was completed three years later.

THE 1995 MIRACLE[1,2]

In 1941 Japanese artillery destroyed the church. A new church was built in 1991, which was one-third larger than the original and could accommodate three thousand people. On May 23, 1995, thirty thousand Catholics gathered for Mass at the Dong Lu shrine on the vigil of the Feast of Our Lady, Mary Help of Christians. Four bishops were concelebrating the Mass in the presence of 110 priests when the sun suddenly lost its overpowering brightness so that people could look directly at it. The center of the sun was covered by a host (the Eucharist Bread). People observed the sun spinning, first to the left and then to the right. It was surrounded by a variety of colors. People saw different apparitions, including the Holy Cross, the Holy Family, and Mary. The sun would approach the participants and then retreat. Then following a sudden white ray the sun returned to normal. This all lasted for about twenty minutes.

These are simply the facts.

The next day security forces barred more pilgrims and started sending them away. Still, about one hundred thousand pilgrims found alternative ways to get to the shrine.

In April 1996, the government forbade anyone from going to the Dong Lu shrine. Soon thereafter, the Chinese government mobilized five thousand troops, supported by dozens of armored cars and helicopters, annihilated the shrine, confiscated the statue of the Blessed Virgin Mary and arrested many priests.

Some miracles have been ruthlessly suppressed by government officials, and Our Lady of China is a prime example.

1. Miracle Hunter website, "Dung Lu."
2. Feain, "Marian Shrine #21."

19.4

Cokeville, Wyoming

Some alleged divine interventions just leave us scratching our heads. They either occurred as they were described at the time or they are the product of conspiring minds to spiritually defraud. Can Wyoming children reporting independently of one another the saving hand of God to avert a disaster be anything but true? Cokeville, Wyoming tells us that miracles don't stop at the Catholic or Orthodox door; God doesn't impose any limitations on his grace because of our individual theological positions.

HEAVEN INTERVENES

In May of 1986 a heavily armed deranged man and wife entered Cokeville's elementary school, took 136 children and eighteen teachers and adults hostage, and herded them into a thirty by thirty-two-foot classroom. The wife was connected to a homemade bomb and inadvertently detonated it. The explosion engulfed her in flames and burned many nearby children. The bomber husband had been in the restroom at the time of the explosion, and when he returned he shot and killed his wife. Students and the adults frantically exited the building, with teachers helping many of the children escape through the windows. The bomber then killed himself. He and his wife were the only two fatalities.

Investigators found that the bomb's blasting cap wires had been mysteriously cut before detonation and that a gasoline leak prevented explosive powder from setting the air on fire. Moreover, despite a great deal of shrapnel, no one had been hit. The blast should have leveled the entire wing, but instead had gone straight up.

So far, it sounds like everyone was just lucky. But when we examine the explosion and hear what the children independently tell of that day, we again see the divine protecting the most innocent and least pretentious. While no one was killed, an extraordinary event by itself, the real miracles were not revealed until later. Children separately began to describe to their parents, police, and counselors how events unfolded and how angels and deceased relatives protected them.

One example: Ron Hartley was the lead investigator for the Sheriff's office. His six-year old son was one of the hostages. The boy had confided to a psychologist that he had seen angels. Hartley tried to set the boy straight. In his own words:

> "I came home with the intent of factually proving to him that he couldn't have seen angels," Hartley recalls. "I asked him who he saw, and he said, 'I don't know. She didn't tell me her name, but I think it was Grandma Meister.' This was exactly what I was looking for. I told him, 'It wasn't Grandma Meister because she's alive and living in Pinedale.'"
>
> But the young boy insisted that his story was true. That's when Hartley asked his wife to get out the family photo album.
>
> "We put it on the table right in front of him, and I started flipping through the pages. I flipped to one page when suddenly he put his little hand on a photo and just beamed," Hartley shares.
>
> "When you do interrogations in law enforcement, you watch for body language. You can tell through physical reactions when someone is lying and when they are not," he continues. "When my son saw that picture, he just brightened up and said, 'That's her! That's my angel!' And it wasn't Grandma Meister—it was my Grandma Elliott. How do you argue that? She'd been dead for three or four years."
>
> Hartley's son told him there were angels for everyone in the room that day, and just prior to detonation, the angels joined hands around the bomb and went up through the ceiling with the explosion.

"When he said that, it lined up with the physical evidence. That, in addition to the fact that he picked out Grandma Elliott, is evidence I can't deny," he says.[1]

Other children gave detailed accounts of how the angels or other spiritual beings directed and saved them just prior to the explosion and during the chaotic fireball and immediate aftermath. Detailed accounts are easily accessible on the internet. Since the Cokeville children were predominately Mormon, it is not surprising that a complete description of what they saw is written on an LDS (Latter Day Saints or Mormon) website.

MOVING ON

The number and diversity of miracles and visions granted by Our Lord is staggeringly high and are easily accessible on the internet. Read about them with an open mind and heart.

It is time to move on. If you have come this far and remain *certain* that the God of Christian theology is a fiction, there is no point in continuing to read. Your door is nailed shut against Christ and, absent some spectacularly dramatic event (and probably not even then), you will never permit the nail-pierced, risen Jesus to enter. If on the other hand you are willing to accept the notion that perhaps God has and continues to reveal himself, but believe the Bible is a fabrication, then it is time to move to the next few chapters.

---

1. Armstrong, J., "Cokeville Miracles."

PART III

The Trustworthy Bible

20

The Word of God?

SKEPTICS AND THE BIBLE

Skeptics tells us that the Bible cannot be the word of God. It contains too many contradictions and internal inconsistencies, precluding it from being the infallible word of an omniscient creator. The God it reveals, particularly the God of the Old Testament, is just plain mean. Additionally, the New Testament wasn't written until decades after the supposed events it describes. And we don't even know who wrote the Gospels of Mark, Matthew, Luke, and John. Moreover, there is no extrinsic evidence supporting the New Testament's central teachings about the life, death, and resurrection of the Son of God, who is named Jesus. That is because the Bible is essentially a propaganda piece and a masterful work of fiction (masterful except for its inherent inconsistencies and weird stories).

THE CAPRICIOUS GOD OF THE OBSOLETE BIBLE AND ITS TEACHINGS

An eternal God should mean unchangeable values and teachings, but there is a distinct shift from the Old to the New Testament. We believe God's values should be ours and are perplexed by some of the biblical stories and teachings that fly in the face of what we know is right. We are confused as to the authenticity of the Bible as the Word of God. Shouldn't we believe "objective" scholars and theologians who have studied these issues (as opposed to Christian clergy and theologians who are just trying to prove their pre-determined conclusions)? The objective scholars tell us that the existence of the omniscient and omnipotent being we refer to as God is illogical and that all his attributes and the story of Jesus are fictions created by mendacious zealots. In the face of such overpowering erudition, how is it possible to believe?

THE ESSENTIAL ISSUE

These questions of authorship, dates of writing and other corollary issues relating to the four Gospels and other books of the Bible would be important if we didn't have Jesus revealed to us in no uncertain terms by his mother at Fatima and elsewhere, as well as by his Turin photograph. Still, these issues are debated by different factions within academia and by scholars of different stripes. Neither side can convince the other and so it seems that everyone runs around in circles jabbering. How can you and I know who is correct from a scholarly point of view?

We can't—and they can't.

The antagonists can dance around as much as they like, honing their debating skills, but in the end, their conclusions and arguments are meaningless. What matters is the powerful evidence that God has laid out for us to see if we but look with an open mind. When you consider the numerous appearances by Mary, miraculous healings, the physical evidence, and other miraculous events, all questions about the veracity of the four Gospel accounts of the life, teachings, death, and resurrection of Jesus Christ should dissipate. But they don't, and that is why we will briefly look at these questions and offer some insight that you may not have considered.

Skeptics claim that the four accounts of the Resurrection contained in Matthew, Mark, Luke, and John contradict one another, thereby proving their falsity. The Resurrection (see next chapter) is, of course, the *sine qua non* of Christianity. Absent other compelling evidence, inconsistent accounts could be a problem for the believer. In fact, a cursory reading of the four Gospel accounts of the Resurrection could lead one to conclude they are inconsistent and even contradict one another. But we will show that a reasonable reading of these Gospels is that they in fact complement one another. Chapter 22 offers a chronology of what happened on that first Easter Sunday by integrating all four Gospel accounts into one narrative.

We use the language of the Gospels and some background information, along with a few reasonable premises, to present one alternative of how the Resurrection occurred. This account harmonizes the four Gospels and at the same time reveals a remarkably cohesive account written from four different vantage points.

Additionally, the objective evidence in the person of the man on the Shroud of Turin and the Sudarium tell us that the Gospel accounts of torture and pain he endured are painfully accurate.

The fact is that most of the events described in the Gospels are stunningly unexpected, imaginative, and incongruous (see chapter 23). If these events, such as the Transfiguration, are fictional we are forced to accept the notion that the early Gospel writers took the long way around to create a completely unbelievable religion that flew in the face of Judaism, and yet flowed directly from the Old Testament. The Transfiguration is but one example and its details and the details surrounding the other events within the Gospels demand that we recognize either its truth or a level of conspiratorial sophistication on the part of the apostles or early disciples that would have been quite beyond the reach of these humble Palestinians some two thousand years ago. To drive home the point, see chapter 24 for a fictionalized meeting of the apostles showing how they concocted all the cutting-edge Christian beliefs and stories about the life of Jesus such as the Transfiguration, the Virgin birth, walking on water, etc.

21

The Resurrection

Unless Peter, Mark, John, Matthew, Paul, and others were absolutely convinced that Jesus rose from the dead his legacy would long ago have dissolved; he was dead and gone—another charismatic flop. His teachings, his parables, his life would merely be another tiny footnote in history with no one paying any attention to him other than a few dust-encrusted scholars writing Doctorate Theses titled "Ancient Religions" or "Jewish Sects that Aborted." There would be neither a New Testament nor Christianity. Western civilization would be in a form that none today could recognize. Almost surely Islam would be the dominant religion of the world (and perhaps the only one). Jesus would be just another obscure prophet that preceded Mohammad.

THE APOSTLES KNEW

To make sure everyone should hear the good news of Jesus' infinite love, and that he suffered, died, was buried and rose from the dead, Jesus gave us the apostles. They were witnesses to the Resurrection. They left their homes, their families, their loved ones and traveled throughout the known world teaching and baptizing. Their only gain was the knowledge that they were doing what Jesus had commanded. Their reward? Eleven died gruesome deaths as martyrs and the twelfth (John) died an old man after years of exile.

From the earliest traditions:

Peter	Crucified upside down in Rome
Andrew	Crucified on an "X" shaped cross in Greece
Thomas	Speared by four soldiers in India
Philip	Either beheaded or crucified upside down in Turkey
Matthew	Thrown off a precipice and beheaded in Egypt
Bartholomew (Nathanial)	Skinned alive in Armenia
James the Greater	Beheaded in Jerusalem
James the Less	Stoned and clubbed to death in Jerusalem
Simon the Zealot	Sawed in half in Syria or Iran
Jude (Thaddeus)	Axed to death in Lebanon
Matthias	Stoned and decapitated in Jerusalem
John	Died in exile in Turkey
Paul	Beheaded in Rome

Would you permit yourself to be tortured and die for a cause that you *knew* was a lie? If you would, do you think you could persuade eleven other fake witnesses to be tortured and die for a lie—without dissent? I think not. The apostles didn't believe that Jesus rose from the dead; they knew.

CONTEMPORANEOUS WRITINGS

Witnesses to the Risen Christ were talking about what they had seen. Baptisms and conversions were taking place with unending frequency. The Christian movement, based upon the singularly unlikely event that a man had risen from the dead, was gathering speed and substance. Yet there is no account of Jewish or Roman historians presenting facts or witnesses to dispute these claims. Instead, and as discussed in Chapter 9.4, "Our Lady of Fatima: The Effects of Her Appearances," there are important references in contemporaneous non-Christian writings describing the rapidly growing Jewish sect called Christians who preached a new and dangerous religion.

Since the facts were on their side, the apostles and other witnesses were vigorously proclaiming what had happened. On the other hand, the antagonists were silent. Jesus had disappeared and there was no evidence to support their claims of fraud or error. Their only recourse was to persecute.

Fear, repression, and even torture and death would await those who believed in the resurrected Christ.

IGNORING THE EVIDENCE

And this brings us to the present. Non-Christians argue that there is no evidence of a resurrected Jesus. For the good faith skeptic such an argument can only be made if he is unaware of Fatima, Lourdes, Knock, the Shroud of Turin and other information presented in Part II that demonstrate the reality of the biblical Christ. The general response of nonbelievers is to ignore this evidence and shrug their shoulders to the effect of "So what?" The described events and evidence seem too strange and outside their core of experience to be taken seriously. There is no need to explore further.

RESURRECTION ELIMINATES ALL OTHER THEOLOGIES

Some say that even if we can prove that a god or gods exist, why the Christian God? Why not Allah, HaShem, Rama, Krishna, Brahma, Vishnu, Maheswara, Ahura Mazda or the myriad other gods that have been worshipped over the centuries? The answer is easy. If we know that Mary appeared with objective certainty at Lourdes, Fatima, or other places and directed us to her resurrected son, we needn't explore any further. Moreover, and quite apart from the claimed manifestations of Mary, if we can demonstrate Jesus died and was resurrected as described in the Bible, there is no reason to consider other potential gods. The Resurrection resolves the issue once and for all.

FREE WILL TO BELIEVE OR NOT BELIEVE

God doesn't push himself on us. He approaches with the gentle persuasion of whispering hope, much as the Shroud of Turin. The Shroud is at first fuzzy and indistinct and its real power becomes evident only when it is studied. As is the case with the Shroud, the Gospel accounts of the Crucifixion and Resurrection need to be studied. Quick glances at the Shroud and superficial readings of the Resurrection are not sufficient. God expects us to devote time, thought and prayer towards him and his gifts. We can't just occasionally glance his way and expect him to force himself into our lives. He may do this, but it's not the norm. Jesus will present himself to us, perhaps subtly, but we need to respond. You will not find God by testing him, but only by trusting him.

One final thought regarding the Resurrection. Regardless of our Christian denomination or church we attend and doctrinal differences, even going as deeply as the nature of the Trinity, or whether there is even a Trinity, or whether we are saved by faith alone or need to prove that faith by keeping the Lord's Commandments, regardless of all these we still can lock arms and thank God for the gift of eternal life that the Christ gave and proved to us by his resurrection. Whatever differences exist among us, we are all united by a common and fundamental belief that God loved us so much that he gave his only begotten son to die for us and that his life did not terminate in that Jerusalem tomb two thousand years ago.

22

The Resurrection

Complementary Gospel Accounts

Non-Christians maintain that the Books of Matthew, Mark, Luke, and John contradict one another in terms of how the Resurrection events unfold, thereby proving that it is a fabrication. And in fact, as you read the Gospel accounts, they may appear on their face to be at the very least inconsistent and at worst hopelessly self-contradictory. We must address these issues.

EXAMINING THE RESURRECTION AND THE BIBLE'S NARRATIVE

We are going to offer a chronology of what happened on that first Easter Sunday by integrating all four Gospel accounts into one narrative. We will use both the language of the Gospels and some background information, along with a few reasonable premises, to present one alternative of how the Resurrection occurred. This account will harmonize the four Gospels and at the same time reveal a remarkably cohesive account written from four different vantage points. The pieces of the puzzle fall into place. There are alternative explanations, but for right now we'll explore this one.

DIFFERENT VANTAGE POINTS

If your twelve-year-old daughter (let's call her Freda) visited Disneyland with her friends Joanna, Edith, and Nicole, as part of a church group, you might write in your annual Christmas letter or on Facebook that Freda went to Disneyland with some friends and had a great time. Or if you were writing to Freda's grandmother you might just say that Freda went to Disneyland and had a wonderful trip. If you were also the church group leader you would probably tell the world that you took your daughter and your church group to Disneyland, etc. Vantage point and your audience and why you're telling them crucially guide your narrative. Keep this in mind as you piece together the events surrounding the Resurrection, the descriptions of which were undoubtedly written at least fifteen years after the event. It is generally believed:

- Mark witnessed much of what happened during the passion and later became a disciple of Peter. He listened to Peter describing Jesus and his ministry, the Passion, and the Resurrection. When you read Mark, you are for the most part reading the recollections of Peter through the pen of Mark. Much of the Resurrection account, however, may have been written later and not directly by Mark, and would have incorporated in part the Resurrection narratives of Matthew and Luke, and possibly John.

- Matthew was one of the original disciples and his Gospel reflects his recollections, as well as other sources.

- Luke was a historian and accompanied Paul on his many travels. His motivation was to provide a careful, accurate and historical record. He gathered his information from diverse sources, including the Blessed Virgin, and may have had either or both Matthew's and Mark's Gospels in front of him.

- John was the beloved disciple. It is generally acknowledged that his was the last Gospel account written and he almost certainly had access to those written by Mark, Matthew, and Luke. John's Gospel reflects his experiences and recollections.

If these four (or their followers) were silent conspirators to present a fictitious Resurrection account, they failed miserably. You would have thought they would have presented a storyline which on its face would be consistent. Instead, they present descriptions which could be confusing and inconsistent to the casual reader. By exploring the subtleties, however, a different picture emerges. What unfolds is a mosaic of Resurrection accounts that weave together a profound and powerful story.

Jesus taught in parables so that the truth would be revealed to those who cared enough to take the time to reflect upon these stories to uncover and retain the messages and the truths they taught. Perhaps the different ways the writers describe Resurrection history is intended to be consumed by those who wish to take the time to reflect and understand.

A LIKELY TIMELINE

With this brief introduction we can now reconstruct a possible, and perhaps likely, timeline of events following the Resurrection.

First, except for Peter and John, the Bible doesn't mention the whereabouts of any of the apostles immediately after Jesus is arrested. They fled, but to where? One logical answer would be away from Jerusalem and to the safe harbor of someone they knew. That could very likely be the home of Mary of Bethany, Martha, and Lazarus. These were siblings who lived in Bethany [now Al-Eizariya or el ʿAzareyeh (there are other different spellings as well)]. Bethany had been used as a base by Jesus when he was near Jerusalem and is located about two miles east of Jerusalem and about two and one-half miles east of Jesus' tomb.

Second, only Peter and John remained in Jerusalem following Jesus' arrest. Tradition has always held that John had a home in or near Jerusalem, a fact that Jesus would have known when he entrusted his mother to John's care. Peter remained in Jerusalem during the Passion, denying the Lord three times. When all was lost and in his moral agony, he could have traveled to Bethany to join the other disciples. Another and more likely alternative, however, would be for him to go with John and stay with him in his Jerusalem house along with the Blessed Mother and possibly Mary Magdalene. These were the other two witnesses who are recorded as remaining close to Jesus throughout his crucifixion.

All four Gospels describe the resurrection of Jesus. The complete accounts of the burial, resurrection, and aftermath are contained in Matthew 27:57—28:20; Mark 15:42—16:20; Luke 23:50—24:53; and John 19:38—20:31. The following chronology is supported by scripture and by common sense. Type in regular font indicates that the statement is directly supported by scripture, giving chapter and verse; *italics indicate reasonable inferences from the context.*

1. Following Jesus' crucifixion, the grieving women that had accompanied him from Galilee continued to follow him after his body was taken down from the cross. They saw the tomb in which he was laid

and *agreed to meet at the tomb at the break of day following the Sabbath* to anoint his body (Luke 23:55–56).

2. *Departing from John's house,* Mary Magdalene arrived early while it was still dark and saw that the stone had been taken away from the tomb (John 20:1). *Shortly thereafter and* as dawn approached, the *other* women arrived, and they saw that the stone sealing the tomb had been rolled back (Mark 16:2–4; Luke 24:2). Matthew explains that there was a great earthquake; for an angel of the Lord descended from heaven and came and rolled back the stone (Matthew 28:2).

3. Fearing that someone had taken the body of Jesus, all the women approached the tomb. There an angel told them that Jesus had risen and pointed to the tomb so they could see for themselves. He told them to go and tell the disciples and Peter (Matthew 28:5–7 and Mark 16:3–7). *The fact that the angel separately referred to Peter and the other disciples seems to imply (and that's all) that Peter was in a different location than the other disciples. Since John was with Peter he would hear the news at the same time.* Mary Magdalene immediately ran off to tell Peter and John, *both of whom were at John's house in Jerusalem with the Blessed Virgin* (John 20:2).

4. *When Mary Magdalene departed,* and following the angel's instructions, the other women entered the tomb and there was no body. They were now completely perplexed, but two men in dazzling attire stood by them and asked why they sought the living among the dead, and reminded them of how Jesus said that he must die and rise again (Luke 24:2–7).

5. Mary Magdalene *arrived at John's house and* told Peter and John that the body was missing. They immediately departed for the tomb, with John running ahead of Peter (John 20:2–3), *followed by Mary Magdalene.*

6. *By the time John and Peter arrived at the tomb* the other women *had* left to tell the *other* disciples of what they had seen and what the angels (men) had told them. They were immersed with joy and fear. *They knew Mary Magdalene was going to tell Peter and John and so* they went *east to Bethany* to tell the other disciples, but no one else (Matthew 28:8 and Mark 16:8).

7. John "outran Peter and reached the tomb first; and stooping to look in, he saw the linen cloths lying there, but he did not go in. Then Simon Peter came, following him, and went into the tomb; he saw the linen cloths lying, and the napkin, which had been on his head, not lying with the linen cloths but rolled up in a place by itself. Then the other disciple [John], who reached the tomb first, also went in, and he saw

and believed; for as yet they did not know the scripture, that he must rise from the dead." (John 20:2–9).

8. *After a short time spent in wonderment and disbelief,* Peter and John went back to their homes. John believed (John 20:10) *and a short time later Peter joined John at his home.*

9. *Mary had followed Peter and John back to the tomb. When she arrived, they were gone.* She stood outside the tomb weeping, not yet understanding that Jesus had risen. Jesus then appeared to her, but she did not recognize him until he turned to her and said, "Mary!" He then told her, "Do not hold me, for I have not yet ascended to the Father; but go to my brethren and say to them, I am ascending to my Father and your Father, to my God and your God." (John 20:11–17 and Mark 16:9).

10. Shortly thereafter, *and somewhere on their journey to Bethany,* Jesus appeared to the other women and said, "Hail!" And they came up and took hold of his feet and worshiped him. Then Jesus said to them, "Do not be afraid; go and tell my brethren to go to Galilee, and there they will see me." (Matthew 28:9–10).

11. Jesus had appeared to Mary Magdalene and the other women. They *arrived in Bethany and* told the other disciples of what had transpired at the tomb and of their meeting with Jesus on the road to Bethany. None of this made sense to the disciples, *but they knew they had to be with Peter and John.*

12. *Also staying in Bethany were Cleopas, the husband of the other Mary, who was one of the women at the tomb and telling them this fantastic tale. Consequently, Cleopas and some other disciples accompanied the women to John's house to be with Peter and John.*

13. All the disciples now gathered *at John's house* in Jerusalem. Mary Magdalene told the disciples what had occurred at the tomb and that she had seen Jesus (John 20:18). "They told all this to the eleven and to all the rest. Now it was Mary Magdalene and Joanna and Mary [wife of Cleopas] the mother of James and the other women with them who told this to the apostles; but these words seemed to them an idle tale, and they did not believe them." (Mark 16:10–11; Luke 24:8–11; and John 20:18). *They all wanted to believe, but how could they? This was just too fantastic!*

14. At some point some of the disciples also went to the tomb and found it empty but did not see the Risen Lord (Luke 24:23). *This was reported to the disciples, including Cleopas and another disciple.*

15. *For unknown reasons* Cleopas and another disciple left the group and journeyed to Emmaus, which is about seven miles northwest of John's house. As they walked they discussed these recent events and the stories given by Mary Magdalene and the other women, including Cleopas's own wife. Then they were joined by a stranger, who after explaining the Scriptures and breaking bread with them, was revealed as Jesus. They too had seen the Risen Lord (Luke 24:13–32 and Mark 16:12).

16. Cleopas and the other disciple returned to Jerusalem and there excitedly told the disciples and the others who were then present that "The Lord has risen indeed, and has appeared to Simon!" Then they told what had happened on the road, and how he was known to them in the breaking of the bread." (Luke 24:33–35). But still the disciples didn't believe (Mark 16:13). *[Note: Mark's Gospel is really Peter's Gospel, but the final verses in Mark describing the resurrection events are thought to have been added at a later date, and not by Peter (writing through Mark) so none of the Gospels state directly the appearance(s) by the Lord to Peter as related by Cleopas.]*

17. In the evening of that first day the Lord appeared to the disciples (except Thomas who was not present) as they gathered together (Luke 24:36–49 and John 20:19–23).

18. The following Sunday when all the disciples were gathered Jesus appeared again and Thomas believes. Jesus says, "Have you believed because you have seen me? Blessed are those who have not seen and yet believe." (John 20:24–29).

This reconstruction weaves together all four Gospels and reconciles supposed discrepancies. The truth is that when you view the four Resurrection accounts, they all supplement one another and present a magnificently thorough but condensed account of what happened. To be sure there are other possible scenarios to explain what on their face appear to be contradictions or inconsistencies, and you need to look at them. The point is that the Gospel accounts of the Resurrection can be trusted as a chronicle of that sacred event as viewed and reported by four disciples of Jesus and his church.

GOD'S LOVE AND THE RESURRECTION

Lest we forget: The Resurrection tells us, profoundly and unequivocally, that God loves us with a love that is eternal and deep.

23

The Unexpected, Imaginative, and Incongruous

ALTERNATIVE EXPLANATIONS FOR THE GOSPELS

It is argued that the Books of Matthew, Mark, Luke, and John (the Gospels) cannot be trusted as historical records for the birth, life, death, and resurrection of Jesus. Instead, skeptics alternatively assert that:

1. Jesus never lived;
2. Jesus was never crucified, but a replacement victim was substituted;
3. Jesus was crucified and survived the ordeal; or
4. Jesus was crucified and died, but his body was secretly removed from the tomb.

It is further argued that the Gospel authors could honestly have thought Jesus was resurrected, but it is more likely that the entire resurrection story was a deliberate lie. In other words, the Gospel writers were either duped or liars.

We will begin by noting that there is no objective evidence to support any of these claims. None. They are conclusions presented in the form of argument or evidence. There is general agreement, however, that the identity of the authors is, in fact, uncertain. Were they the men whose Gospels bear their name? Their scribes? Their immediate followers or students? Were they written by followers of a later generation?

RED HERRINGS AND THE REAL ISSUE

A red herring is a false issue or a diversionary one, and the question of human authorship is a red herring. The real question is whether God is the author using humans (whoever they might be) as his instruments to communicate his word. I can't say what other Christian churches teach, but the Catholic Church clearly holds that the Gospels are of apostolic origin—whether directly from the apostles themselves or through the apostles. The identity of the person God used to write the Book of Luke, for example, is of secondary importance. The overriding issue is whether the New Testament faithfully hands on what Jesus Christ did and taught for our eternal salvation.

IGNORING THE OBVIOUS

Christian and non-Christian scholars unanimously agree that the Gospels were written in Palestine sometime between A.D. 40—125. If you are a skeptic, pick whatever dates you like within that spectrum, and you are still faced with the issue of explaining how the early authors, assuming events described in the New Testament were lies, were able to piece together a narrative of incredible love, complexity and deep theological significance and teaching in all their parts. You need to explain how literally overnight a new religion, called Christianity, could have been created by Jews which flew in the face of Judaism and its expectations of the Messiah. Additionally, even while this new Christianity was forging a new and completely unanticipated path to salvation, you need to account for the fact it was simultaneously continuing and augmenting the Old Testament story of salvation.

Rejecting the Gospels requires us to accept the notion of incredibly gifted scholars and logicians never before heard of (or after unless they were the named authors, Matthew, Mark, Luke, and John) breaking away from their Jewish heritage to introduce a new theology centered around an insidious superstition of resurrection and eternal life for Jew and Gentile, made possible by the life and death of a carpenter. This would be a carpenter born in the hinterlands of the Roman empire, into poverty, who never wrote a book, never went to a university, and just walked around for three years in a limited geographical area telling everyone that he was the Son of God. Then to prove his point, he suffered a tortuous death and came back to life. This deceitful story would have been created overnight; this would be your fake religion.

If we were to make up a religion, this would not be what we would devise. We would create a belief system that everyone would expect, be simple to explain, and an easy sell. Christianity doesn't do that—in fact, it is just the opposite.

Here is a great irony. The Resurrection is the core event of Christianity. Skeptics attack it as an historical event, but rarely attack the reality of other Gospel events which, if true, would substantiate the Resurrection and that Jesus was the Son of God. The intricate web of lies and the strange events the writers of the Gospels and other New Testament books would have to have devised to trick the gullible is ignored.

THE CONSPIRACY IS HATCHED

Put yourselves in the shoes of the earliest disciples, particularly the apostles. If you were going to start a new Jewish cult based on nothing but your imagination or wishful thinking, how would you try and convince others as to the veracity of your claims, especially the one about a Nazarene who was brutally crucified and then rose from the dead. How could you possibly persuade others?

The next chapter describes a fictitious meeting of the apostles and some of the weird beliefs and doctrines they created.

24

The Apostles Conspire

PRELIMINARY CONSIDERATIONS

Leaving their motivations aside, let's assume for the moment that the disciples of Christ decided to launch a new religion based upon a fictitious resurrection of Christ. We'll take it one step further and assume that they in all honesty, but erroneously, thought he rose from the dead. They wanted others to believe that Jesus was the Son of God who gave us the gift of eternal life by dying on the cross.

Imagine a meeting among Peter, James, John, Paul, Mark, Luke and Matthew.[1] The agenda has been prepared by Peter and the top of the scroll reads, "Convincing Jews that Christ was the Promised Messiah and Convincing Gentiles to Accept the Reality of Jesus as their Saving God and Creator." The time is some years after the Holy Week events and the place is Jerusalem.

---

1. If you prefer, imagine a meeting consisting of men not with these names, but others who, for the purposes of this story, we would deem the real authors of the Gospels.

THE FIRST MEETING

Peter opened the meeting, "Friends, we've been through a lot together. We thought Jesus was the Messiah, but when he was executed it looked like we were wrong. Then, as I told you some time ago, Jesus appeared to me in a dream and I then knew that he had been raised from the dead." Nodding towards Paul, he continued, "Paul affirmed his resurrection when he had that vision of the resurrected Jesus on the road to Damascus. We've made remarkable progress in spreading the gospel of the Lord and the story of his life, death, and resurrection, but we need to do more. So now the question is what can we do to make people believe that he actually rose from the dead?"

It was Paul who responded, "I think it's time we seriously consider writing a history of Jesus' life. We need to commit in writing what he said and taught. But even that's not going to be enough to convince succeeding generations of his life and that he died and was resurrected. I've given this a lot of thought and we're simply going to have to include stories about healings, miracles—you know, that sort of thing. The story of Jesus needs legs and to solidify our position and the attractiveness of our message we need to expand the message to include the Gentiles. That means we must proclaim that Jesus was the fulfillment of the Old Covenant and that God's mercy as first envisioned by us, the Jews, is now available to everyone, and in a simplified format."

Peter was doubtful, "I don't know. That sounds pretty intellectual. Can we handle that?"

Paul continued, "Stay with me. I think it's time we introduce the written word. This will expand the reach of our teaching dramatically. But our life of Jesus must include details of his teachings, events leading up to the crucifixion, about his being resurrected and his second coming. These teachings should differentiate us from the rabbis and help solidify our position. Sure, we'll take some grief, but we need to expand our message so that we can start building our church to include Gentiles as well."

Peter now saw where Paul was heading and turned to the group, "What can we say that would convince others of the reality of his resurrection? It's not going to be enough to say that I had a dream and Paul had a vision. How can we convince others that Jesus was the Son of God and rose from the dead?"

It was Matthew who responded first, "I think one thing we can do is to declare that Jesus was born of a virgin. This should help convince the Jews at least that he is the promised Messiah because of Isaiah's prophecy. I know our rabbis here in Palestine aren't sure whether Isaiah explicitly said that his mother was to be a virgin or whether they implicitly said the same thing when he said he would be born of a young woman because Isaiah knew that a young woman in our Hebrew tradition would necessarily be a virgin. But on the other hand, our rabbis in Alexandria are not the least bit uncertain. They know that the Christ was to be born of a woman who had never known man."

Luke picked up on this, "I think Matthew is right. We need to make up a story on how Mary miraculously conceived him and develop supporting details."

Paul broke in, "Matthew is the one to run with this story. I know he wants to write about the life of Jesus, primarily for the Jews. He can go back into the Scriptures and weave a story which fits nicely into our Hebrew tradition. The key is to develop something they'll believe.

Mark was puzzled, "Do you think Jesus would want us to lie about his life and teachings? I mean just to make up a story about how he was born...."

Luke interrupted him, "Mark, don't be so naïve. We've got a hard sell here. I can put together a really great story about how an angel visited Mary and then add all kinds of miraculous things to convince the so-called rational Greeks that Jesus was in fact God. Wise men coming from the east will persuade them of his reality and kingship. I can have them following a star that only they can see or discern its significance. The Gentiles will love it!"

Matthew agreed, "Mark, you need to write a story about the life of Jesus, his teachings and everything else from the time he started teaching. Stay away from anything doing with his childhood. Luke and I will take care of that. Just work with Peter and he'll be able to give you the basics. No disrespect, Peter, but you're just an uneducated fisherman and nobody would take your written story seriously. Let Mark handle this for you. He's educated and pretty smart. Luke, go with the complete infancy narrative and I'll supplement it in a way that may be more palatable to the Jews.

John had been quiet. He was the youngest and sometimes was reluctant to offer his opinions. After all, Matthew used to be a tax collector and had been around. Then there was Luke. Luke was a physician and historian and knew how to gather stories from various witnesses to narrate a story about Jesus. Finally, however, John could no longer contain himself, "Luke you weren't there so you couldn't really be a witness to our Lord's death so despite your academic credentials, what you say may be somewhat suspect. Mark, you have the same problem, but somewhat mitigated by the fact that you were there as a young man during the trial of Jesus and have been associated with Peter for so many years. . ."

Mark interjected, "I see what you're saying. Maybe I should make up some more personal stories and include them in my writing. What if I were to include a story about how the night Jesus was arrested, I followed him and then the guards grabbed me, tore off my garment and I had to flee naked. That's weird enough to add a sense of realism."

Peter thought for a moment, "I think that's a great idea! Also, maybe introduce some other personal touches like maybe how Jesus said I would deny him three times and how bitter and remorseful I was when these instant prophecies all came true."

Paul had been silent a while, but now he came forward with what can only be described as a stroke of genius, "Listen, all of you except Luke claim to have been with Jesus when he preached the coming of the Kingdom. You all saw him taken away to be tortured, crucified, and die. Peter saw him resurrected in a dream, which is a clear message from God. Plus I saw him. We all are pretty well convinced that he rose again. We need to create events in the life of Jesus which will enable our fellow Jews to see how Jesus was the fulfillment of the scriptures. That's a big task, I know, but it's an important one."

The group fell silent, and after a short pause, James offered a suggestion, "We should claim that Jesus spent forty days with us after his resurrection teaching and explaining and applying the scriptures so that we could understand how he was the fulfillment of the Old Covenant. Think about it! This would tie in nicely with how Moses remained on Sinai for forty days[2] and the forty years our ancestors were in the desert being tempted.[3] We can claim he told us what to do and then rose bodily into the sky."

Luke then put the finishing touches on this scheme, "Maybe we can make up a story about how Satan tempted Jesus at the beginning of his ministry and how Jesus spent forty days in the wilderness fasting and then arguing with the devil. That should start tongues wagging! Plus, his forty days of our being fed his word following the Resurrection would be a nice counterbalance to his forty fasting days when he first got started."

Paul continued, "Then I think we should make up a story about how ten days after he ascended into heaven, and when you were all in Jerusalem, tongues of fire descended upon you. I doubt that kind of event has ever been recorded before. I know in the Old Covenant, fire from Heaven came down and consumed the offering made by Elisha, but for fire to land on each of you and not burn you would be great—kind of like the time when God appeared to Moses in the burning bush. The possibilities are endless.[4]

---

2. Exod 24:18.

3. Deut 8:2.

4. I wonder if the Holy Fire described in chapter 19.1 is an extension or continuation of the Pentecost holy fire."

"Don't forget, when I saw him on the road to Damascus he made it clear that he was the resurrected Lord and that my job was to spread his gospel as best I could to the whole world. That's what I've been doing and will continue to do. But we really need to come up with some more fabulous events and new teachings and history that would prove he was the Son of God. We'll start of course with the resurrection and the aftermath. But we need more. Let's think about all this and get together in a week."

THE STORY EMERGES

Seven days later they convened, and it was agreed that they would build a New Testament to join with the Old. The New would be anchored by Mark, Matthew, and Luke who would write in roughly parallel fashion. Either Mark or Matthew would write first and then the other two could use that as a starting point and modify as they thought best to reflect their own thoughts and to avoid the charge of collusion.

One thing they had to be careful about was describing events and stories that other people who could have been there might look at and say, "No—never happened!" Additionally, they decided to make up some stories that were so miraculous they would have to be believed on the grounds that no one could conceive of such wildly improbable events. As part of the overall planning it was decided that John would author a separate testimonial. He was, after all, closest to Jesus and pretty imaginative. He could make up some great stories that were so outside the mainstream that they must in fact be accepted as true.

After a lot of give and take they decided that some of the stories they would create would include:

- Mary was approached by the angel Gabriel and told her she would conceive the Son of God but without having any sexual relations with Joseph. They'd have to bring Mary on board, of course, but that shouldn't be a problem;
- Mary visited Elizabeth who had conceived a few months earlier. It was good luck that she was so old since that plays right into their scheme that with God nothing is impossible. We could say that her son became John the Baptist and pointed towards Jesus as the savior;
- And we could say how John, while still a baby in the womb, leaped with joy as Jesus arrived in the womb of Mary;

- They would figure out how to have Jesus born in Bethlehem in fulfillment of the Messianic prophecies because everybody knew that Jesus was from Nazareth. Luke could probably come up with a believable story;
- They needed to make up a couple of childhood stories about Jesus—maybe they could say that Jesus was presented to the Lord in the temple when he was an infant and how an old Jew prophesied about how Jesus and Mary would suffer, and that Jesus would be a light to the world;
- Then demonstrate that Jesus knew he was the Son of God even when he was only twelve. Make up a story about staying in Jerusalem, and his parents losing him, and then finding him three days later (ties in neatly with his being lost in the tomb for three days) in his "Father's house" (not Joseph's) to be about his business. This would add a sense of realism to the story and constitute a great continuation of the theme presented earlier at his birth;
- Even though Jesus would not have sinned since he was the Eternal One and of necessity sinless, he should still be baptized by John the Baptist (Elizabeth's son) dressed in a weird outfit. At the baptism the voice of God would be heard from heaven and a dove alight upon Jesus, representing the Holy Spirit (they still hadn't figured out what that was, exactly);
- Jesus spent forty days fasting and then winning an argument against the devil;
- Jesus told them to eat his body and drink his blood. This may be going a step too far, alienate the Jews (and maybe just about everyone else), and possibly lead to future persecution. No one likes cannibals. Still, they decided to go with it;
- Jesus stood up in a boat and calmed a raging sea;
- Miraculous healing after miraculous healing, and incorporate theological lessons in the miracles (but keep them subtle so their meaning wouldn't necessarily leap out at the reader);
- Jesus raised people from the dead. John would take it a step further and describe how Jesus raised one of his friends four days after he died;
- Jesus would commit the ultimate blasphemy and actually forgive sins. Only God could do this, so this would be a huge step toward showing that Jesus was actually God—the creator of the universe, omniscient, omniscient, but who still lived within Mary's womb for nine months;

- Jesus turned water into wine, but only after his mother told him to do something to help out at a wedding;
- Jesus walked on water, and so did Peter when he had a sufficient amount of faith—for a little while anyway;
- Jesus fed 5,000, and then 4,000 with a few loaves of bread and a few fish;
- After he died he would rise from the dead and later fly into heaven; and
- Tongues of fire would descend upon the apostles about ten days after he ascended into heaven.

They agreed to create stories and sermons from Jesus with a subtlety that could only be appreciated after many years of study. One example that came to mind was having Christ preach as he suffered on the cross.[5] Also, they thought it would be helpful always to incorporate the unexpected, such as having women discover an empty tomb. They all agreed this was a good start but would require a lot of coordination and communication among the group to be able to develop a consistent story line, particularly when it came to the details of the resurrection.

MATTHEW INTRODUCES THE TRANSFIGURATION

It was then that Matthew elevated the level of enthusiasm to new heights when he introduced a story that would put to rest all doubt. He called it the Transfiguration, and they all loved it. They would say that Jesus went to the top of a mountain and there his face and garments would transform into a dazzling white. Elijah and Moses would appear with him. A voice from heaven would declare that Jesus was "His Son." They would also be enveloped by a cloud. All of this would incidentally tie in neatly with another story about a similar voice from heaven when Jesus was baptized. Peter, James, and John agreed that they should be shown as the witnesses to this transfiguration. It was also decided that these three should be shown as the apostles with Jesus in the Garden of Gethsemane. They would actually be bold enough to proclaim that Jesus prayed to himself (since he was God and there was only one God) to release him from his journey to the cross.

After a bit of give and take, Matthew sat down and penned the story:

---

5. These are known as the Seven Last Words of Jesus from the Cross. See Luke 23:34, 43; John 19:26,27; Matthew 27:46; John 19:28, 30; Luke 23:46.

> And after six days Jesus took with him Peter and James and John his brother, and led them up a high mountain apart. And he was transfigured before them, and his face shone like the sun, and his garments became white as light. And behold, there appeared to them Moses and Elijah, talking with him. And Peter said to Jesus, "Lord, it is well that we are here; if you wish, I will make three booths here, one for you and one for Moses and one for Elijah." He was still speaking, when lo, a bright cloud overshadowed them, and a voice from the cloud said, "This is my beloved Son, with whom I am well pleased; listen to him." When the disciples heard this, they fell on their faces, and were filled with awe. But Jesus came and touched them, saying, "Rise, and have no fear." And when they lifted up their eyes, they saw no one but Jesus only.
>
> And as they were coming down the mountain, Jesus commanded them, "Tell no one the vision, until the Son of man is raised from the dead." And the disciples asked him, "Then why do the scribes say that first Elijah must come?" He replied, "Elijah does come, and he is to restore all things; but I tell you that Elijah has already come, and they did not know him, but did to him whatever they pleased. So also the Son of man will suffer at their hands." Then the disciples understood that he was speaking to them of John the Baptist."[6]

Paul recognized the genius behind the Transfiguration story. First, introducing Moses and Elijah into the story was first rate. Moses represented the Law, and Elijah was the greatest of the prophets. Now Jesus would replace them. They would disappear and God Himself would tell Peter, James, and John that they needed to listen to Jesus. This was His Son. Pretty powerful stuff. This would plow new ground. Not only that, but Moses had died and so he represented those who were waiting to hear the Salvation message which would be delivered by Jesus. They could later say that Jesus descended to the dead when he had been crucified. Elijah came from heaven to confirm that all heaven joined in this event–that heaven and earth were bound together by this one unifying act. Jesus harmonized all of creation.

Second, Christ wouldn't appear as just being illuminated. He would be described as the illumination itself. This they could say was the glory of God. Later, in his gospel, John could say that the Word had become flesh and dwelled among us, full of grace and truth and that "we beheld his glory, glory as of the only Son from the Father." We would say that Jesus shined like

---

6. Matt. 17:1–13. The other accounts of the Transfiguration are at Luke 9:28–36 and Mark 9:2–13.

the sun. In other words, Jesus was the source of his illumination and not just the reflection as if he were to be illuminated by the sun. Because he was the source of the light this meant that he was the creator of the light. This was the same concept introduced by Moses in Genesis when he said that God created light. Finally, God permitted the apostles to see that Jesus had both a human nature and a divine nature. Jesus illuminated from within as the Creator, but then this energy was transmitted to matter when his clothing took on a brilliance never seen. The apostles recognized that the importance and significance of the Transfiguration as they had made it up wouldn't be understood by many—and perhaps for years—but it was worth inserting this story along with all its improbable details. Were they subtle or what!?

They all agreed that this wasn't too bad for a bunch of mostly ignorant village people.

FUTURE PLANNING

They could leave it to their successors (assuming they had any because they all held varying degrees of confidence that Jesus would soon return) to puzzle through the issue of the Trinity. That was really complicated and they were uncertain how they could actually convince people that God was Three Persons in One and One Person in Three, but they decided to be bold and include in the gospels and in Paul's writings enough information that would lead people to accept a concept created by the apostles and which would be completely alien to the thinking of Jewish and Gentile scholars and totally incomprehensible to the average person. They could at least get the ball rolling by alluding to a Three Person Godhead at the Baptism and at the Transfiguration.

Finally, they concluded that since Paul was going to continue his significant travel schedule he should be the most prolific writer. Besides, he was good at that—being a Jewish scholar and all.

There was a lot of coordination and creativity required to implement their new religion. And for the most part, these were just a bunch of ordinary guys from Palestine, and their leader was a fisherman! They had to keep their stories straight.

It is self-evident that such a meeting never took place and never could. The intricate machinations, coordination, and cover up lies required to devise the story of Jesus as we now have in the Bible would have been completely beyond the abilities of this small cadre of Palestinians and their first century followers.

A RATIONAL PERSPECTIVE

The fact is that most of the events described in the Gospels are stunningly unexpected, imaginative, and incongruous. The Transfiguration is but one example, although admittedly an especially powerful one. Skeptics attack the Resurrection, the core belief of Christianity, but the reality of the Transfiguration is never attacked, other than to contend that it is but one more fanciful creation of early Christians. Yet the Transfiguration and its details demand that we recognize either its truth or a level of conspiratorial sophistication on the part of his apostles that would have been quite beyond the reach of these humble Palestinians some two thousand years ago. In fact, the Transfiguration eliminates the possibility of fraud, as well as mass delusion, unless of course the delusion and hallucinations continued unabated in a very ordered and logical manner from before the Transfiguration and continued through the Transfiguration and into the Passion, the Crucifixion, the Resurrection, the Ascension, and Pentecost.

With this in mind, consider the alternatives explaining the New Testament origins:

1. The New Testament accurately reports what Jesus said and did;

2. It is a series of fictitious narrations and letters created by unidentified zealots for reasons now unclear to us;

3. It is a series of narrations and letters written by unidentified authors that reflect events and teachings they thought or hoped occurred some twenty to a hundred years earlier. If that's the case, and if Jesus was not who he said he was, the reported events which can only be described as miraculous or strange must have been fabricated; or

4. Jesus' teachings and what he said about himself were generally accurate as reported. This means, however, that he was who he said he was or he was lying or delusional. And if he was lying or delusional, this would also mean that the reported miraculous events during his life were inventions of the authors since they could not have occurred without his being the Son of God.

There are no other alternatives.

PART IV

A God of Love

25

God's Love

OUR IDEA OF CREATION AND LIFE

The concept of a loving God is hard for many to accept because of the evil, suffering, and pain we see. After all, a loving God would have created a world free of pain, evil, suffering, and death—in other words, a world with the characteristics of what Christians call heaven. In all honesty, however, to deny God because one may believe that God could have done a better job building the universe and our world if only he had accepted our model of the way things should be is simply silly. Our goal, and admittedly a difficult one to reach, should be to surrender our idea of how things ought to be and trust Jesus. When we do this, we will find the loving biblical God. To fight or deny him because things aren't the way you think they ought to be raises stupidity to a new level.

We will consider these issues in this Part IV.

EVIL AND SUFFERING

In chapter 26 we address the problem of evil, etc. by recognizing that our concept of time is not God's. As the *Catechism of the Catholic Church*[1] points

---

1. Retrievable online at many sites, including http://www.scborromeo.org/ccc.htm.

out, God's creation is unfolding to perfection and he has asked us to help, just as he asked Mary to bear his Son. When we don't, we impede his will with the disastrous consequences of the evil and suffering we see about us.

UNANSWERED PRAYERS

The issue of unanswered prayers is addressed in chapter 27 by recognizing that God's objective is our eternal salvation. Suffering and our unanswered prayers should be accepted as God's way (not ours) to help us find God and remain in his presence.[2] We need to trust God, just as Alexandrina da Costa of Balasar did (chapter 28). Her prayers to be relieved of her intense physical suffering were never answered. While the miracle of physical healing never occurred, a far greater miracle took place—thirteen years of being nourished only by the Eucharist—no sustenance of any kind from 1942 to 1955. Her faith conquered her suffering and she was clearly brought to the gates of heaven.

THE SAVIOR'S INCREDIBLE LOVE

The details of Christ's agony during his passion are given in chapter 29 and correlated with the Shroud of Turin so that the reader can see that Christ understands our suffering. This is the suffering of love. When Jesus suffered and died on the cross, he declared with acts that can never be diluted his incredible love for man. He had said that no greater love can there be than to give one's life for another. And that's what he did.

WHY DID JESUS HAVE TO SUFFER AND DIE? (CHAPTER 30)

When Jesus suffered and died the way he did, he eliminated all doubts about his divinity. There can be no certainty about his resurrection if there is uncertainty about his death—and the cross removes all uncertainty. A sacrifice is intended to bring us closer to God, and that's what Jesus' sacrifice did. He suffered and died not because God needed a sacrifice, but because we did.

---

2. See, for example Wis 3:4–6: "For though in the sight of men they were punished, their hope is full of immortality. Having been disciplined a little, they will receive great good, because God tested them and found them worthy of himself; like gold in the furnace he tried them, and like a sacrificial burnt offering he accepted them."

HELL: A LOVING GOD AND ETERNAL PUNISHMENT?

The concept of a loving God permitting the very people he had created to spend an eternity in agony and punishment flies in the face of logic. We address this dilemma in chapter 31 by first noting, with one key exception, that there is no single Christian doctrine regarding the concept of hell and who gets to go there. But whatever hell is, a universal Christian teaching is that a place or state of eternal punishment awaits those who, with full knowledge, deliberately and with malice reject Jesus. What about just regular atheists and agnostics? Opinions vary. Perhaps their ultimate destination will be precisely what they had expected and, in some cases, even hoped for—eternal death. What about others who never gave any thought to the eternal or who never had the opportunity to know Jesus? We can't judge but must rely upon the mercy of Jesus. He understands us, our problems, and issues. His life, teachings, death, and resurrection tell us that he will judge each of us with love and understanding.

26

Evil and Suffering

A LOVING GOD?

How does Christianity deal with the question of suffering and evil? We look about us and see children starving in Africa, a killer tsunami in Japan, a lion maliciously attacking and killing a leopard, hopeless alcoholics and drug addicts wasting their lives away on skid row. We see one human beheading another in the name of Islam, and we see a child suffering the ravages of war clutching her dead mother. Disease and pestilence ravage. It is easy to conclude that the continuing presence of evil and suffering belie the existence of the Christian God, or any other.

GOD'S PLAN

Unbelievers hold to the unstated position that God's rational process must reflect ours. The underlying premise (and quite often subconscious) is that if cosmic and earthly events don't unfold the way we think they should, well, then, quite likely there is no God and certainly the God of the Bible is a fiction. Yet Scripture clearly anticipates this mindset and teaches that God wants us to trust him and not ourselves.

In the beginning God could have created a world that was good and devoid of evil, or a world which allowed evil to roam freely. He chose to create a world that was good and without evil or suffering. He also could have created man to walk lockstep with God and without any free will. Instead, he created us with the ability to make choices, and gave us the dignity of acting on our own.

Whether we believe that Adam was an actual person with a sign hanging around his neck saying, "My name is Adam," or a metaphorical allusion to mankind, Christianity teaches that man elected to use his free will to ignore God and pursue his own objectives. Evil was introduced; don't blame God. He made us above the animals and gave us domain over the earth, and we elected to pursue lives in complete or partial absence of God. That's called evil and, consequently, suffering and pain were introduced.

Consider the possibility that God did in fact create a perfect world, but that the creative process didn't occur in an instant, as we record time, but over thousands, millions, and even billions of years. From our perspective there is no perfection but only turmoil and imperfection. For God, however, who is the creator of time, all is but an instant. He can see yesterday, today, and tomorrow without the interference of a timeline of A preceding B, which precedes C, etc. In other words, from our point of view we are on a journey to perfection.

The *Catechism of the Catholic Church* succinctly tells us (footnotes deleted):

> 310 But why did God not create a world so perfect that no evil could exist in it? With infinite power God could always create something better. But with infinite wisdom and goodness God freely willed to create a world "in a state of journeying" towards its ultimate perfection. In God's plan this process of becoming involves the appearance of certain beings and the disappearance of others, the existence of the more perfect alongside the less perfect, both constructive and destructive forces of nature. With physical good there exists also *physical evil* as long as creation has not reached perfection.
>
> 311 Angels and men, as intelligent and free creatures, have to journey toward their ultimate destinies by their free choice and preferential love. They can therefore go astray. Indeed, they have sinned. Thus has *moral evil*, incommensurably more harmful than physical evil, entered the world. God is in no way, directly or indirectly, the cause of moral evil. He permits it, however,

because he respects the freedom of his creatures and, mysteriously, knows how to derive good from it . . . .

EVIL AS A PREREQUISITE TO GOOD

"In time we can discover that God in his almighty providence can bring a good from the consequences of an evil, even a moral evil, caused by his creatures. . . ."[1] The scourging, crowning, mocking, abuse, and crucifixion of Jesus is the greatest moral evil ever committed. Yet the Passion is the perfect example of events that initially appeared to thwart our journey to perfection but were prerequisites for the resurrection and glorification of Christ and our redemption.

As creation unfolds, God gave us the power to cooperate with him, ignore him, or even oppose him. God created a world which from our point of view is not yet perfect, but is journeying to God's goal of perfection. "Only at the end, when our partial knowledge ceases, when we see God 'face to face', will we fully know the ways by which—even through the dramas of evil and sin—God has guided his creation to that definitive sabbath rest for which he created heaven and earth."[2]

EVIL AND OUR SELF-INFLICTED SUFFERING

God created a perfect world, pronounced it good, and gave man the opportunity to live free from strife and in constant companionship with him. Instead, we elected not only to disobey, but also to outwit and second-guess him. God gave us a simple commandment in the Garden of Eden, but we disobeyed. Our attack upon God didn't stop there. Our arrogance has led us to believe that there are no absolutes and that we are endowed with the exclusive ability to determine what is right and wrong. Arrogance leads us to conclude that scripture is archaic and of no further use other than as a source of amusement and incredulity as to the naiveté of believers.

Unfortunately for us, when we block God's teachings and substitute ours—just as Adam did—we really revert to the most ancient of all mistakes. We introduce our own teachings and standards of belief and conduct with the inevitable consequence of ever more egregious error and misery. Think of all the diseases and horror that could be eliminated if we adhered to the teaching of Jesus that sex is within marriage only and his teaching

---

1. *Catechism*, par 312.
2. *Catechism*, par 314.

about divorce. The wedding at Cana tells us that marriage between a man and a woman was so sacred that it was blessed by the presence and participation of Jesus (he turned the water into wine). Within the Church, matrimony became a sacrament filling the man and woman with God's graces. Now we have attempted to undo God's love by not only ignoring his teachings, but actively rejecting and countermanding them. Ergo, the sky-high divorce rate, the number of men and woman ignoring the sanctity of marriage and the increasingly successful drive to legitimize homosexual acts and marriage.

Because we have rejected God and his absolutes and bring in our own relative assessments of what's right and wrong, only God could set us straight, and then only through Christ's suffering. We may find this concept of vicarious suffering difficult to understand and somehow think that it can't possibly be right—but then, there we go again—substituting our own judgments for those of God.

Consider the sufferings we endure. Nearly all could be prevented or significantly mitigated if we but cared enough for each other. If we followed the example set by Jesus and his teachings, man's inhumanity to man and to animals would be eliminated. Murder, theft, religious persecution, malice, envy, aggrandizement, and a host of other man-made or induced sufferings would not exist. We would be miles further along in our journey to perfection.

NATURAL DISASTERS AND UNAVOIDABLE MISERY

Still, while we may be able to accept that man's inhumanity to man is the consequence of our turning away from God, it remains difficult to accept earthquakes, fires, tsunamis, unanticipated accidents and misfortunes whereby even the most innocent and faithful are killed or suffer, as anything but events meted out or at least tolerated by a mean god. And since the God of Christian theology is supposed to be loving and caring for us, these sufferings belie his existence.

Two points are to be made here.

First, these tragedies warn us about how fragile and short life is. When we least expect it, we may be taken. Pay attention! Life is short, eternity forever and none of us knows when we will make this inevitable transition. Natural disasters and unexpected suffering, whether through disease or accident, tell us we should never delay our examination of Christ's life, teachings, suffering, death, and resurrection. When we delay, we effectively reject him.

Second, even the suffering caused by natural disasters could be significantly reduced if we cared enough to develop early warning systems for tsunamis, hurricanes, etc. and build organizations and infrastructure to provide safety and relief for all peoples, whether living in North America, Africa, Asia or anywhere else. That, however, would require us to love one another as ourselves. Apparently, we're not ready to do that.

Through science and a sustained effort, we could eliminate nearly all disease and hunger. But that would require a giving and sacrifice that would interfere with our individual taking. Our continuing rejection of God assures us that while progress may be made, such progress will always fall short. We have the collective ability, but unfortunately not the desire, to obey God and be stewards of each other and nature.

Don't blame God for our unwillingness to be his instruments and help move his creation along towards perfection. Don't deny God because you don't like the way he set things up.

DRAWING CLOSER TO GOD

Finally, as you contemplate the problem of suffering and unanswered prayers, consider the possibility that individual suffering may in fact illuminate the path to eternal life with God.

How often do you think about God when things are going swimmingly well? We know the answer. The irony is that while pain, sense of loss, remorse, uncertainty, humiliation, fear all reduce us to the horror of suffering, it is when we suffer that we turn to God most often and with the greatest intensity. It is then that we try to draw closer to Jesus. It is then that we intensely seek his presence and help. Perhaps that is why Jesus told us how difficult it is for a rich man to enter his kingdom. A self-satisfied, self-congratulatory arrogance quite often accompanies riches. Suffering, on the other hand, is an opportunity to grow in faith and in our love for God. So, and as difficult as it may be to accept, perhaps unanswered prayers aren't so bad after all. Perhaps God uses suffering to give us the opportunity for humility and to understand that we are completely dependent upon him. And it is only through humility that we can draw near to him.

27

Suffering and Unanswered Prayers

When we need help in our lives—what can we do?

We can pray for God's help.

That sounds a bit ambitious. Yet, God does answer prayers. Miracles (particularly miraculous healings) bring home the point that every now and then God unmistakably reveals himself. Nevertheless, we know that when we pray for miraculous healings 99.9897 percent of the time the requested miracle or healing didn't occur. We may have petitioned Jesus for help in reliance upon his promise that whatever we ask for will be granted. But nothing happened, or if it did, we just didn't recognize his intervention. It was an unanswered prayer. The insidious cancer striking down our loved one continues to progress. I didn't get that promotion; instead, it went to that guy who we all know is a first-class phony with not nearly the knowledge of the company's operations. The girl of my dreams left me for that creep in Texas.

The list of unanswered prayers is endless. The upshot is that when prayers are answered the intervening hand of Jesus is quite often ignored, soon forgotten, or explained away as a non-miracle since the prayed for result would have happened anyway.

THE END OF THE WORLD

Before we go any further about unanswered prayers we should listen to C.S. Lewis. He reminds us of something that *always* slips our mind. The world as we know it would cease to exist if our prayers were always or mostly answered. Here is what he tells us:

> I wonder whether people who ask God to interfere openly and directly in our world quite realise what it will be like when he does. When that happens, it is the end of the world. . . .[B]ut what is the good of saying you are on His side then, when you see the whole natural universe melting away like a dream and something else—something it never entered your head to conceive—comes crashing in; something so beautiful to some of us and so terrible to others that none of us will have any choice left? For this time it will be God without disguise; something so overwhelming that it will strike either irresistible love or irresistible horror into every creature. It will be too late then to choose your side. . . . Now, today, this moment is our chance to choose the right side. God is holding back to give us that chance. It will not last for ever. We must take it or leave it.[1]

If you have chosen the side that will be overwhelmed with agonizing and eternal distress once God reveals himself, you may want to reconsider.

GOD TELLS US HE UNDERSTANDS

Here is something else we often overlook. When Jesus took upon himself the human condition he became subject to the same emotions and feelings we have. He became angry; he felt sorrow; he endured agonizing pain and suffering. His life tells us that he understands. He knows our individual pain, agony, suffering, and distress.

That brings us to the events of that first Good Friday weekend and his brutal execution and the excruciating anguish and pain he suffered, to be discussed in chapter 29. Consequently, when you suffer or see others suffer, and prayers appear to be unanswered, don't conclude that we've been abandoned or that God is just a myth. Whatever your circumstance, and through the life and death of Jesus, God knows about your situation and understands. His creation and plan of salvation tell us we cannot emerge from the back door of this life without suffering or without causing others to suffer (perhaps just the mere fact that we die and leave grieving loved ones).

---

1. Lewis, *Mere Christianity*, 65.

Perhaps your unanswered prayer is his way of telling you to look more deeply into your heart for the Eternal Jesus and his love. On that first Holy Weekend, Jesus teaches by example. In the Garden he accepted God's will and knew how excruciating his physical and moral pain would be. As he pressed on towards Calvary, he knew the depth of his mother's anguish as she saw her beloved son in such torment, but he didn't relieve her of this burden. Mary must have suffered with a despair we cannot imagine as she saw the Romans drive the nails through his hands and feet. Jesus didn't relieve her of this anguish. The darkest hour is, however, just before dawn and he triumphed on that first Easter Sunday, as did his mother, apostles, disciples, and everyone else (including you) who acknowledges what he did and why. It is not so difficult. Jesus is not forcing us to believe and accept him. He has given us free will and is asking us to follow him by praying and submitting to God's will even if this requires pain and suffering culminating on our cross at calvary. What Jesus desires is your ultimate triumph for all eternity, just as he triumphed on that first Easter Sunday. Perhaps your prayers are being answered, but you just don't know it —at least for right now.

TRUSTING GOD

As followers of Christ, we must trust God, just as Jesus did from the time he was first conceived in the womb of Mary until the close of his earthly life. Despite all this we know from personal experience that our faith can be severely tested. We may struggle and have issues of pain and sickness and we pray and pray for relief, but nothing seems to happen. We must never forget that Jesus is seeking our eternal soul. For some reason, relief is not deemed conducive to Jesus' objective—and what should be ours. Farther along we'll understand, but not right now. We must simply trust that whatever God permits to happen to us or our loved ones, or others, is permitted for our eternal salvation.

For example, God allowed his son to suffer and die on the cross. We call this day of agony and torture Good Friday because the cross tells us victory over death is available to all. Perhaps God permits us to suffer so that we can draw closer to the cross of Jesus and achieve our victory over death. Despite our sufferings we can never say that God doesn't know what our suffering is like because, as we shall see in chapter 29, he does. Jesus never promised us freedom from suffering. What he promised was our resurrection and life eternal with him.

Let's see if a dog can shed more light on the apparent dilemma confronting us when we try to square God's unconditional love with our suffering.

A dog lives in the present. What happened a week ago has no meaning except as to how the experience prepares him for a future response to a similar situation. The world as it will exist in five months or five weeks, or even five minutes is of no consequence or concern. What exists is what is happening now. He does not get the big picture.

The pain he feels as the veterinarian performs a procedure to restore his well-being is very real, but temporary. He doesn't know what's next on the agenda, but as long as you are beside him he knows it's going to be ok. Your dog trusts you even though he cannot possibly understand. And you love him more because of his trust. Your mission is to take care of him.

Our relationship with Jesus and our lives bear a deep similarity. We need to recognize that our perspective of reality is but an infinitesimal segment of eternity. Compare our suffering of ten minutes, ten years, or a lifetime with Jesus' promised eternity of happiness in a place of love beyond our earthly ability to comprehend. The essence of Christianity is trusting God.

Imagine a pane of opaque glass one mile high and one mile wide. Now imagine a clear spot the size of a pin prick in the lower left-hand corner. That's what we know of God. He is the creator of all that is seen and unseen, of all that is visible and invisible, of the tiniest microbe as well as the complex complementary living cells within it, and of the most ferocious and magnificent galaxies billions of light years distant. And you think you should understand why we suffer and that no loving God could ever permit evil as we interpret it to roam our world! And you think you can see the relationship of all that has gone before, goes on today, and all future events and creation! And you think you could put all of time and eternity and all creation together in way superior to what God has done! And you think God needs to prove himself by directly answering all your prayers!

Give it a rest!

God made us so that we could choose to spend eternity with him. To reach the finish line we have to trust him. We have a choice. When we suffer we can trust him and accept that his will is for our benefit, or we can curse or ignore him. When we do the latter, we in effect are saying that we and not he should be the captain of our ship.

Perhaps we need to regroup and understand that the deepest level of our prayers should be to thank God for his creation, our lives, and the gift of Jesus and the acceptance by Mary to become the mother of our Saving Grace. Only when we recognize and acknowledge God's love should we present our petitions, and then always with the caveat that his will be done. Having done this, our job then becomes to trust Jesus. Above all, our prayer should always be, first and foremost, for the Holy Spirit. This prayer will always be answered because the will of God is for us to live in his presence and for his presence to be within us. Jesus' kingdom is not of this world, and he makes himself available with a richness beyond comprehension if we merely ask for it and open our heart. He is waiting to enter.

ALEXANDRINA DA COSTA OF BALASAR

Because we can only see a slice of eternity we can't know what has gone before or what is yet to come. Our myopic vision is compounded by the fact that God is and must, of necessity, be incomprehensible. Nevertheless, he has spoken to us in deed and language which proves he understands and loves us with a powerful enduring love. When we recognize and accept his demonstrated love, then we can begin to understand why we have unanswered prayers. Through it all we need to remain faithful, just as Alexandrina da Costa of Balasar did.

28

Alexandrina da Costa of Balasar

Sometimes miracles reveal themselves in the most unexpected ways. If the petitioner asks for a cure when medical science says none is possible, and is then healed, that's a beautiful and glorious miracle that all can see. Sometimes, however, the miracle arrives quite unexpectedly and in contravention of our request. Blessed Alexandrina da Costa of Balasar in Portugal (1904–1955) gives us a perfect example.

When Alexandrina was fourteen she was sexually assaulted. Rather than submit she leaped out a window and fell thirteen feet to the ground. She suffered severe injuries and the doctors diagnosed her condition as irreversible and they correctly stated that the paralysis she suffered would only get worse. As the years progressed her paralysis and pain steadily intensified and finally in 1924 at the age of nineteen and until her death thirty one years later, she would remain bedridden, suffering agonizing pain, and completely paralyzed.

Alexandrina was intensely spiritual and prayed for a miracle. She and the villagers and her family and friends prayed and prayed that her pain be relieved and that she be cured and her paralysis lifted. The prayers were never answered. Instead, her condition became more desperate over the years and she was always in constant and severe pain. There was never any relief. Finally, she concluded that her vocation in life was to suffer. By so doing she would join her pain with that of the Savior for the salvation of souls. In other words, she would "offer it up." This means that when we suffer we join our suffering with that of Jesus. Since we are all part of the Body of Christ, we offer our pain and sacrifice to the Lord to help in the salvation of others. Her physical pain and suffering was intense and never ceased. Through it all her faith continued intact and strengthened as the years progressed. Her prayer life was ceaseless, and she was devoted to the Eucharist.

Finally, in 1942 Jesus told her in an ecstasy, "You will not take food again on earth. Your food will be My Flesh; your blood will be My Divine Blood, your life will be My Life. You receive it from me when I unite My Heart to your heart. Do not fear, my daughter...."[1] Consequently, beginning on Good Friday, March 27, 1942, and until her death in 1955 Alexandrina received no nourishment of any kind except the Holy Eucharist.

In June 1942, she was admitted to a hospital to be studied under strict observational controls to determine the veracity of her claims. For forty days while in the hospital she was certified by attending physicians to have not eaten or drunk any liquids. Her only food was the daily Eucharist—the body and blood of Christ.

Her pain and suffering continued unabated for the remainder of her life, but she was always secure in her faith and a joy and inspiration to others. The miracle of physical healing never occurred, but a far greater miracle took place—a lifetime of being nourished only by the Eucharist. Just as Jesus' love and presence was demonstrated by the Miracle of the Sun at Fatima and the physical cures in Lourdes, so there could be no doubt that he continues to be with us, not just spiritually but physically in the Eucharist.

God doesn't hide, and he answers prayers in ways we may not understand at the time. Alexandrina could easily have told you this.

SUFFERING AS A TEST

Is our suffering nothing more than a test from God? Someday we'll know, but in the meantime, we can follow the example set by Jesus the Christ: Never waver and try always to remain in the presence of God through prayer. Our job is to try and ascertain and follow the will of God. We must do our best to follow his commandments, whatever the cost, just as Jesus did. Love does conquer all.

---

1. Mystics of the Church website, "Blessed Alexandrina."

JESUS' INCREDIBLE AND DEMONSTRATED LOVE

To gather a glimpse of his incredible love and how he has spoken to us, we need to return to that Holy Friday in Jerusalem some two thousand years ago, and we shall do so in the next chapter.

29

The Savior's Incredible Love

KNOWING THAT GOD KNOWS

The Shroud of Turin, Lourdes, Fatima, and other manifestations of God provide us with overpowering evidence that we have an eternal loving God. Nevertheless, and notwithstanding our philosophical musings and the most airtight logic, common sense tells us that this can't be possible because evil and suffering could not co-exist with an eternal loving God. Consequently, based upon our own personal pain and suffering, as well as the suffering we see in others, we can be led to the conclusion that the God of Christian theology must be the product of wishful thinking. Alternatively, we speculate that if there is a God, he can only be the aloof deist watchmaker with no interest in our lives. This would be the same as no God.

If only we knew that God understands the horror of fear, pain, suffering, and despair, then perhaps we could make sense of this apparent dilemma. As briefly alluded to in the preceding chapter, he does, and the intense suffering of Jesus during the Passion confirms this with profound certainty. But I think we need to understand the depth of his physical suffering.

JESUS CHRIST AND THE PASSION

The Bible offers an understated description of what happened during the Passion. It merely says that Jesus was scourged, mocked, beaten, crowned with thorns, taunted, and crucified. Finally, a spear was run into his side to confirm he was in fact dead. While all of this sounds horrible beyond description (and it is) the reality of the evil and pain which befell Jesus is infinitely greater.

The mother of Jesus is often forgotten when we consider his suffering. Yet, her suffering and anguish must have been at least equal to that experienced by Jesus, and you can be sure Jesus knew her suffering. We can better understand Mary's agony and live the Passion of Christ more deeply if we make one adjustment to those scenes of pure brutality. Do you have a six-year-old son or grandson? Perhaps an eight-year-old or ten-year-old son or daughter, grandchild, brother, or sister? Every now and then when you visualize Jesus being whipped, spat upon, beaten, or suffering through any of the events on that first Good Friday, try substituting your loved little boy or girl in the place of Jesus. It is impossible because seeing your loved little innocent one terrorized and in agony being whipped or nailed to a cross takes the definitions of "gut-wrenching" and "distress" to unacceptable levels. The mind automatically rejects such an attempt to relive the Passion because the recollection is just too painful and agonizing to consider. Mary saw and lived those events of her cherished child being tortured and executed. Jesus knew her despair and anguish. His suffering wasn't limited to his physical and spiritual pain. As a loving son the torture experienced by his mother became his suffering.

To understand our Savior's love, it is important that we witness the brutality of Jesus' sufferings. What follows is a brief description of that nightmare.

THE SCOURGING

Jesus would have been repeatedly lashed (probably thirty nine times, and possibly even more) by whips tipped with iron balls or sheep bones which would have cut into his skin and rip into the underlying muscles. The Roman scourging of Jesus was a bloody and painful endeavor, which we should never forget. The Alpha and Omega suffered intensely. In our artistic depictions, we can put a loin cloth on Jesus to make him more presentable, but he was in fact stripped naked. We can show a bloodless passion and crucifixion. By doing so, however, we dishonor the immensity and horror of his sacrifice.

THE CROWN OF THORNS

Think about how the soldiers maliciously and gleefully put a wreath of long sharp thorns in the form of a hemispheric crown on Jesus' head. Visualize and feel the pain and anguish suffered by Jesus as the soldiers pressed the thorns into his head and repeatedly strike him. Jesus' physical pain would have exponentially intensified as the minutes and hours dragged on.

MOCKING AND DEGRADATION

Degradation and insult were heaped upon Jesus. They tore off his garments and arrayed him in a purple robe. They mocked him, beat him, and spat upon him. They placed a reed in his hand as a scepter and continued their mocking and ridicule. Jesus' excruciating pain must have become even more hideous as the taunting and beatings continued unabated. They even whipped him with the reed they had placed in his hand. They beat this imposter creator and king of the universe with his own scepter!

BEHOLD THE MAN

The torment and pain Jesus suffered before he began his agonizing climb to Calvary continued. He was brought before the crowds clothed in a purple robe, adorned with a crown of thorns, spittle on his face, blood oozing from his uncountable stripes and wounds, wrapped in intense pain and Pilate said, "Behold the man!" as if to say, "Look at this miserable thing! Doesn't this satisfy you?" The crowd responded by demanding crucifixion, and Jesus is led away to the cross.[1] The mother of our Lord watches; his apostles watch; and his friends watch. They are all helpless. Jesus is the Son of God and he knowingly accepted this torment and the imminent excruciating pain, with patience, forgiveness, and love.

---

1. *Scarlet Purple Robe* by Ralph Stanley https://www.youtube.com/watch?v=zNgxuzFFAUI (YouTube search words: scarlet robe Stanley).

ABANDONED

Except for his mother, John, and a few others all his relatives and followers deserted him, a fact Jesus would have known as evidenced by his prophecy that Peter would deny him three times.

THE WAY OF THE CROSS

The Gospels provide almost no detail regarding Jesus carrying the cross to Golgotha.[2] Matthew, Mark, and Luke tell us that Simon of Cyrene was pressed into helping Jesus carry his cross. Mark goes one step further and tells us that Simon was the father of Alexander and Rufus. John makes no mention of Simon. That's it!

While the Gospels provide little detail, the Shroud of Turin tells us much more. The image shows the agonizing pain Jesus would have suffered as he began his journey to Golgotha dragging the cross from which he would hang. Recent research shows that the physical damage to the man on the Shroud confirms the following account of the Way of the Cross:

1. Jesus, weakened from the trauma and blood loss from the scourging, would have collapsed under the weight of the cross (approximately 140 lbs.). He fell forward and was severely injured when he hit the ground.

2. The cross would have crushed down upon his back between the neck and right shoulder as he fell, thereby dislocating his shoulder and paralyzing his right arm. This further caused the displacement of the head from the left side. The nerve tree running from his shoulder would have been violently stretched causing intensely severe and continuing pain.

3. The fall explains why "the right shoulder is lower than the left by 10±5 degrees" and why the right eye is retracted or displaced in the eye socket.

4. The pain would now have been extreme and Jesus would have completely lost the function of his right arm.

5. The Roman soldiers now tried to have him carry the cross supported by his left shoulder, but he would have been unable to do so. His

---

2. Matt.27:31–32; Mark 15:20–22; Luke 23:26–32; and John 19:17.

physical inability to carry the cross explains the biblical account of Simon being pressed into service.³

We can easily visualize Jesus agonizingly struggling on the road to Calvary. Surely Mary must have waited for him as he approached. As the by-standers gathered around her, she would have listened in horror to the hate and calumny uttered against her son. The Romans probably led the procession, carrying nails, hammers, ropes, and other requisite instruments to torture and kill Jesus. They would have passed by Mary, followed by Jesus, unrecognizable and covered with blood and wounds from head to foot, a crown of thorns piercing his head.

How can we measure the anguish Jesus must have felt when he saw his mother looking upon his bloodied, disfigured, and dying form? Can there be any more suffering than what Jesus endured as he made his way up the hill? Yes, and it's called . . . .

CALVARY

When he arrived at Calvary, nails were driven through his hands and feet to secure him to the cross. There he hung for six hours gasping for breath and in unspeakable pain. Finally, he died. Once again, the Shroud provides us with more detail.

1. The nails were pounded through the wrists (or at least exited through the wrists), and not the palm of the hands as traditionally represented.
2. The disappearance of the thumbs in the Shroud is linked to the trauma caused by the nailing.
3. It appears that Jesus suffered a right ankle dislocation during nailing.
4. One nail was driven through one foot and the other ankle to attach them to the cross. The researchers concluded that there probably was first a 5" nail driven through one of the feet to act as a pilot hole, followed by a 10" nail pounded through the heel. Interestingly, the Roman Catholic Church believes there was one nail used to affix both

---

3. The academicians Matteo Bevilacqua, Giulio Fanti and Michele D'Arienzo conducted a detailed study of the man on the Shroud and the trauma he suffered. Their paper, "New Light on the Sufferings and the Burial of the Turin Shroud Man," appears in the May 19, 2017 issue of *Peertechz*, a peer-reviewed platform of scientific articles providing a global platform for open journals to promote qualitative research publications for Science, Engineering, Technology and Medicine.

feet, while the Orthodox believes there were two. It looks like they both are correct.

The pain and trauma suffered by Jesus as he hung on the cross are beyond our comprehension. Because of the (a) scourging, (b) his carrying the cross and the injuries he sustained as he struggled towards Calvary, (c) the crown of thorns pressed upon his head, (d) his dislocated ankle, and (e) the nails embedded in and through his wrists and feet, every slight movement of Jesus on the cross produced intense pain and trauma. To breath it may have been necessary for him to push his body down upon his ankles and feet fastened to the cross so as to lift his body up to allow passage of air in and out of his lungs.

This is the suffering of love. When Jesus suffered and died on the cross, he declared with acts that can never be diluted his incredible love for man. He had said that no greater love can there be than to give one's life for another. And that's what he did.

Jesus understands your pain and suffering.

30

Why did Jesus have to Suffer and Die?

Some years a radio commentator confidently stated that she had made a thorough examination of Christianity and could report with absolute certainty that Christianity was a hoax. She couldn't worship any god that demanded a bloody sacrifice in the form of Jesus' crucifixion. It was simply too barbaric and made no sense. Christianity was obviously a fiction and merely an extension of earlier pagan religions.

SOME ALTERNATIVES

Why did Jesus suffer and die the way he did. After all, God is God and can do whatever he wishes. Surely God could have redeemed us without ravaging his only begotten Son. And, since God is omnipotent, he was not under any compulsion. Not only that, but since Jesus is God he didn't have to consent at Gethsemane. He could have terminated the proceedings then and there and declared a universal or selective salvation. Or, since all things are possible with God, he could have undergone the Passion painlessly. There are plenty of approaches that God could have taken. Another would be for each of us to be individually punished or suffer a horrible death so that we could expiate and redress our own sins. But that would still involve immense pain and individual horror. On the other hand, God could have merely chosen to appear in the sky every month or so and say, "You're all forgiven for whatever you've done and for the times you turned your back on me. I'll appear again next month and forgive you again—or better yet I'll just rearrange things to let you do whatever you want. Whatever you do is ok as long as you think it's ok."

Let's see if we make sense of this dilemma.

THE CERTAINTY OF JESUS' DEATH

Calvary didn't occur because God demanded a bloody sacrifice. Calvary occurred because we demanded it. How else could we believe in the eternal mercy and love of our Lord? Without it Jesus would have been just another philosopher and do-gooder whose mission would have dissipated with the passage of time. But Jesus was not just another teacher or prophet. To prove his Divinity for people throughout the ages the fact of his death would have to be unassailable. Quite simply there could be no certainty of resurrection unless there was first a certainty of death. And the events of that Good Friday would prove with absolute certainty that Jesus did indeed die. Whipping, scourging, beating, thorns pushed into his head, spikes driven into his hands and feet, hanging on a cross for hour upon hour, capped by a spear thrust into his side could only mean certain death.

God in his wisdom knows the frailties of men. We can never understand God and why he selected a certain course of action, but we can see the results. For example, the brutality of the crucifixion and its aftermath drives home the point that physical death does not snuff out life. If Jesus had merely appeared on the scene and taught for a few years—or a lifetime—and then mysteriously disappeared into the sky, we would now be talking about the charming story of this fanciful guy that supposedly lived so long ago, affirmed most of the Jewish law, made some other lovely but unprovable promises such as how God loved us and the gift of eternal life, etc. But all of that would have been universally rejected as cult fodder.

Instead, Jesus affirmed his Godhood and love by teaching, suffering, dying, and coming to life again, all in plain view of the Jews. This was no mere philosopher who would be remembered only because of what he said, but a historical figure who would be remembered for what he did and what he promised all humanity. There could be no doubt but that he died, was resurrected, and told his disciples to tell the world about him, even unto death. Then and only then was Jesus lifted from the bottomless agony of his passion to the glory of his ascension. The Creator loved us so much and even with all our blemishes and weaknesses that he performed an act of atonement that would live and be remembered through the ages.

THE SACRIFICE OF LOVE

Consider the possibility that we are looking at the concept of "sacrifice" incorrectly. This misunderstanding can lead us to misinterpret the meaning of Jesus' death—of his sacrifice. We are all accustomed to using the word "sacrifice" to mean giving up something that we want or performing an act which we would prefer to avoid, and generally accompanied by discomfort or even outright pain. That is not the intended meaning. In the Old Testament God said he desired the sacrifice of prayer and love, and not the death and blood of animals. That's because sacrifice really means any act that brings us closer to God. Prayer and love should more effectively accomplish this objective than blood or pain. As the Old Testament tells us, however, it appeared that we were not ready for the sacrifice of love and prayer but had to resort to animal sacrifice to underscore the brutality of sin and draw closer to God.

At Calvary we have the ultimate Sacrifice, which combines love, death, pain, joy, in the person of Jesus in crippling agony stumbling to the cross, there to have his hands and feet pierced by big blunt nails. This is the meaning of sacrifice. This is pure love. If the Passion doesn't draw you closer to God, then nothing will. It was said of Brother Lawrence, "While meditating on . . . the passion of Jesus Christ (about which he never thought without being inwardly moved) he was changed into another man. The humility of the Cross seemed more beautiful to him than all the glory of the world."[1]

What higher purpose could there be for us than to search for God, and to realize that he gave his only begotten son so that whosoever believes in him will not perish but have everlasting life. God loves us with a love so infinite it cannot be measured or even described. The closest we can come is to recall what he did for us, and the intensity of his passion and death enables us to do precisely that. This was the ultimate sacrifice; it was an act intended to bring us ever closer to God's redeeming love.

REMEMBERING JESUS

What could God have done for us that he has not done? When we knowingly ignore the cross, we ignore the crucial element of why Jesus walked the earth and we make God a liar and a useless dilettante. God does not pursue actions which are meaningless. His demonstrated love is available to all who desire it.

The radio commentator I referred to at the beginning of this chapter was wrong—dead wrong. We (that includes you) sent Jesus to the cross. The Catholic mystic, St. Faustina, said that one day she "saw Jesus at her side

---

1. Helms, *Brother Lawrence*, 26.

racked with pain, stripped of his clothing, all covered with wounds, who spoke these words to me: 'How long shall I put up with you and how long will you keep putting me off?'"[2] The steep price Jesus paid to reconcile us with God demonstrates with unparalleled certainty how evil disobedience to God is and how much he loves us. If we don't cringe whenever we visualize or even think about those two days beginning in the Garden of Gethsemane and culminating on the cross, it is because we do not understand the magnificent love that took place to set us free. We do not understand the pain and torment which the Lord suffered for us. We do not understand this sacrifice of love. We keep putting him off.

GOD'S LOVE

This is God's love. Once we fully consider what Jesus has done, and relate it to the empirical evidence God has given us of his existence and love, how is it possible to reject Jesus?

Jesus was fully human, fully the Messiah, and fully God. His life, teaching, suffering, death, resurrection, and ascension prove the point. Because Jesus suffered and died in such a dramatic and gruesome fashion his death can be affirmed even now—two thousand years following the event. Jesus was born to die, and the manner of his death should erase any doubt that this in fact occurred. When someone understands the brutality of the Passion and still argues that Jesus really didn't die, but merely "swooned," you may be sure that an agenda other than uncovering the truth is in play.

GOD'S PLAN OF SALVATION

The sacrifice on the cross gives us a clear opportunity to accept God's invitation to live in his presence. Was there no other way for God to reconcile us to him other than the Cross? The answer is that the question is irrelevant. The Cross is God's plan and that is all that matters. By it he demonstrated a love which is quite beyond our comprehension. To accept, reject, or ignore is our choice. If you decided to ignore or reject you may wish to reconsider after you have read the next chapter.

---

2. Tassone, *Jesus Speaks*, 210.

31

A Loving God and Eternal Punishment

THE PROBLEM

Christianity teaches that our final destination will be either heaven or hell. These are places or states far beyond our human capacity to understand, and anything we say about them is mostly speculative. Nevertheless, the prevalent perception of hell is that it is a place where the damned will burn and be in physical and spiritual torment for all eternity.

And that is the problem. How could a loving God consign most, many, some, or merely a few of us to a place or state of eternal torment? If Jesus is love and came to save the world and not condemn it, how can this be? Even assuming a justification for the existence of hell and eternal punishment, why should a single act or an honest belief that Christianity is false, land a person in hell for all eternity? How does one balance the equities—seventy years of disbelief or wrongdoing versus one hundred million years and more of intense suffering. That equation makes no sense.

NO SINGLE CONCEPT OF HELL

To address this issue, we need to correct a pervasive misconception. The popular characterization of hell as a fire that burns and torments the damned for all eternity is not a universal Christian belief. While all Christians accept the concept of hell (Jesus was quite clear on this subject), the description of what hell means varies across the Christian sub-faiths. This tells us that no one knows for sure. Here are some theological opinions—and that's all they are—opinions:

1. The damned will burn and be in physical and spiritual torment for all eternity.
2. After a period of suffering, the damned will suffer eternal separation from God by being extinguished. They will suffer eternal death.
3. God is present in both hell and heaven. In heaven he is experienced as pure love and paradise; in hell the lost soul cannot withstand the fire of God's presence and love, and experiences eternal and unspeakable anguish.

There are other variations as well, but the common element is that while we may not understand the details of eternity, we do know that Christianity teaches that hell will be a place or state of eternal punishment, and that this punishment will, at a minimum, be eternal separation from God or an inability to experience the love of God.

REJECTING GOD BECAUSE OF HELL

Carefully consider the wisdom of rejecting Christ because you don't like the concept of hell. To shut down belief because you think God would never establish a plan of eternal punishment for those who reject him or a plan contrary to what you think that plan should be is vacuous, silly and a poor excuse (and that's all it is; it's not a reason) to ignore Fatima, Lourdes, Turin, miraculous cures, and the numerous other proofs of God's love.

First, your opinion of eternity is almost certainly wrong. Second, stop trying to prove that you are smarter and more merciful than Jesus by asserting that your concept of the eternal right is better than his. Third, you display no honor and achieve nothing by joining those on the wrong side of the great chasm separating heaven from hell (I'm speaking both literally and figuratively, depending on your view as to whether heaven and hell are places or states). Wouldn't it make more sense to stay on the side Jesus died for and try to bring others over?

FREE WILL AND ETERNAL CONSEQUENCES

God created us in his own image. He gave us intelligence, will, and the freedom of choice. He offered his love, first to and through the ancient Israelites and then through Jesus. But since his love included the gift of free choice, we can either accept that love, disbelieve, resist, or simply refuse it. We push him aside when we disbelieve or reject his love.

When we accept God's love, however, we have accepted his continuing offer to live in his presence. When we die, our existence will then be elevated to an infinitely higher plane when we come into his celestial presence. We call this "heaven." When we say "no," God respects our choice because he gave us freedom of choice, and a necessary element of this gift is the ability to choose wrongly. Hell is the final and definitive "no" to God's love, and the wrong choice.

In other words, God doesn't send people to eternal punishment; they send themselves. Free will includes a key to the doors of hell. We may be tempted to conclude that God is a cruel God (and, therefore, non-existent) because he allows this eternal separation from him, but in all honesty if we couldn't make that decision we would be mere animals, not made in the image of God. If one knowingly turns from Christ in this life, he is really telling God that his preference is to continue that non-relationship for all eternity.

WHY CHOOSE HELL?

But why would anyone choose hell? How about this quote from a person who was outraged that a film critic actually gave a positive review of Mel Gibson's film, *The Passion of Christ*:

> You accept all of this Biblical brutality and bloodshed as "normal" only because you want to believe your life to be sooo important and special, that you will be granted immortality. Do you really want to spend the next million years on bended knee, in constant adoration? Is that why you were created, for eternal appeasement and glorification?

It is hard to see anything but hate in the heart of this writer, and it looks like hate directs his beliefs and actions. I'm not judging, but only reporting what appears to be the case. Contrition and conversion may be in his future, and if he reverses course we know that Jesus will welcome him to paradise.

Here is another answer: Look at our daily lives and the people around us. They choose to ignore God and pursue their own self-involved agenda.

While many of us wonder what awaits when our earthly journey is over, many don't seem to care. In fact, a 2014 poll said that 47 percent of Americans (arguably the most Christian nation in the world) never think about their eternal destination. God became man and assumed human nature in the body of a poor Palestinian carpenter. He knows our story, our temptations, our lives, our uncertainties, insecurities, pains, anger, love, hurt—everything about each of us. His life and Passion tell us of the enormity of his love. Our lethargy tells him of our disdain for what he did. If we deliberately ignore our Creator during this life, does it seem unreasonable for our decision to continue throughout all eternity? Should we expect God to overrule our decision, much like the Supreme Court would reverse a lower court's ruling?

The Old Testament tells us that when the law was given and the Israelites rejected or ignored it they suffered terrible consequences. If that was the case at a time when much less revelation was given, then think of the consequences of our rejecting or neglecting the great salvation offered by Christ.

TRUSTING JESUS

Who does Christianity say will spend eternity in hell? I think it is fair to say that virtually all of Christianity believes that those who with full knowledge reject Christ and attack him to the end of their days are doomed. After these cases of extreme hate there is disagreement so there is no point speculating about this subject. The fact is that it is Jesus who judges and so we are led once again to the nexus of all Christianity. Trust Jesus.

THE WAGES OF SIN ARE DEATH

Still, there is a deep gnawing within us that keeps saying that no one in control of his senses would deliberately reject God, knowing that an eternity of torment and pain awaited him. Similarly, it seems hard to accept the notion that God would condemn him to eternal torment for some wrong choices made during our fleeting lives.

On the other hand, anyone who deliberately rejects God clearly believes that when he dies, his life is snuffed out forever. That is his expectation and choice. Does it seem unfair for Jesus to honor that decision? I wonder, then, if the eternal punishment that Jesus referred to is the complete annihilation and extinction of the person—an eternal separation from God. Their eternal fate would be exactly what they anticipated; they would disappear into non-existence and thereby eternally removed from the presence of God. There is certainly scriptural basis for this position (as there are for other more traditional positions), but it is interesting that the Bible generally tells us that those who are not saved suffer eternal death. For example:

> John 3:16. "For God so loved the world that he gave his only Son, that whoever believes in him should not perish but have eternal life."

> Romans 6:23. "For the wages of sin is death, but the free gift of God is eternal life in Christ Jesus our Lord."

Perhaps, then, "hell" as referred to by Jesus does not mean a place of eternal torment and suffering, but rather punishment until the close when the existence of the individual, body and soul, is extinguished. This position is not inconsistent with Christianity in general, or Catholicism in particular. The *Catechism* states:

> 1056 Following the example of Christ, the Church warns the faithful of the "sad and lamentable reality of eternal death" (*GCD* 69), also called "hell."

> 1057 Hell's principal punishment consists of eternal separation from God in whom alone man can have the life and happiness for which he was created and for which he longs.

One interpretation, then, is that the fires of hell burn the body and soul so that the person and the disobedience he carries with him is removed from God's creation, and because the flame never dies, they are extinguished for all time and eternity.

It is interesting that the one place in the New Testament that specifically speaks of an eternal torment is found in Revelation 14:9–11.

> 9 And another angel, a third, followed them, saying with a loud voice, "If any one worships the beast and its image, and receives a mark on his forehead or on his hand, 10 he also shall drink the wine of God's wrath, poured unmixed into the cup of his anger, and he shall be tormented with fire and sulphur in the presence of the holy angels and in the presence of the Lamb. 11 And the smoke of their torment goes up for ever and ever; and they have no rest, day or night, these worshipers of the beast and its image, and whoever receives the mark of its name.

If someone worships the beast with full knowledge [as evidenced by the fact that he receives a mark on the forehead or hand] he shall be tormented forever. This seems quite different from the fate of those who have rejected Christ or the evildoers that are separated out at the last judgment. While we don't know who or what the beast is (a pretty good guess is Satan or his derivatives), the action of the individual is the same: worshiping a creature with full knowledge of their actions and an attempt to undermine God and substitute a mere creature for him.

There is no need for speculation, however, as to what hell is like or is. We know from the best of authority that it is eternal punishment. The specifics may vary by individual or it could be the final and irrevocable extinguishing of the body and soul. We just don't know, but when we evaluate the alternatives the prospect of it should be horrifying beyond description and we need to understand and help others understand the consequences of their decisions in life. We do know that God does not want hell as our final destination, and this was told to us by Our Lady of Fatima, when she asked the three shepherd children to include the following prayer in the Rosary: "Oh my Jesus, forgive us our sins, saves us from the fire of hell, lead all souls to heaven, and help especially those most in need of your mercy."

IGNORANCE

But what if the Lord never entered our crowded lives? What if we never really heard about Him? Or effectively heard about Him? What if we are born and live in country or culture where Christianity is an anathema and even to pray in the name of Christ is blasphemy punishable by death? What about even those most subtle of situations where through family history, or other factors a child grows up in an environment of latent hostility or apathy towards Christianity. We must accept the fact that there are plenty who die without the opportunity, through no fault of their own, of knowing Jesus.

We don't know on an individual basis, but we do have guidance from both the Bible and the teaching of the Catholic Church. Paragraph 847 of the *Catechism*:

> Those who, through no fault of their own, do not know the Gospel of Christ or his Church, but who nevertheless seek God with a sincere heart, and, moved by grace, try in their actions to do his will as they know it through the dictates of their conscience—those too may achieve eternal salvation.

Paul tells us in Romans 2:14–15 that knowledge of good and evil is built into the heart of everyone. God's inherent gift to each of us is a conscience of what is good and what is evil. Reason should tell us about the existence of a God and the acts that are against the laws of nature. Deep down we all know those actions which are proper such as taking care of the less fortunate and honoring parents. We don't know, of course, which of us will receive the grace of heaven. We can only trust Jesus and try to follow his commandments.

OUR CHOICE—ETERNITY WITH GOD, OR APART FROM HIM

God's love is the overriding principle of Christianity. Another is the freedom God gave us to accept or reject that love. These two principles lead to what appears to be an inevitable consequence. We can reject God's love and remain outside his presence. When we do that, we willingly accept the pain and suffering which accompanies such rejection. We will have exiled ourselves from God's saving love and grace. Christ came to save us, not condemn. He opened the doors for all of us, but here's the catch: He doesn't force us through that door, and we can make the imbecilically poor decision to remain outside. Nevertheless, to remain outside would be our decision and the consequences of that decision would be a necessary corollary of God's love. The Lord makes himself available in our crowded lives and we can accept, ignore, resist, or reject.

The bottom line is that God wishes no one to spend eternity in hell, but that through free will we have been empowered to make this choice. This is your decision, not his. God wants only those who love him to spend eternity with him.

OUR PLACE IN ETERNITY

Christianity teaches that God's love and mercy are universally available and fall upon the rich and the poor, the wise and the ignorant, the good and the bad, upon all of us like a gentle rain. If we live in a house with the blinds drawn shut, we will never see the sun. We need to open them and allow light and warmth to enter. God's love is out there waiting for an invitation.

God loved you so much that he gave you the choice. If I were you, I would want to be sensible and carefully consider the meaning of Jesus' words when he said that the greatest commandment was to love God with all your heart, mind, and soul. There is a reciprocity at play. Jesus took time out for us, so shouldn't we take time for Jesus?[1]

Believe to understand.

---

1. *Time out for Jesus* by Charley Pride https://www.youtube.com/watch?v=4BjsM3E JozE&list=RD4BjsM3EJozE&start_radio=1 (YouTube search words: time out charley).

PART V

Personal Experiences

32

Glimpsing Eternity

Mystical personal experiences are sometimes offered as proof of God. I think this goes a step too far simply because they are private and cannot be independently verified. There are numerous experiences, however, that ring true and deserve our attention as de facto glimpses into eternity. These are incredibly special gifts to individuals, possibly to be shared with others.

NEAR-DEATH EXPERIENCES

Numerous people (perhaps thousands) have lived through near-death experiences. They were clinically dead, or close to it, and reported what they describe as encounters with eternity. Typical experiences include being outside their body and witnessing events around them. Many report going through a tunnel, being enveloped by a glorious light and love, meeting departed loved ones, heavenly beings, beautiful scenes and indescribably beautiful colors, being enveloped by incredibly beautiful music, feeling they belong there, conversations with heavenly beings (including Jesus), and being told it was not their time, and a return to their body—sometimes painfully.

What are we to make of these reports? Some are fabrications, and some undoubtedly are hallucinations or dreams. It appears that some may be the result of physiological and chemical changes as the brain shuts down. But there are numerous events that cannot be so easily dismissed, and many occur in the presence of reliable witnesses. We briefly describe two in Chapter 33, "To Heaven, Hell, and Back" and Chapter 34, "*Heaven is for Real.*"

While visions of the afterlife may vary, one common characteristic is that those who have undergone a near-death experience are never the same. Dreams and nightmares may haunt you for a while, but you know they are imaginings. Drug induced euphoria or horror are later recognized by the person as not real. That is not the case with those who have been to heaven or hell and back when they were clinically dead or approaching death. They all remember the event as a real event, and their lives are changed forever.

PERSONAL EXPERIENCES

It is my firm conviction (just an opinion) that at least once in our lives God opens a heavenly door and allows believers and those seeking him to directly experience his love and presence. These personal experiences have no explanation other than a divine intervention. I describe one very personal and unexpected event in Chapter 35, "Waco, Texas."

VERIFICATION

I can't tell you how to determine which near-death-experiences, visions, or personal encounters are true and which are not. We must bear in mind, however, that revelations or visions such as those described by Father Jose Maniyangat in chapter 33 and four-year-old Colton Burpo in chapter 34 are "private revelations," as are the many revelations that saints and mystics have had over the years. Paragraph 67 of the *Catechism of the Catholic Church* makes it clear that "private revelations" (which means that they have been given to help the recipient or perhaps people of a certain time or culture), do not belong to the deposit of faith. Consequently, they can vary and so it is difficult to know their meaning or application, if any, to each of us. The experiences we describe are for your consideration, meditation, and prayer.

FURTHER ACTION

I would encourage you to dig more deeply into the matters discussed here, as well as other claimed divine interventions, bearing in mind that some (or perhaps many) are not real. Do not allow the false ones to taint the real ones. They are separate events or claimed events and need to be examined independently of one another. All it takes is but one event that is real to close the door on atheism.

33

To Heaven, Hell, and Back

When we talk about heaven we are speaking of the unknowable, and biblical descriptions are appropriately vague. First Corinthians 2:9 tells us that "no eye has seen, nor ear heard, nor the heart of man conceived, what God has prepared for those who love him." When we speak of hell we contemplate the unthinkable, and biblical descriptions are brimming with pain and punishment. We like to ignore these descriptions.

Maybe that is why God has permitted some to glimpse heaven and hell, and tell us about them—the best they can. There are those whose credibility cannot be attacked who claim to have been granted the visions of heaven, hell, and even purgatory.

FATHER JOSE'S ACCOUNT

Father Jose Maniyangat was born in India in 1949 and was ordained a Catholic priest in 1975. In 1985 he was riding his motorcycle in Kerala, India on his way to celebrate Mass at a mission when he was hit head-on by a jeep driven by a drunk driver. He was rushed to a hospital about thirty five miles away. He died enroute and was pronounced dead at the hospital by a doctor. Because the hospital did not have air conditioners, they were concerned that the body would decompose quickly, and his dead body was transported to the morgue.

This is Father Jose's account of what happened, retrieved directly from his website:

> On the way my soul came out from my body and I experienced death. Immediately I met my Guardian angel. I saw my body and the people who were carrying me to the hospital. I heard them crying and praying for me. At this time my angel told me: "I am going to take you to Heaven, the Lord wants to meet you and talk with you." He also said that on the way he wanted to show me hell and purgatory.
>
> First, the angel escorted me to hell. It was an awful sight! I saw Satan and the devils, an unquenchable fire of about 2,000 Fahrenheit degrees, worms crawling, people screaming and fighting, others being tortured by demons. The angel told me that all these sufferings were due to unrepented mortal sins. Then, I understood that there are seven degrees of suffering or levels according to the number and kinds of mortal sins committed in their earthly lives. The souls looked very ugly, cruel and horrific. It was a fearful experience. I saw people whom I knew but I am not allowed to reveal their identities. The sins that convicted them were mainly abortion, homosexuality, euthanasia, hatefulness, unforgiveness and sacrilege. The angel told me that if they had repented they would have avoided hell and gone instead to purgatory. I also understood that some people who repent from these sins might be purified on earth through their sufferings. This way they can avoid purgatory and go straight to heaven.
>
> After the visit to hell, my Guardian angel escorted me to Purgatory. Here too, there are seven degrees of suffering and unquenchable fire. But it is far less intense than hell and there was neither quarreling nor fighting. The main suffering of these souls is their separation from God. Some of those who are in Purgatory committed numerous mortal sins; but they were reconciled with God before their death. Even though these souls are suffering, they enjoy peace and the knowledge that one day they will see God face to face.
>
> I had a chance to communicate with the souls in Purgatory. They asked me to pray for them and to tell the people to pray for them as well, so they can go to heaven quickly. When we pray for these souls we will receive their gratitude through their prayers and once they enter heaven their prayers become even more meritorious.

It is difficult for me to describe how beautiful my Guardian angel is. He is radiant and bright. He is my constant companion and helps me in all my ministries, especially my healing ministry. I experience his presence everywhere I go and I am grateful for his protection in my daily life.

Next, my angel escorted me to heaven passing through a big dazzling white tunnel. I never experienced this much peace and joy in my life. Then immediately the heaven opened up and I heard the most delightful music, which I never heard before. The angels were singing and praising God. I saw all the saints, especially the Blessed Mother and St. Joseph, and many dedicated holy Bishops and Priests who were shining like stars. And when I appeared before the Lord, Jesus told me: "I want you to go back to the world. In your second life you will be an instrument of peace and healing to my people. You will walk in a foreign land and you will speak in a foreign tongue. Everything is possible for you with my grace." After these words, the Blessed Mother told me: "Do whatever He tells you. I will help you in your ministries."

Words can not express the beauty of heaven. There we find so much peace and happiness, which exceed a million times our imagination. Our Lord is far more beautiful than any image can convey. His face is radiant and luminous and more beautiful than a thousand rising suns. The pictures we see in the world are only a shadow of His magnificence. The Blessed Mother was next to Jesus; she was so beautiful and radiant. None of the images we see in this world can compare with her real beauty. Heaven is our real home, we are all created to reach heaven and enjoy God forever. Then, I came back to the world with my angel.

As they were moving my dead body to the morgue, my soul came back to the body. I felt an excruciating pain because of so many wounds and broken bones. I began to scream and then the people became frightened and ran away screaming. One of them approached the doctor and said: "the dead body is screaming." The doctor came to examine the body and found that I was alive. So he said: "Father is alive, it is a miracle, take him back to the hospital."

A HEALING MINISTRY

Father Jose was in the hospital for two months, undergoing surgeries to repair the broken lower jaw, ribs, pelvic bone, wrists, and right leg. His orthopedic doctor said that he would never walk again, and Father Jose replied that the Lord who gave me his life back and sent him back to the world would heal him. He continues:

> Once at home we were all praying for a miracle. Still after a month and with the casts removed I was not able to move. But one day while praying I felt an extraordinary pain in my pelvic area. After a short while the pain disappeared completely and I heard a voice saying: "You are healed. Get up and walk." I felt the peace and healing power on my body. I immediately got up and walked. I praised and thanked God for the miracle."[1]

Following his healing, Father Jose's Hindu doctor converted and was baptized into the Catholic faith by Father Jose.

Father Jose came to the United States in 1986 as a missionary priest, working in the Diocese of Boise, Idaho (1987–1989) and Director of Prison Ministry in the Diocese of Orlando, Florida (1989–1992). He has since served in various parishes in Florida. Among other spiritual activities, he has served as the Catholic Chaplain in various state prisons, as well as the Diocesan Spiritual Director of the Legion of Mary. Father Jose retired effective April 15, 2016 from active parish duties and now shares his Healing Ministry on a full-time basis with people throughout the world.

In other words, Father Jose's actions and life are 100 percent consistent with the vision he received in India in 1985 and his miraculous cure. His actions following his encounter with the Risen Lord confirm the sincerity of his beliefs and special gifts which were conferred upon him.

It is hard to separate real visions or revelations about heaven and hell from the imaginary (but believed by the visionary to be true) and fraudulent claims. If you are a Christian you tend to accept them, particularly when they conform to your understanding of these eternal destinations. If you are non-Christian, you have no option but to disbelieve all of them.

Why would one not believe Father Jose's story?

---

1. Fr Maniyangat, "Life after Death Experience," selected paragraphs. Be sure to read Fr Jose's complete account at his website. http://www.frmaniyangathealingministry.com/.

34

Heaven is for Real

A near death experience that lends itself to objective confirmation was reported by a four-year-old child as he lay on an operating table fighting for his life. What is striking is that the reality of his event was independently confirmed by a four-year-old girl living half a continent away. Later, at the age of eight she painted an incredibly powerful portrait of the Jesus she visioned in heaven.

We will first consider the vision of heaven from this little Nebraska boy and described in the book, *Heaven is for Real: A Little Boy's Astounding Story of His Trip to Heaven and Back*. In 2003 little Colton Burpo nearly died on an operating table while undergoing a major operation. Over the following months he gradually revealed to his minister father, Todd Burpo, in bits and pieces and in the vocabulary of a four-year-old what happened on that operating table and his visit to heaven and being with Jesus. Since his father is a minister, that by itself is not terribly surprising.

But what is surprising are details of his family and other information that four-year-old Colton should not have known. Moreover, this little child of a Protestant minister saw Mary, the mother of Jesus, kneeling before the throne of God and standing next to Jesus. The favored place of Mary in heaven is a concept either ignored or rejected by Protestants. Colton's description of Mary's place flew in the face of what he would have learned. Colton said that Mary "still loves him [Jesus] like a mom."[1] Mary's presence in heaven close to Jesus would be a dogma or teaching quite alien to little Colton.

Over the next few years, Colton was asked if any painting or representation of Jesus that he looked at accurately depicted Jesus. None of them did; there was always something wrong. That is, not until he saw the *Prince of Peace*,[2] a painting by eight-year old Akiane Kramarik.

THE PRINCE OF PEACE

Colton is the son of a minister. Akiane Kramarik was the daughter of non-religious and lived hundreds of miles from Colton. When she was four, she started having visions of heaven, and they sound remarkably like Colton's. Over a three-year period Colton's parents had shown him various paintings of Jesus, and Colton told them that none of them were right. When Colton was seven, Todd Burpo (Colton's father) had just learned of the child prodigy Akiane and her paintings, including her portrait of Jesus, painted when she was eight years old. Todd called his son to the computer where the full front face painting appeared and asked him what was wrong with this painting. Colton studied it for a bit, looked at his father and said, "Dad, that one's right."

Prince of Peace by **Akiane**

1. Burpo, *Heaven is for Real*, Epilogue.
2. Kramarik, *Prince of Peace*, scroll down https://akiane.com to view her paintings at the age of eight.

Todd explains, "We were pretty sure no painting could ever capture the majesty of the person of the risen Christ. But after three years of examining Jesus pictures, we did know that Akiane's rendering was not only a departure from typical paintings of Jesus; it was also the only one that had ever stopped Colton in his tracks. Sonja and I thought it was interesting that when Colton said, "This one's right," he hadn't known the portrait, called *Prince of Peace: The Resurrection*, was painted by another child—a child who had also claimed to visit heaven."[3]

AKIANE PAINTS THE PORTRAIT OF JESUS

The website, God Reports, provides some detail.

> At eight-years-old, Akiane decided she wanted to paint the face of Jesus, based on the visions she received. She looked for a person she might use as an artist's model for a long time, and finally told her family they should pray for God to send someone.
>
> On the day they prayed, a mysterious carpenter showed up at their front door looking for work. Akiane took one look at the man's facial features—remarkably close to the vision she received—and told her mother he was the one.
>
> In humility, the man initially said he was not worthy to represent his Master. But reluctantly, the man agreed, although he asked to remain anonymous.
>
> Akiane's painting of Jesus was a painstaking effort. "The 'Prince of Peace' took me 40 hours to paint and another 20 hours of working with model sketching," Akiane says. Akiane deftly works with light and shadows to create powerful impressions. "The light side of his face represents the truth, the dark side represents suffering," she notes.[4]

HEAVEN IS LOVE

The trouble with heaven, eternity, and God's plan of salvation is that they are way beyond our ability to understand them. When visions of heaven and hell are given, or ostensibly given, they sometimes differ. What is interesting is that they are given in terms that the recipient can relate to, but do not conflict. It is kind of like the old story of two blind men running their hands

---

3. Burpo, *Heaven is for Real*, chapter 27.
4. Ellis, "*Akiane, Jesus is for real.*"

over different parts of an elephant and describing what they think the creature looks like. In effect, this is precisely what Jesus told us. Heaven and eternity are far beyond our ability to see, much less understand. Consequently, we are left again with the fundamental premise or theological underpinning of Christianity: We need to trust Jesus and hold on to a child-like faith.

I think that is the reason scoffers scoff. They rely upon their own intelligence and logic (but with unacknowledged biases) and are unable to see. For them, that which cannot be seen, touched or is apparent to the senses is a fiction. They stumble because self-reliance is inadequate. Consequently, when the witnesses describe what they have seen, and felt, and heard, these experiences are dismissed by the scoffer as hallucinations, dreams, lies, chemical imbalances, etc. because according to the metaphysical world of the skeptic, these visions or experiences simply cannot be real.

What do all these witnesses say about heaven? What is the one characteristic that permeates all descriptions? Everyone says they experienced a profound sense of love and beauty that are impossible to describe. The love and beauty of heaven and Jesus are overpowering and indescribable. That is precisely what the Bible tells us.

Believe to understand.

35

Waco, Texas

PERSONAL EXPERIENCES

The experiences and visions of heaven described by visionaries share the commonality of a profound and overpowering sense of love. Let me describe a personal incident which has no explanation other than a divine intervention. It wasn't a miracle; it wasn't a vision; it was merely an event where God opened a heavenly door to just a regular guy and allowed me to experience the outflow of his love in a subdued but very real manner.

THE EUCHARIST

Years ago, my wife and I were visiting one of our sons near Waco, Texas, where he was an undergraduate at Baylor University. I can't remember the precise circumstances, but I do recall that we were to meet him at the local Catholic Church where he would be participating in the Perpetual Eucharistic Adoration.

During Eucharistic Adoration, the Communion Bread (a thin unleavened wafer) which Catholics believe had been consecrated into the Real Presence of Jesus is displayed in a monstrance and adored by the faithful. When the Eucharist is exposed twenty-four hours a day, seven days a week, the practice of adoration is called Perpetual Eucharistic Adoration. In a typical parish (which is large enough), parishioners volunteer to devote at least an hour a week at specific times in the chapel containing the exposed Eucharist, so that there will always be somebody present with the Lord. When one enters the chapel containing the Eucharist, you are literally entering into the physical presence of Jesus. You are with Jesus himself.

When I arrived at the church I asked for directions and was directed to a door. I entered, and there before me were about seven or eight pews facing the monstrance. My son was in one of the rear pews and there were several other worshipers there as well.

What happened next will be burned into my memory forever. When I entered the chapel, I was immediately overwhelmed by the most powerful feeling of love and peace I have ever experienced. It was as though another dimension of senses had opened. The sensation and emotions were not just quantitatively superior to anything I thought was possible, but qualitatively on an entirely different plane.

This was completely unexpected. The reverence, joy, love, and awe which flooded my senses were unanticipated and spontaneous. I knew that the resurrected Savior was in that room. Twenty-five years later I remember the event and the sensations as though it occurred twenty-five minutes ago. I don't remember the details of the events leading up to or following the encounter, but I am absolutely certain that the Baylor chapel event occurred just as I have described.

VERIFICATION NOT POSSIBLE

This event can never be objectively confirmed. Some of you are nodding your head and thinking, "Yes, I believe that happened." Some of you, however, will reject my description of what happened as a lie, a delusion, or an optimistic memory. That is understandable because there are enough frauds in this life to spill over and taint the real. All I can say is please consider the possibility that while Jesus does not force himself upon anyone, he will at least once in our lives make his presence known (sometimes at the most unexpected of times), particularly when you call upon him with a deep desire and humility.

Father Jose's vision is supported by his subsequent miraculous healing and his healing ministry that followed. The heavenly visit granted to Colton Burpo is verified by the portrait of Jesus painted by the eight-year old Akiane Kramarik. Additionally, there are numerous aspects about Colton's vision which could only have occurred if the story he tells is true.

These stories, as well as my personal experience in Waco, have not been narrated to convince you of the reality of the risen Lord. They could never do that, but they might help you or your loved ones keep an open mind (and heart) and keep you from drifting too far from the shore.

Try to keep an open mind and heart.

PART VI

Quo Vadis?

36

Portrait of Jesus, Ruler of All

You will recall from chapter 14.1 that in 544 the Mandylion was discovered, hidden away in Edessa. Shortly thereafter, a new common image of Jesus emerged and dominated in the Middle East. The earliest extant example of this bearded Jesus was uncovered in 1962 at St. Catherine's Monastery in the Sinai desert. This icon is called *Christ Pantocrator* and is dated to around 550, or about six years after the discovery of the Mandylion. The fact that this icon survived the destructive forces of iconoclasm is probably attributable to the Monastery's remote location, just as the fact that the Shroud of Turin survived the iconoclastic period is probably attributed to the fact it was hidden away.

Christ Pantocrator

As with all icons (they are described as writings because they impart theological lessons) the *Christ Pantocrator* declares profound theological teachings about Christ. It is not just a nice picture. You can see that Christ's face is in two halves, merged seamlessly. His left side holds the Bible and he presents a severe and powerful Christ; he is the eternal judge. His right side is calm and serene; he is the savior. This is the dual nature of Christ. Moreover, and as portrayed in the icon, Jesus is the perfect union of both divine and human nature. These are fundamental teachings of all Christianity regardless of sect or sub-faith.

Now, go back to chapter 34 and look again at the *Prince of Peace* painted by eight-year-old Akiane Kramarik. This is not an icon but her incredibly gifted rendering of Christ as she saw him during her heavenly vision and as confirmed by Colton Burpo when he was seven years old and recalling his heavenly visit three years earlier. Akiane essentially tells us that her painting represents the divine nature of Christ (the light side of his faith representing truth) and the human nature of Christ (the dark side representing suffering and, by implication, Calvary).

Finally, and to bring together some loose ends, return to chapter 14 and the Shroud of Turin. Compare the face of the dead but resurrecting Christ on the Shroud with that of the *Pantocrator* and then again with the *Prince of Peace*. You will see startling similarities.

The Christian faith is truly universal. In the *Pantocrator* we see a visual portrait and theological lessons presented through Eastern Orthodox eyes but expressing the universal Christian teaching about the dual nature of Christ as savior and judge and as divine and human. We see a slightly different perspective from the Shroud of Turin, commonly associated with Catholicism. There we see the suffering and glory of Christ—again a universal Christian teaching. Finally, we see Christ as seen by the child of a Protestant minister and the child of atheists (now Christians). The *Prince of Peace* reveals, yet again, the dual nature of Christ and his love.

The Shroud of Turin, the *Pantocrator*, the *Prince of Peace*. They are one; they are Christ.

Clearly, the Mandylion was the model for the *Pantocrator*, and just as clearly the Mandylion was the Shroud of Turin hidden away for centuries because of the assault by pagans, Muslims, and iconoclasts against all images Christ. Then, to make Christ more understandable for all Christianity and the modern world we have a little girl gloriously painting the Christ she saw in her visions confirmed by a mysterious carpenter who appeared one day at her front door in answer to her prayers.

Who at your door is standing?[1]

---

1. *Who at my door is standing?* Sung by Johnny Cash https://www.youtube.com/watch?v=pLLAAD2KqeY (YouTube search words: Cash door standing).

37

One Christian Mansion

Some arguments to disprove Christianity are not really arguments; they are nothing more than observations or puzzling reflections. One is that if Christianity were true it wouldn't be so fragmented, as evidenced by the thousands of denominations we see. Moreover, there wouldn't be the verbal attacks by one group of Christians against others because some beliefs differ.

Don't be diverted by these red herrings. I say this for a couple of reasons, best summed up by C.S. Lewis in his Preface to *Mere Christianity*.

> But in this book I am not trying to convert anyone to my own position. Ever since I became a Christian I have thought that the best, perhaps the only, service I could do for my unbelieving neighbours was to explain and defend the belief that has been common to nearly all Christians at all times. I had more than one reason for thinking this. In the first place, the questions which divide Christians from one another often involve points of high Theology or even ecclesiastical history, which ought never to be treated except by real experts. I should have been out of my depth ins such waters: more in need of help myself than able to help others. And secondly, I think we must admit that the discussion of these disputed points has no tendency at all to bring an outsider into the Christian fold. So long as we write and talk about them we are much more likely to deter him

from entering any Christian communion than to draw him into our own. Our divisions should never be discussed except in the presence of those who have already come to believe that there is one God and that Jesus Christ is His only Son.

There are questions at issue between Christians to which I do not think we have been told the answer. There are some to which I may never know the answer: if I asked them, even in a better world, I might (for all I know) be answered as a far greater questioner was answered: "What is that to thee? Follow thou Me."[1]

Look upon Christianity as a mansion with a hallway and many rooms. First, come into the building and then find the room that makes the most sense for you. If you are outside and trying to decide whether to enter, do not be distracted or repelled by the squabbling that seems to occur within this house of many rooms. And once you find your room don't devote your energies to attacking those who have selected other rooms. You're not infallible and whatever your fine-tuned Christian beliefs, some of them (or maybe all) are almost certainly wrong or at least off the mark. It's nice to know that the first sermon Jesus spoke while hanging from the cross was, "Father, forgive them; for they know not what they do."[2]

If you're trying to help someone with their faith, stay focused on our common bond and bring the nonbeliever in from the cold. They can fine-tune their beliefs later and figure out what room to enter once they're in the hallway.

One final thought on this subject: Jesus started carrying the cross to Calvary by himself, but he couldn't make it and Simon was forced into helping our Savior. We all carry our individual crosses and struggle. We always need the help of others even though we may not acknowledge our need or be willing to accept an offering of help. In fact, some Christian denominations seem to spend an inordinate amount of time separating themselves from others by drawing upon various biblical passages to support doctrines that everybody else has got wrong. They wish to carry the cross by themselves and everyone else must fall in line or risk eternal damnation.

Clearly this is not what Jesus desired. In the seventeenth chapter of John, Jesus prayed to the Father that his disciples and all believers be one, just as Jesus and the Father were one. He prayed for them and he prayed for those that would believe in him because of their teaching and that all who believed in him would be one.

---

1. Lewis, *Mere Christianity*, IX. The biblical quote is John 21:22.
2. Luke 23:34.

Maybe it's time we as Christians seriously start to follow Christ's admonishments. We must understand that we need to carry the cross together. This is what the Lord prayed for just before Gethsemane. If you are about to be beheaded by a Muslim jihadist, he is not going to ask you if you are Episcopalian, Evangelical, Catholic, or Orthodox. He's going to identify you as a person of the cross to be dispatched accordingly.

We are one Christian faith, just as the *Prince of Peace*, the man on the Shroud, and the *Pantocrator* are one Christ; just as God the Father, God the Son, and the Holy Spirit are One.

Let's stick together.

38

If Jesus Comes Tomorrow, What Then?

GOD'S LOVE AND OUR FREE WILL

God's grandeur, majesty, power, knowledge and love are infinitely beyond the power of human comprehension. Despite his being as far above us as the heavens are above the earth, he has made himself available to each of us.

He gave us his creation, the universe, life, the revelation of himself to the ancients and to the Jews. He gave us the Old Covenant and allowed us to demonstrate that without his guidance and grace we would never reach his Heavenly Kingdom. He gave each of us a conscience and a knowledge of right and wrong. When we kept denying him, he finally gave us his Son. Jesus demonstrated the meaning of love and empowered us to stay in his presence and follow his commandments. He told us how to become a channel for his peace. We received the gift of the Holy Spirit and he gave us the tools to build a huge mansion with doors open for everyone.

He gave us the wisdom to identify those things which are from God and those which are not. Our free will allows us to accept, reject, or ignore him. He gave us pain, suffering and doubt for us to overcome. He allowed us to be tempted by false gods and, when we devolve into ourselves, we alienate God through our pride, arrogance, and self-involvement. Still, God has freely provided the grace for us to re-connect with him.

OVERPOWERING EVIDENCE

He gave us overpowering evidence. The next time your faith begins to soften or someone says they can't believe in God or the resurrection of Christ, try to maintain your equanimity and direct them to the two thousand year old love letter called the Shroud of Turin. Then you might mention:

Chapter	
17	The incredible complexity of life.
9–9.6	Our Lady of Fatima and the Miracle of the Sun and other associated miracles.
9.4	Early non-Christian writers such as Pliny describing the early Christians and their practices.
10, 18–18.3, 18.5	Our Lady of Lourdes and the miraculous instant healings of Jack Traynor, Gabriel Gargam, Marie Bailly, and Francis Pascal.
19.1	The Miracle of the Holy Fire.
11, 18.4	Our Lady of Knock and the miraculous instant healing of Marion Carroll.
16	The Holy House of Loreto.
19.2	The Great Peshtigo Fire and the oasis of green.
13.1, 13.2	The image of Our Lady of Guadalupe. While we recognize possible uncertainties, we also understand that divine intervention is often assisted by human instruments. The present image of Our Lady of Guadalupe may be a perfect example.
12	Our Lady of Zeitoun in Cairo.
19.3	Our Lady of China.
19.4	Cokeville, Wyoming and the saving interventions of heavenly beings.
20–22	The Four Gospels incredible compilation and complementary accounts of the Resurrection.
14–14.4	The negative photographic image of Jesus on the Shroud of Turin imprinted at the instant of resurrection.
15	The Sudarium and how it correlates and completes the picture given us by the Shroud of Turin.
23–24	The impossibility of the apostles and their followers concocting strange Christian beliefs such as the Transfiguration, the Virgin birth, and other completely inexplicable events.

Chapter	
7	Our tiny place in the universe of space and time, God's incomprehensibility, and our need to turn over everything to him, and to trust him.
25–27	Evil, suffering, and unanswered prayers as a beacon illuminating God's love.
28	The story of Alexandrina da Costa of Balasar and how she survived on the Eucharist alone for 13 years.
29, 30	God's incredible love as demonstrated by Jesus' suffering, passion, crucifixion, and the suffering of his beloved mother.
31	Eternal death or an eternity of hell tell us that our choices matter, and that if we ignore him and his love, he will honor our desire to remain separate from him from all eternity. How we choose to live our earthly lives has eternal consequences.
21	How eleven of the original apostles died horribly cruel deaths because they had witnessed the life, death, and resurrection of Jesus. They knew with a certainty that Jesus was the Son of God. They didn't die for a philosophy; they died for the Savior and his promise, which they personally witnessed.
32, 33	Near death visions such as that of Father Jose Maniyangat in 1985.
34	The *Prince of Peace* Portrait of Jesus and the confirming experience of four-year-old Colton Burpo.
35	Personal experiences.
36	The Mandylion and the *Pantocrator*

God showered us with gifts to help us in our journey. He gave us the Bible, the apostles, their successors, the Church, lives to emulate, each other, and miracles. He gave us his mother to be our mother. Her job is to bring us closer to Jesus. Above all, he gave us prayer. He gave us all of this to show that he is available for all time to all people. These are powerful allies, but they are useless if we do not call upon them.

WHAT ELSE COULD GOD HAVE DONE?

What would it take to convince you or the world that God exists? How about the hypothetical cross in the sky visible throughout the world simultaneously as described in Chapter 12, "Our Lady of Zeitoun." Would all of us now believe? Would you believe? Would all atheists, or even 97 percent of them, convert? 60 percent? Would Islam and other religions watch a mass emigration to Christianity? The answer, of course, is no.

COMING TO BELIEF

As you examine the question of Christianity, you must remember that, despite all the evidence, belief in the resurrected Jesus is not purely an intellectual affair. Logic and traditional apologetics don't work, except as a starting point. Belief generally requires (1) a desire to believe, (2) personal experiences or an awareness of the events and evidence described in Part II and (3) prayer. This triage should produce a firm belief for anyone who has an open mind.

A common perception in the USA is that faith should come instantly. "I was born again!" or *I Was There When It Happened.*[1] Without doubting the reality of immediate conversions, I would expect that many come by their knowledge of God through a more gradual process. The shepherds on the hill on Christmas night received instant knowledge of the Savior. The magi from the east came by their knowledge through a longer and more tedious process. Even Mary Magdalene at the empty tomb didn't recognize the Risen Jesus at first. It was only after Jesus called her name that she recognized the Lord.[2] Maybe the same will be for you or the person to whom you are speaking. Jesus is always searching for his sheep; sometimes it appears he's just waiting for them to look for him.

JESUS IS FORGIVENESS

Our dog poops and pees where he shouldn't. Barks when he shouldn't, and even sojourns in the neighborhood when he escapes the yard. But if he comes back wagging his tail and looking at us with his brown eyes for love and forgiveness, well, we love and forgive. I wonder if it's the same with God and us. If our dog just took off and avoided us, we may become angry but if he came back, we would forgive. But if he decided to leave us forever we would be sad, but we would honor his decision even though we knew it was self-destruct. Is this what happens to those who decide to forsake the Lord?

We all falter and do or think things that we know we shouldn't. And we repeat our mistakes repeatedly despite our pledges not to. If we are truly

---

1. *I Was There When It Happened* sung by Johnny Cash. https://www.youtube.com/watch?v=8yyzsgHb6rU (YouTube search words: there happened cash).

2. John 20:11–18

sorry Jesus has promised forgiveness. Don't hesitate to return to the Lord in prayer and ask for forgiveness and help even as you continue to stray. If it is helpful, open your prayer with, *Jesus, It's Me Again*.[3] We need to have sufficient courage to trust in God and his love for us. We need to stay the course even in the face of the most discouraging of times. Never became discouraged and, when we do, embrace the guidance of Mother Teresa of Calcutta who told us that discouragement is a sign of pride because it shows you trust in your own powers. We need to be humbly obedient and trust God.

THE HARD-CORE NONBELIEVER

Here is a sad reality. We need to acknowledge the unfortunate fact that there are hard-core nonbelievers who would reject the Risen Christ even if Jesus emerged from the tomb in front of them. Regardless of the evidence or even a cross in the sky as described in chapter 12, they will not accept any conclusion except that Christianity was built upon a foundation of lies or legend. If this describes someone you're trying to help, maybe at some point you need to back off.

If you have seen the "Dog Whisperer" on TV you know that Cesar Millan spends a lot of time training dogs who misbehave badly, while at the same time rehabilitating their owners. After instruction by Cesar and sometimes months of implementation by the owners, we have a dog that now fits into the family and can be trusted (I wonder?!). The dog's life has been saved and the sanity of the owners preserved. But think now about all the loving dogs abandoned in animal shelters who are denied a home because of the time and energy diverted from them to the recalcitrant one. Perhaps Cesar should tell the owners that if his plan does not result in a loving and trusting dog within a specified period of time, the effort should be abandoned, and the owners need to rescue another dog trembling in an animal shelter. When it comes to proclaiming and defending the Gospel maybe we need to recognize that our individual resources are limited and curtail the amount of time spent with hard core skeptics so that we can bring those who are graced with a receptive mind to accept the gospel.

There are those who do not want to accept the biblical Jesus. This may seem strange to you and me, but it is a sad fact. Paraphrasing Jesus, "Even if one were to rise from the dead they would not believe."

---

3. *Jesus, It's Me Again* sung by Dick Damron. https://www.youtube.com/watch?v=ywvm8ujTx74&ab_channel=LonnieRatliff (YouTube search words: Jesus again Damron).

THE QUESTION THAT TRUMPS ALL

If Jesus comes tomorrow, what then?[4] If the sky turned black as midnight in the middle of the day and you knew that Jesus would return within 24 hours, what would you do?

Don't be left standing at the station when the gospel train pulls out. You have been given a ticket to ride. Discarding it is an eternal mistake. Remember, we have nothing without God, and that's what he's been trying to tell us for uncounted thousands of years. Hollywood celebrities have everything, and yet they have nothing. Suicide, drugs, sexual abuse, and trouble are the natural consequence of turning to ourselves for pleasure, ego stroking, all the answers, and to our fellow creatures for adulation. Instead of loving God and our neighbor we love ourselves and try always to fill the void created by a spiritual vacuum. That void can never be filled except by God and through his grace.

But first we must ask. We should consider doing this.

When you do, you will be able to join Johnny Cash and tell the world, *I Came to Believe*.[5] You don't want to cross Jordan alone.[6]

---

4. *If Jesus Comes Tomorrow (What Then)?* sung by Daniel O'Donnell https://www.youtube.com/watch?v=9cVHdZdrryQ (YouTube search words: Jesus tomorrow O'Donnell).

5. *I Came to Believe* sung by Johnny Cash. https://www.youtube.com/watch?v=PCb-JJ7bPE4&t=17s (YouTube search words: came believe cash).

6. *I Won't have to Cross Jordan Alone* sung by Daniel O'Donnell. https://www.youtube.com/watch?v=-qiVMUJlZtg&ab_channel=IsanLife (YouTube search words: cross Jordan o'donnell).

Bibliography

Aleteia website. "New Study: The Shroud of Turin and the Sudarium of Oviedo Covered the Same Person" (April 11, 2016). https://aleteia.org/2016/04/11/new-study-the-shroud-of-turin-and-the-sudarium-of-oviedo-covered-the-same-person/.

Anderson, Mary Jo. "The Other Shroud of Christ." *CatholicCulture.org*. https://www.catholicculture.org/culture/library/view.cfm?recnum=3953.

Armstrong, Jamie. "The Astonishing True Stories Behind the Cokeville Miracle Movie" (September 10, 2015). LDSLiving website. https://www.ldsliving.com/the-Cokeville-miracle/s/79933.

Armstrong, Mark & Patti. "A Miraculous Healing" (January 31, 2016). Catholic News & Inspiration website. http://www.pattimaguirearmstrong.com/2016/01/a-miraculous-healing.html.

Barnett, Paul, *Is the New Testament History?* Ann Arbor, Michigan: Servant, 1986.

Bevilacqua, Matteo, et al. "New Light on the Sufferings and the Burial of the Turin Shroud Man." *Peertechz* (May 19, 2017). Peertechz website. https://www.peertechz.com/articles/new-light-on-the-sufferings-and-the-burial-of-the-turin-shroud-man.pdf.

Boissarie, George. *Heaven's Recent Wonders or The Work of Lourdes.* Translated by Rev. C. Van der Donckt. New York: Frederick Pustet & Co., 1909. https://archive.org/details/HeavensRecentWonders. The complete account can also be retrieved from http://miraclesoflourdes.blogspot.com/p/marie-bailly.html.

Burpo, Todd. *Heaven is for Real: A Little Boy's Astounding Story of His Trip to Heaven and Back.* Nashville: Thomas Nelson, 2010. Available online at http://outpouring.ru/file/Heaven_is_for_Real_Todd_Burpo.pdf.

Carroll, Robert T., "Zeitoun." In *Skeptic's Dictionary.* http://skepdic.com/zeitoun.html.

Castellano, Daniel J. *Historiography of the Apparition of Guadalupe* (2013, rev. 2018). http://www.arcaneknowledge.org/catholic/guadalupe.htm.

Catechism of the Catholic Church. Retrievable online at many sites, including http://www.scborromeo.org/ccc.htm.

Churchill, Rhona. "Blind, Paralyzed Cured at Grotto." *Ottawa Citizen* June 19, 1957. https://news.google.com/newspapers?nid=2194&dat=19570619&id=2tIxAAAAIBAJ&sjid=he.FAAAAIBAJ&pg=7236,1004931&hl=en.

BIBLIOGRAPHY

Digisound Hearing website. "How does our ear work?" In *Hearing & Hearing Loss*. https://www.digisoundhearing.com.sg/how-do-our-ears-work.

Ellis, Mark. "For child art prodigy Akiane, Jesus is for real" (January 4, 2012). God Reports website. http://godreports.com/2012/01/for-child-art-prodigy-akiane-jesus-is-for-real/.

Encyclopedia.com, "Knock." https://www.encyclopedia.com/places/britain-ireland-france-and-low-countries/british-and-irish-political-geography/knock.

Estrade, Jean-Baptiste, *The Appearances of the Blessed Virgin Mary at the Grotto of Lourdes: Personal Souvenirs of an Eyewitness*. Westminster: Art & Book Company Ltd, no publication date given, but the Nihil Obstat and Imprimatur are dated June 12, 1912. https://archive.org/stream/appearanceofmaryooestruoft?ref=ol#mode/2up?ref=ol.

Fatima website. https://fatima.org/.

Feain, Fr. Andre. "Marian Shrines of the World #21: Our Lady of China" (August 8, 2015). https://www.youtube.com/watch?v=e_o8dKiCMpI.

Good Shepherd Film Productions. *Bible Reference to Shroud of Turin* (2013). https://www.youtube.com/watch?v=b2T2rn-i1X8.

Grace Gateways website. "The Poignant Prayer of a Soviet Soldier" (21 November, 2016). https://gracegateways.com/soviet-soldier-prayer/.

Helms, Hal M., ed. *The Practice of the Presence of God—Brother Lawrence*. Translated by Robert J. Edmonson. Orleans, MA: Paraclete, 1985.

Holy Fire website. "Description of the Miracle of Holy Light (Holy Fire) that happens every year in Jerusalem." http://www.holyfire.org/eng/.

Keating, Karl. *Catholicism and Fundamentalism*. San Francisco: Ignatius, 1988.

Kelly, Brian. "First Approved Marian Apparition in the US, Champion, Wisconsin" (December 23, 2010). Catholicism.org website. https://catholicism.org/first-approved-marian-apparition-in-the-us-champion-wisconsin.html.

Knight, Kevin. "The Martyrdom of Polycarp." *The Fathers of the Church*. In New Advent Website. https://www.newadvent.org/fathers/0102.htm.

Knock website. "Knock Apparition Witnesses' Statements 1879." https://www.knockshrine.ie/downloads/?v=7516fd43adaa

Kramarik, Akiane. *Prince of Peace*. https://akiane.com/.

Lewis, C.S. *Mere Christianity*. San Francisco: Harper Collins Edition, 2001.

Longnecker, Fr Dwight. *Catholic Herald*. "Turin Shroud: the latest evidence will challenge the sceptics" (August 3, 2017) https://catholicherald.co.uk/turin-shroud-the-latest-evidence-will-challenge-the-sceptics/.

Maniyangat, Fr Jose. "Life after Death Experience," Fr. Jose Eucharistic & Charismatic Healing Ministry website. http://www.frmaniyangathealingministry.com/Content/View_Content.aspx?linkid=16.

Marchi, John de. *The True Story of Fatima*. Constable, NY: The Fatima Center, booklet is undated, but originally published in 1947. https://fatima.org/wp-content/uploads/2017/03/The-True-Story-of-Fatima.pdf.

Miracle Hunter website. "Dung Lu, China (1900, 1995)." http://www.miraclehunter.com/marian_apparitions/approved_apparitions/donglu/index.html.

Mystics of the Church website. "Blessed Alexandrina da Costa of Balasar (1904–1955)—Extraordinary mystic and victim soul." https://www.mysticsofthechurch.com/2009/11/blessed-alexandrina-da-costa-mystic-and.html.

Nican Mopohua. University of California San Diego website. http://pages.ucsd.edu/~dkjordan/nahuatl/nican/NicanMopohua.html.

O'Conner, Patrick. "I Met a Miracle—The Story of Jack Traynor." *The Faith, the Family . . . Future* website. http://www.faithandfamily.org.uk/publications/jack_traynor.htm.

Our Lady of Mercy Lay Carmelite Community. "The Mystery of the Trinity." https://olmlaycarmelites.org/reflections/mystery-trinity.

Our Lady of the Rosary Library website. "Miracles of Lourdes." http://www.olrl.org/stories/lourdes.shtml.

Pope John Paul II. "Apostolic Letter *Rosarium Virginis Mariae* of the Supreme Pontiff John Paul II to Tthe Bishops, Clergy and Faithful on the Most Holy Rosary" October 16, 2002. Vatican website. http://www.vatican.va/.

Pope, Msgr. Charles. "Our Lady of Fatima—Her Prophecies and Warnings Remain as Essential as Ever!" (October 12, 2015), *Msgr. Pope blog*: http://blog.adw.org/2015/10/our-lady-of-fatima-her-prophecies-and-warnings-remain-as-essential-as-ever/.

Rogers, Raymond N. "Studies on the radiocarbon sample from the shroud of turin." *Thermochimica Acta* Volume 425, Issues 1–2 (2005)189–194. https://www.sciencedirect.com/science/article/abs/pii/S0040603104004745.

Scavone, Daniel C. *//acheiropoietos jesus images in constantinople: the documentary evidence* (2006). https://shroudstory.wordpress.com/about/acheiropoietos-jesus-images-in-constantinople-the-documentary-evidence/.

Servants of the Pierced Hearts of Jesus and Mary. "The Virgin Mary and the Holy House of Loreto." https://www.piercedhearts.org/treasures/holy_sites/loreto.htm.

Shroud of Turin Facts Check. "Second Face on the Shroud of Turin." http://www.factsplusfacts.com/second-face.htm.

Shroud of Turin, The: A Critical Summary of Observations, Data and Hypotheses (1978). https://www.shroudofturin.com/Resources/CRTSUM.pdf.

Shroud of Turin website. "The Second International Conference on the Sudarium of Oviedo." https://www.shroud.com/pdfs/n65part6.pdf.

Tassone, Susan. *Jesus Speaks to Faustina and You*. Manchester, N.H: Sophia Institute Press, 2020.

Tour Egypt website. "Christ Pantocrator—Icon in the Monastery of St. Catherine." http://www.touregypt.net/featurestories/catherines2-1.htm.

Wikipedia. "Basilica of the Holy Trinity (Fatima)." In *Wikipedia The Free Encyclopedia*. https://en.wikipedia.org/wiki/Basilica_of_the_Holy_Trinity_(Fátima).

Subject Index

Aaron Arrogance, 18–19
Abortions, 99
Acheiropoietos Jesus Images in Constantinople: the Documentary Evidence, 108
Administrator (Chief Magistrate) of Fatima, 46–47
Alexandrina da Costa of Balasar, 19, 214, 225–228, 273
Angel Gabriel, 70, 126, 265
Annals of Imperial Rome, 55
Annunciation, 60, 70, 126, 127, 129, 131
Apologetics, Traditional, xii, 6–8, 11
    Abstractions vs. evidence, 7–8
    Inadequacy, xii, 8, 11
    Vision of St. Augustine, 6–7
Apostles, 29, 35, 79, 187–189, 194–197, 199, 201–210, 231, 272, 273
Aquino, Marcos Cipac de, 94
Atwell, Father, 139
Azores, The, 40, 62
Aztecs, 86–88, 95–97, 99

Bailly, Marie, 14, 138, 148–157, 272
    After her healing, 155
    Illness, 151–153
    Miraculous healing detailed, 151–155
Barnett, Paul, 55
Barta, César, 124
Belgium, 174–175

Belief, Coming to, xiii, 9–10, 274
    Desire, 9
    Heart and mind, 10
    Prayer, xiii, 10
    Recognizing suffering of cross, 10
Benford, Sue, 116
Bernadette Soubirous, See Our Lady of Lourdes
Bevilacqua, Matteo, 233
Bible, xi, 4, 16–18, 185–210, 243, 244–245, 259, 273
    Attacking, 185–186, 198
    Defending, 186–187, 199–200, 201–210
    Heaven, 259
    Hell, 243
    Ignorance of the Gospel, 244–245
    Red herrings, 199
    Resurrection of Christ, 188–197
    Shroud of Turin, 104–105, 108
    Stunning Gospel events, 201–210
Bible Reference to Shroud of Turin, 108
Bishop of Leiria, 41
Boissaire, Dr., 148
Boxer Rebellion, 178
Brise, Adele, 174–177
Burpo, Colton, 250, 256–259, 267, 273
    Mary next to Jesus, 256–257
    Near-death experience, 256–257
    Prince of Peace verified, 257–258, 267

Burpo, Todd, 256–258
Byrne family members, 84, 79

Calvary, 26, 29, 223, 231–237, 267, 269
Carrel, Alexis 14, 138, 148, 155–156
Carroll, Marion, 14, 80, 81, 138, 161–162, 272
Castellano, Daniel J., 92
Catechism of the Catholic Church, 213, 217, 243, 244, 250
Cathedral of St John the Baptist in Turin, 101
Catholic Church, xii, 22, 29, 34, 63, 70, 86, 162, 168, 177, 180, 199, 213, 217, 233, 243, 244, 250, 260
Charney family, de, 117
China, See Our Lady of China
Christ Pantocrator, 20, 265–267, 270, 273
Christ, Ruler of All, 20, 105, 265–267
Christian divisions, 20–21, 191, 268–270
    Argument against Christianity, 268
    Jesus' prayer, 269
    One Christian faith, 268–270
Church of the Holy Sepulchre, 168–171
Church of the Most Holy Trinity, 57, 98
Clari, Robert de, 106
Cokeville, Wyoming 15, 166, 180–182, 272
    Mormons, Identified with, 182
    Spiritual beings protect, 181–182
Communion, Holy, 29, 57, 127, 159, 162, 260, See also Eucharist, Holy
Constantinople, 106, 108
Coptic Orthodox, 34, 83, 170
Cortes[z], Hernan, 86, 87, 96
Cova da Iria, 44, 46–49
Creation unfolds, 216–220, 238
    Plan of Salvation, 238
Croatia, 127–128

Daily Telegraph, London, 77
Dalmatia, 127–128

Damen, Father Arnold, 177
d'Arcis, Bishop Pierre, 117
D'Arienzo, Michele D'Arienzo, 233
Diodor, Orthodox Patriarch, 170
Divine Redeemer, 41
Dong Lu, China, 178–179

Egypt, 13, 20, 34, 83, 114, 122, 123, 189
Elijah, 105, 107–108, 207–208
Elisha, 107, 204
Emperor Constantine VII, 106
Estrade, Jean-Baptiste, 64–69
ETH Zurich, 115
Eucharist, Holy, 29, 79, 130, 160, 179, 214, 227, 260–261, 273, See also Communion, Holy
Evidence for Jesus, Physical, 13
Evidence for Jesus summarized, 272–273
Evil and suffering, xi, 3–4, 18–20, 213–214, 216–234, 271, 273
    Drawing closer to God, 220
    God's Plan, 216–218
    Jesus understands, 222–223, 229–234
    Natural disasters, 219–220
    Prerequisite to good, 218
    Self-inflicted suffering, 218–219
    Test, 227
Evolution, See Science and Evolution

Faith and miracles, 46, 97–98
Fanti, Giulio, 116, 233
Fatima children, See Our Lady of Fatima
Fatima miracle of September 13, 48–49
Fatima, Portugal, See Our Lady of Fatima
First Cause, 27–28
Free will, xiii, 5, 8, 11, 17, 28–30, 190, 216–218, 223, 241–242, 245, 271, 276
Flury-Lemberg, Mechthild, 113
France, 13, 14, 34, 63, 106, 123, 127, 141, 156, 157
Francisco [Fatima visionary], 36, 37, 41, 43, 44, 46, 52, 53, 57

SUBJECT INDEX 283

Gargam, Gabriel, 14, 138, 158–160, 272
Garrett, Almeida Dr., 39
God, 27–30, 52–53, 79–80, 103, 124, 138, 222–224, 228–238, 271–275
    God's love, 52–53, 79–80, 103, 124, 138, 222–224, 228–238, 271–275
    Incomprehensible, 27–28, 224
    Omniscience and omnipotence, 28–30
Great Chicago Fire, 177
Great Peshtigo Fire, 15, 166, 173–177, 272
    Adele Brise, 174–175
    Firestorm, 175–176
    Great Chicago Fire, 177
    Wisconsin apparition approved, 177
    St. Polycarp, 173–174
Green Bay, Wisconsin, 174, 176, 177
Guadalupe River, 96
Guadalupe tilma, See Our Lady of Guadalupe

Hall, Edward, 15
Hartley, Ron, 181
Hawking, Stephen, 28
Heaven, xiii, 65, 241, 254, 258–259
    Described, 254, 258–259
Heaven is for Real, 20, 250, 256–259
Hell, xi, 3–4, 16, 18–19, 44–45, 53, 215, 239–250, 253, 258, 273
    Choosing hell, 241–242, 245, 273
    Described, 253, 258
    Father Jose's account, 253
    Fatima prayer to Jesus, 44
    Hell is real, 53
    Ignorance of the Gospel, 244–245
    No single concept, 215, 239–240, 242–244
    Rejecting God because of hell, 240
    Vision of Fatima children, 44–45
Hill, Patrick, 74–76
Historiography of the Apparition of Guadalupe, 92
Holy Family, 40–41, 179

Holy House of Loreto, 13, 126–131, 272
    Description, 126
    Documented history, 127–128
    Evidence for Nazarene house, 129–131
Holy Spirit, 51, 68, 80, 83, 99, 206, 224, 270

I Came to Believe, 276
I Was There When It Happened, 274
Image Not Made By Hands, 105
Immaculate Conception, 70–71
Immaculate Heart of Mary, 45, 51–52
India, 20, 189, 252, 255
Ireland, 13, 34, 73, 138, 161
Is the New Testament History?, 55
Islam and Fatima, 59–60

Jacinta [Fatima visionary], 36, 37, 41, 43, 44, 46, 52, 57
Jerusalem, 15, 105, 112, 120, 122, 125, 166, 169–172, 189, 194–197
Jesus, 10, 24, 54–56, 101, 191, 213, 214, 216, 223–225, 229–234, 235–238, 242, 245, 259, 273, 274–275
    Historical Jesus, 54–56
    Jesus' love, 10, 214, 229–234, 235–238, 274–275
    Jesus' suffering, 10, 101, 214, 229–234, 235–238
    Passion, The, 230–234
    Shroud of Turin confirms the Passion, 232–234
    Reasons Jesus suffered and died, 214, 235–238
    Trusting Jesus, 24, 191, 213, 214, 216, 223–225, 242, 245, 259, 273, 275
Jesus, It's Me Again, 275
Jewish Antiquities, 56
Jews, 33, 34, 53, 55–56, 60, 83, 156, 199, 201–204, 206, 236, 271
Josephus, 56
Juan Diego, 13, 86, 88, 89, 91, 94, 97, 99

SUBJECT INDEX

Keating, Karl, 40
Knock, Ireland, See Our Lady of Knock
Koran, 60
Kramarik, Akiane 20, 257–258, 261, 267

Lady of Knock, 80
Lamb of God, 65, 75–77, 79, 80, 243
Lewis, C.S., xiii, 29, 222, 268, 269
Lirey, France, 106
Lords Prayer, xiv, 26
Loreto, Italy, See Holy House of Loreto
Lourdes, France, See Our Lady of Lourdes
Lucia [Fatima visionary], 36–38, 41, 43–46, 48, 49, 52, 57

Mandylion, 105, 108, 265, 267, 273
Maniyangat, Father Jose, 250, 252–255, 273
    Guardian angel, 253–254
    Life after NDE, 255
    Miraculous healing, 255
    Near-death experience, 252–254
Marchi, John de, 38, 40, 49
Marian apparitions, 12–13, 33–35, 93, 161, 177
Marino, Joe, 116
Mary, the mother of Jesus, 22, 26, 33–35, 36, 42, 45, 50–52, 56, 57–60, 62, 67, 70–71, 79, 83, 89–90, 96–97, 99, 126–131, 190, 223, 224, 230–234, 256–257
    Annunciation, 224
    Appearances eliminates all other religions, 190
    Bogus apparitions, 62
    Confirms Jesus' love, 52
    Directs us to Jesus, 22, 26, 35, 50, 56, 60, 67, 79, 97, 99, 224
    Ever-Virgin, 89
    Guadalupe image, 96–97
    Holy Family fleeing to Egypt, 83
    Honoring Mary redirects to Jesus, 57–58
    Immaculate Conception, 70–71
    Immaculate Heart of Mary, 45, 51–52
    Intercessions, 60
    Islam, 59–60
    Marian apparitions, 33–35
    Mary in heaven, 36, 42, 256–257
    Mary praying, 52
    Mary's house, 126–131
    Mary's suffering, 223, 230–234
    Mother of God, 50, 89–90
    Our Mother, 97, 99
    Rosary, 50–51
    Theotokos, 50
Masonic Lodge, 46
McLoughlin, Mary, 73–75
Mexico, 13, 34, 86, 87, 96, 97, 98, 99
Millan, Cesar, 275
Miracle of the Holy Fire, 15, 166, 168–172, 204, 272
    Church of the Holy Sepulchre, 168–169
    Orthodox, Identified with, 168–172
    Timeline, 169–171
    Why West unfamiliar, 172
Miracle of the Sun, 9, 13, 33–34, 36–43, 48, 61–62, 93, 227, 272
    Drying, Instantaneous, 41
    Official recognition, 41
    Skeptics' attacks, 61–62
Miraculous events, 15, 166–167
    Cokeville, Wyoming, 15, 166, 180–182
    Great Peshtigo Fire, 15, 166, 173–177
    Hypothetical cross in the sky, 82–84
    Miracle of the Holy Fire, 15, 166, 168–172
    Our Lady of China, 15, 166, 178–179
Miraculous healings, 14, 63–64, 72, 138–165, 186, 272
    Atwell, Father, 139
    Bailly, Marie, 138, 148–157
    Carell, Alexis, 138, 155–156
    Carroll, Marion, 81, 161–162

Description of seventy Lourdes
 healings, 72
Gargam, Gabriel, 138, 158–160
Lourdes protocol to determine,
 63–64
Pascal, Francis, 138, 163–165
Traynor, Jack, 138, 140–147
Miraculous Mary, 128
Montezuma, 87
Moreno, Juan Ignacio, 124
Mormon, xii, 182,
Mother of God, 49, 50, 72, 76, 89, 98
Mother Teresa of Calcutta, 24, 275
Muslims, 34, 59–60, 83, 106, 122, 127,
 128, 169, 267, 270
Music, Inspirational, xiv, 11, 21, 26, 72,
 80, 231, 245, 267, 274

National Shrine of Our Lady of Good
 Help, 174
Nazareth, 18, 126–130, 206
Near-death experiences, 20, 249–259,
 273
 Burpo, Colton, 256–259
 Maniyangat, Father Jose, 252–255
Nican Mopohua, 88

O Seculo, 38
O'Connor, Reverand Patrick, 146–147
Orthodox Church, xii, 22, 34, 83,
 105, 166, 168–172, 180, 234,
 267–270
Our Lady of China, 15, 166, 178–179,
 272
 1900—Our Lady protects, 178–179
 1995—Confirming miracle of the
  sun, 179
 Boxer Rebellion, 178
 Chinese government response, 179
Our Lady of Fatima, 9, 13, 23, 29,
 33–34, 36–62, 93, 97–98, 158,
 172, 190, 227, 229, 244, 272
 August 13 incarceration of Fatima
  children, 46
 Background, 36–38
 Effects, 54–58
 Fatima Prayer, 44
 First four appearances, 43–47

Hell, Vision of, 44–45
Holy Family, 40–41
Immaculate Heart of Mary, 45,
 51–52
Islam, 59–60
Messages of love, 50–53
Miracle of the Sun, 38–41
Rosary, Instructions to pray the,
 43–46
September 13 miracle, 47–49
Skeptics' attacks, 61–62
Our Lady of Fatima Basilica, 57
Our Lady of Graces, 128
Our Lady of Good Help, 176–177
Our Lady of Guadalupe, 13, 34–35,
 85–99, 272
 Aztec culture, 86–87, 99
 Blessed Virgin appears, 88–91
 Bombing of image, 98–99
 Effect, 95
 Faith and miracles, 97–98
 Image created in two steps, 93–99
 Image revealed, 90–91
 Inculturation, 95–97
 Messages, 89, 95–97
 Our mother, 97, 99
 Spanish conquest, 87–88
Our Lady of Knock, 13, 14, 34, 73–81,
 138, 161–162, 190, 272,
 Lady of Knock, 80
 Marion Carroll's healing, 81
 Messages, 79–80
 Secular explanations, 77–79
 Visitations, 73–76
Our Lady of Lourdes, 13, 14, 29, 34,
 35, 63–72, 93, 95, 138–160,
 163–165, 172, 177, 190, 229,
 272
 Bernadette after Lourdes, 71
 Bernadette's visage, 65–66, 68
 Immaculate Conception, 70–71
 Protocol to establish miraculous
  healings, 63–64
 Rosary, Praying, 68
 Spring revealed, 69–70
 The Village of St. Bernadette, 72
Our Lady of Sorrows, 41

Our Lady of the Rosary, 36, 40, 44, 54, 97
Our Lady of Trsat, 128
Our Lady of Zeitoun, 13, 34, 35, 82–84, 272, 273
    Cairo Coptic Orthodox Church, 83
    Skeptics dismissal, 83–84
Oureana, 59
Oviedo, Spain, 112, 121–122

Pascal, Francis, 14, 138, 163–165, 272
    Blind and paralyzed, 163–165
Paul, 105, 107, 108, 244
Peertechz, 233
Pernin, Reverend Peter, 176
Personal experiences, 20, 247–262, 273
    Burpo, Colton, 256–259
    Eucharist Adoration, 260–261
    Father Jose Maniyangat, 252–255
    Near-death experiences, 249–259
    Waco, Texas, 260–262
Peshtigo, Wisconsin, See Great Peshtigo Fire
Peyramale, Father, 70, 71
Pliny, 55, 272
Pope Clement VII, 117–118
Pope John Paul II, 51
Pope, Monsignor Charles, 60
Pope Stephen II, 105
Portugal, 13, 33, 36, 40, 41, 42, 226
Pray Manuscript, 106, 117
Prayer, xiii, 10, 11, 22–26, 190, 224, 227, 273, 274, 275
    Did You Think to Pray?, 26
    God's gift, 273
    Humility, xiii, 10, 26
    Importance, xiii, 10, 11, 22, 26, 274
    Jesus, It's Me Again, 275
    Mother Teresa of Calcutta, 24
    Nonbeliever praying, 22–23
    Practice, 24
    Prayer of Soviet soldier, 25–26
    Remain in the presence of God, 227
    Simplicity and perseverance, 25
    St. Augustine's conversion, 23
Prayers, Unanswered, xi, 3–4, 16, 18–19, 214, 220, 221–227, 273
    Alexandrina da Costa of Balasar, 225–228
    End of the world, 222
    God understands, 222–223
    Trust God, 223–225
Presse, Alexis, 156
Prince of Peace, 20, 257–258, 267, 270, 273
Protestant denominations, xii, 22, 172, 256
Purgatory, 252, 253

Quaresma, Monsignor John, 48
Queen of Heaven, 41, 66, 175–176

Recanati, Italy, 128
Resurrection of Christ, 4, 17–18, 106, 186, 188–197, 201, 272, 273
    Apostles knew, 188–189, 273
    Apostles martyred, 188–189, 273
    Complementary Gospel accounts, 4, 17–18, 186, 192–197
    Contemporaneous writings, 189–190
    Effects of, 54–56
    Eliminates all other theologies, 190
Rogers, Raymond N., 116
Rosarium Virginis Mariae [*Rosary of the Virgin Mary*], dated October 16, 2002, 51
Rosary, 43–46, 50–51, 67–68, 244
    Our Lady of Fatima instructions to pray, 43–46
    Significance, 50–51
Russia, Consecration to, 45

Sagan, Carl, 28, 83
Scavone, Daniel C., 108
Science and Evolution, xi, 4–5, 14, 16–17, 27–28, 98, 103, 112, 115, 119, 124, 132–137
    Complexity of body systems, 132–137
    Complexity of cells, 135–136
    Hearing system, Description of, 133–134
    Inter-dependence of body systems, 132–137

SUBJECT INDEX 287

Res ipsa loquitur, 14, 132–137
Visual system, Description of, 136–137
YouTube, visual descriptions, 135, 137
Servants of the Pierced Hearts of Jesus and Mary, 131
Sheen, Archbishop Fulton J., 60
Shroud of Turin, 9, 13, 18, 20, 29, 100–125, 187, 190, 214, 229, 232–234, 267
   Bible references, 104–105, 107–108
   Carbon dating, 103, 115–117, 118, 124
   Confirms Christ's suffering, 101, 187, 214, 232–234
   Description, 101–102
   Evidence against Shroud, 115–118
   Features, Inexplicable, 109–114
   God's Eternal Love, 103
   Historical documentation, 104–106
   Mandylion, 105, 108
   Pray Manuscript, 106
   Reversing the Evidence, 103
   Scarlet Purple Robe, 231
   Scientific proof impossible, 119–120
   Secular explanations, 102
   STURP, 102–103
Sisters of Good Help, 175
Skeptics Dictionary, The, 83
Soviet soldier, Aleksander Zacepa, 25
Spain, 96, 112, 121–122, 124
Spiritual dryness, 23, 24
St. Augustine, 6, 7, 23
St. Faustina, 237
St. Francis, 23, 127
St. John, 75–77, 79, 80
St. Joseph, 34, 40–41, 46, 73–77, 79–80, 83, 205, 254
St. Mary's Academy, 175
St. Michael the Archangel, 178
St. Polycarp, 173–174, 176
St. Thomas Aquinas, 7, 8
STURP, 102
Sudarium of Oviedo, 13, 18, 112, 120, 121–125, 187, 272
   Biblical references, 121–122
   Carbon dating, 123–124
   Correlation to Shroud of Turin, 122–124
   Description, 121
   God's love, 124
   Timeline, 121–122
Suetonius, 55
Suffering. See Evil and Suffering

Tacitus, 55
Tepeyac, 88–89
Tersatto, 127–128
The Appearances of the Blessed Virgin Mary at the Grotto of Lourdes: Personal Souvenirs of an Eyewitness, 66
The Passion of Christ, 241
The Shroud of Turin: A Critical Summary of Observations, Data and Hypotheses, (Shroud Critical Summary), 102, 105, 117
The Village of St. Bernadette, 72
Thermochimica Acta, 116
Tite, Michael, 113
Traynor, Jack, 14, 138, 140–147, 272
Trench, Bridget, 76
True Story of Fatima, The, 38, 46, 49, 52
Tsrat, 127–129
Tyrer, John, 113

Unanswered prayers, See Prayers, Unanswered
Unbelief, Reasons for, xi, xiii, 3–5, 9–11, 17–20, 61–62, 83, 98–99, 115–118, 123–124, 158, 163, 172, 185–186, 190, 192, 198–199, 213–215, 219, 221, 239–240, 259, 268–269, 275
   Arrogance, xiii, 18–19, 259
   Biases, xiii, 10–11, 190
   Bible is untrustworthy, xi, 4, 17–18, 185–186, 192, 198–199
   Christian doctrines, xi, 186, 239, 268–269
   Hard-core nonbeliever, 9, 83–84, 275

Unbelief, Reasons for (*continued*)
   Hidden God, 3, 11
   Hostility, 10–11, 61–62, 98–99
   Miracles, No real, 4, 158, 163, 172, 250
   Pride, 10–11
   Resurrection, No evidence, 190
   Science and evolution, 4–5, 16–17, 62, 82–83, 98, 115–118, 123–124, 186
   Suffering, evil, unanswered prayers, hell, xi, 3–4, 18–20, 213–215, 219, 221, 239–240
   Summary, xi, 3–5

University of Arizona, 115
University of Oxford, 115

Waco, Texas, 20, 260–262
Walsh, Patrick, 77
Wisconsin, 15, 166, 174–177
Wyoming, See Cokeville, Wyoming

Zumarraga, Bishop Juan de, 87–89, 94

Scripture Index

Exodus

24:18	204

Deuteronomy

8:2	204

2 Kings

2	107

Wisdom

3:4–6	214

Matthew

27:57—28:20	194–197
27:46	207
27:31–32	232
26:36—Ch 27	101
17:1–13	208
13:54–58	xiii

Mark

15:42—16:20	194–197
15:20–22	232
14:32—Ch 15	101
9:2–13	208
6:1–6	xiii

Luke

23:50—24:53	194–197
23:46	207
23:34, 43	207
23:34	269
23:26–32	232
22:39—Ch 23	101
9:28–36	208

John

20:24–29	101
20:11–18	274
20:6–8	105, 121, 122
19:38—20:31	194–197
19:28, 30	207
19:26, 27	207
19:17	232
17–19	101
10:26	156
3:16	243

2 Timothy

4:13	105, 107

Romans

13	23
6:23	243
2:14–15	244

Revelations

14:9–11	243
12:1	97

www.ingramcontent.com/pod-product-compliance
Lightning Source LLC
Chambersburg PA
CBHW051630230426
43669CB00013B/2243